Karma and Happiness

Karma
and
Happiness

A Tibetan Odyssey in Ethics, Spirituality, and Healing

Miriam E. Cameron, PhD, RN

With a foreword by His Holiness the Dalai Lama

Center for Spirituality and Healing, Minneapolis

Established in 1995 within the University of Minnesota's Academic Health Center, the Center for Spirituality and Healing's mission is to promote interdisciplinary education, research, and patient care that integrate biomedical, complementary, cross-cultural, and spiritual aspects of care.

Library of Congress Cataloging-in-Publication Data
Cameron, Miriam.
    Karma and happiness : a Tibetan odyssey in ethics, spirituality, and
    healing / Miriam E. Cameron
        p. cm.
    Includes bibliographical references.
    ISBN 1-57749-105-X (pbk. : alk. paper)
      1. Religious life—Buddhism. 2. Karma. 3. Buddhism—China—Tibet—
    Doctrines. I. Title.
    BQ7604 .C36 2001
    294.3'923'092—dc21
    [B]   2001023045

First Printing: September 2001

Printed in the United States of America
05 04 03 02 01   6 5 4 3 2

Cover: *Cover design by Laurie Ingram Duren*
Book design: Dorie McClelland, Spring Type & Design

Tibetan organizations receive a portion of the royalties for *Karma and Happiness*.

For a free current catalog of Fairview Press titles, please call toll-free 1-800-544-8207. Or visit our Web site at www.fairviewpress.org.

This book is dedicated to my Tibetan family.

◆ ◆ ◆

"As rain forests are to the earth's atmosphere—
so are the Tibetan people to the soul of this planet
in this time of their desperate ordeal."

Huston Smith,
The Illustrated World's Religions: A Guide to Our Wisdom Traditions

Contents

THE DALAI LAMA

FOREWORD

I believe there is great potential in Tibet's religious culture, its medical knowledge, peaceful outlook and respectful attitude to the environment that can be of widespread benefit to others. For instance, living experience of meditation has given Tibetan practitioners a profound knowledge of the workings and nature of the mind, an inner science to complement the conventional scientists' understanding of the physical world.

In this century in particular, it has become clear that no amount of technological development on its own leads to lasting happiness. What is also required is a corresponding inner development. Many people have remarked that Tibetans seem to have just such a sense of inner peace and hope, even in the face of great adversity. I think the source of this lies mostly in the Buddhist teachings of love, kindness, tolerance and especially the theory that all things are relative.

Nevertheless, although the Tibetan people and I myself have derived great satisfaction from the teachings of the Buddha, I have no intention of trying to convert others to Buddhism. I believe that the ultimate purpose of Buddhism is to serve and benefit humanity, and what actually interests me is the contribution we Buddhists can make to human society according to the ideas and values we believe in.

This book, *Karma and Happiness*, is an account of Miriam E Cameron's dialogue with Tibetans and Tibetan culture. Already concerned with issues of health and ethics, she discusses here what she learned from her visit to Tibet and her growing acquaintance with Tibetans. She describes how these experiences challenged her sense of values, giving her a new perspective on ethics and spirituality in the context of healing. I welcome this kind of openhearted approach to different ideas and practices. I feel it is along such lines that Tibetans and the values we espouse can make a contribution to creating a happier, more peaceful world. I am sure that readers who are interested in the relations between ethical values and the health of individuals and society will find much here to inspire them.

April 13, 2001

Acknowledgments

I am deeply grateful to Michael Ormond, my soul mate and husband, who shared this Tibetan odyssey with me. He helped me to develop my thinking, repeatedly edited what I wrote, and provided financial support.

After delivering the first draft of this book to my friend Rhoda Lewin, I went to sleep feeling vulnerable about her response. I dreamed of a cherry tree in my backyard. Both ripe and rotten cherries had fallen to the ground. I wondered whether to take the time to sort through the cherries and salvage the edible ones. When I woke up, I knew the dream was advising me to identify and use the helpful comments Rhoda would provide, for this would lead to a better book. I reflected on why the dream used cherries as a metaphor; the image came to mind of a hot fudge sundae with a cherry on top.

I had no reason to worry. Rhoda offered delectable cherries by editing the entire first draft. Thankfully, she advised me to steer away from an academic style and write from my heart.

Sherab Dolma, Susan Moch, Ngawang Ngora, Tsamchoe Ngodup, Judy Ormond, Joän Patterson, Kate Pfaffinger, Riki Scheela, Dorjay Thseten, Dorle Vawter, and Dolkar Wangmo handed me delicious cherries, too. They took time to read portions or all of the manuscript at its various stages, and they made helpful suggestions.

Traditional Tibetan physicians Tsering Lhamo and Tsering Dorjee, from the Men-Tsee-Khang in Dharamsala, India, and Yangdron Kalzang from Lhasa, Tibet, corrected errors in the manuscript and assisted me in writing about traditional Tibetan medicine.

Tsewang Ngodup, a Western-trained Tibetan physician from Dharamsala, India, read both the first and second drafts of the manuscript—no easy task, as the first draft was twice as long as the second draft! He helped me clarify my statements about Tibetan culture and values into accurate reflections of so complex a subject.

I'm also grateful for the energy, patience, commitment, and expertise of Lane Stiles, Stephanie Billecke, Steve Deger, and the rest of the staff at Fairview Press.

The National Institute of Nursing Research at the National Institutes of Health; the University of Minnesota Graduate School; and Bethel College of St. Paul, Minnesota, generously funded my research reported in this book. Marjorie Schaffer of St. Paul, Minnesota, and Hyeoun-Ae Park of Seoul, Korea, helped me to conduct the research about nursing students.

Above all, I want to thank the Tibetans who opened their hearts to me, without whom I would not have experienced my Tibetan odyssey, or written this book.

Introduction:
The Relationship between Ethics, Spirituality, and Healing

Tibetan Odyssey

My husband, Mike, and I were on a month-long tour of China when we decided to travel to Tibet. Our tour director, who turned out to be Tibetan, invited us to accompany him the next time he visited his native land set high in the Himalayan Mountains of Central Asia. We accepted his invitation, thinking that going to the "Roof of the World" would be an interesting adventure. At the time, I knew little about the Tibetan people or the wisdom of their ancient heritage. I prepared for the trip to mysterious "Shangri-la" by reading books, attending lectures, and participating in activities put on by the Tibetan community in our hometown of Minneapolis. But it wasn't until I was actually in the "Land of Snows" that I began to realize the extent to which this experience would transform my life. It is this Tibetan odyssey that I share in *Karma and Happiness*.

As Mike and I learned firsthand about the conflict between Tibet and China, we encountered increasingly difficult ethical problems. We came to see that there are no easy answers—for the Tibetans, for the Chinese, or for any of us who want to behave ethically. Ethical conflict isn't unique to Tibet; the search for how best to conduct our lives and heal society is as old as human civilization. In various forms, these ethical problems confront each of us—and society as a whole—generation after generation.

The Tibetan situation is an excellent vehicle for examining both personal and societal ethical problems. Most Tibetans view the Dalai Lama as their ethical, spiritual, and political leader, but these three roles don't exist in simple harmony. As an ethical

1

and spiritual leader, the Dalai Lama guides Tibetans and other Buddhists throughout the world. Because his message is universal, many non-Buddhists also look to him for wisdom. His political leadership, however, extends primarily to Tibetans who support his government in exile. This political role is complex because the values of Tibetans in diaspora are not always consistent with the values of the Tibetans who remain in Tibet.

This is not a social science book. My academic education was in nursing and bioethics; I make no claim to professional expertise in anthropology, political science, or history. No, this book was written as a statement from one human being who, like everyone else, yearns to be happy, to avoid suffering, and to live with meaning and integrity.

I have changed the names of most Tibetans described in this book, and I altered details about their lives and mine in order to ensure our privacy and safety. Of course, I have preserved the name and biographical facts of the most famous Tibetan of all, the fourteenth Dalai Lama, Tenzin Gyatso.

Before describing my Tibetan odyssey, I wish to provide a brief background about ethics, spirituality, and healing—concepts that lie at the core of *Karma and Happiness*.

Ethics

How should I conduct my life, knowing that I will die? This question is an ethical problem, a situation involving conflict about the right thing to do. Ethical problems range from small, personal conflicts to large, societal ones.

We experience many ethical problems throughout life:

> What should I value?
> Who I should be?
> How should I treat other people?
> What kind of a world should I help to create?

Underlying each of these questions is conflict about the right way to conduct our lives.

Perhaps the most common ethical problem is whether to tell a lie, especially if the consequences of a lie seem better than the consequences of the truth. For example, my friend asks if I like her new haircut. Should I admit that I don't like it, or lie to keep from hurting her feelings? I feel conflict because I want to avoid lying, but, at the same time, I don't want to jeopardize our friendship.

Like all other ethical problems, whether or not to tell a lie is much more complicated than it may seem.

Are lies always wrong, or is a "white lie" ever all right?

Is being tactful any different from being evasive?

Can I lie when it will benefit me, but injure others?

Is remaining silent or failing to affirm the truth the same as lying?

Should I lie to thwart the harmful action of another person?

Is it ethical to tell a lie if the consequences are good?

Who determines if the consequences of a lie are good or bad?

To learn more about individuals' experience of ethical problems, I conducted two research projects: one involving persons with AIDS and the other with elders and their families. Colleagues and I conducted a similar research project with students who had nearly completed a bachelor's degree in nursing. The 133 research participants in the three studies came from a wide range of ethnic and economic backgrounds. They described hundreds of ethical problems, all of which consisted of three components: a conflict of values, a resolution to the conflict, and a rationale for the resolution.

The research participants described each conflict as a stressful clash of their deeply held values. They felt confused about how to behave, for their responsibilities and loyalties were unclear. One conflict overlapped another, and a new conflict emerged before a previous one was resolved. Often, superficial conflict hid deeper, more painful conflict. Ethical, spiritual, and psychological conflicts were intertwined.

For example, a young man with AIDS wondered whether to lie to his extended family about his diagnosis. His parents were ashamed that he had AIDS, and they didn't want him to be honest with the rest of the family. He loved his parents, but he also valued honesty. "Is my responsibility to please my parents, or to be true to myself?" he asked me. "If I lie to my family, I'll have to tell other lies to cover up for the first lie. This is very stressful for me, because I don't know if God will forgive me for lying."

The research participants struggled to develop resolutions that helped them to live with meaning (the belief that life has purpose) and integrity (harmony with their best values). They acknowledged that their most effective resolutions were based on an informed, reasoned conceptual framework, often called a *philosophy of life*. Failure to resolve conflict in this way led to stress, burnout, and compromised integrity.

These research results suggest the importance of recognizing our ethical conflicts, examining them carefully, and resolving them in a manner that leads to meaning and integrity. If we base our resolutions on a sound philosophy of life, we'll be more likely to take responsibility for our actions, rather than follow our impulses or do what other people tell us is right. We'll see the overall picture, not just our own needs, and we'll make better choices.

Of course, an informed, reasoned philosophy of life is not a panacea. No one can devise rules to fit all circumstances or resolve every ethical conflict. A formulaic approach does not capture the richness and diversity of human experience. Moreover, rigid principles can lead to close-mindedness and bigotry. Each of us is unique, and one philosophy of life will not fit everyone. As human beings, we have both the capacity and responsibility to grapple with and seek meaning in the particularities of our own life.

A philosophy of life is a work in progress. As we engage in values clarification—the ongoing process of evaluating our values—we discard those values that aren't ethically justifiable, thereby, freeing ourselves to develop better ones. We adapt our philosophy of life as our values evolve. With sound values and an informed, reasoned philosophy of life, we'll effectively resolve our ethical conflicts and conduct our lives well.

Spirituality

But what is the best philosophy of life for dealing with ethical problems and conducting our lives well? Many people turn to wisdom traditions—sometimes called religions—for direction. Christianity, Judaism, Islam, Hinduism, Buddhism, and other wisdom traditions address what is good and right. They help us to see ethical problems in a larger context, which ultimately gives meaning to life.

Some people substitute science for a wisdom tradition. Science may help us to predict and control some aspects of the natural world; however, science doesn't ask, "Is it ultimately good and right to exercise this control?" Science can't tell us the right thing to do.

Wisdom traditions agree that the best way to conduct life is to behave ethically. They advocate goodness, justice, truth-telling, and other positive values. In a nutshell, we are advised to avoid causing harm and, if possible, to give help instead. Even so, adherents to the various wisdom traditions often disagree about why we should act ethically and what it means to hurt and to help. Such differences of opinion have led to animosity and, in extreme cases, even war.

If we attempt to tie ethics to one wisdom tradition, we must ask, "Which wisdom tradition teaches the right view of ethics?" It is an unfortunate fact of history that, too often, believers in a particular wisdom tradition insist that theirs are the only right values. Moreover, adhering to a wisdom tradition is no guarantee of ethical behavior. Throughout history, people with strong religious beliefs have committed terrible acts, with a battle cry shared by kindergartners and dictators alike: "I'm right and you're wrong."

Basing ethics on a single tradition can be hurtful. And given the diversity of humankind, no single wisdom tradition—including science—meets everyone's needs. In fact, many people find that one tradition is insufficient in this complex world.

Throughout history, sages around the world have suggested that we base ethics on spirituality, rather than on a particular wisdom tradition. Spirituality refers to values describing the human spirit, including love, compassion, kindness, contentment, responsibility, altruism, peace of mind, joy, patience, humility, tolerance, and forgiveness. Spiritual practice is the process of developing these values in order to transform ourselves into better people. A spiritual life is not otherworldly, magical, or mysterious. It is simply a reorientation away from our habitual preoccupation with self, causing our actions to become more ethical. By focusing less on ourselves, we can turn toward the wider community and recognize other people's needs as our own.

Of course, ethics and spirituality don't eliminate the need for laws. Although each of us has the potential to improve ourself, we don't evolve ethically or spiritually at the same rate. That's why every society needs effective laws. Ideally, laws will be ethical, but that is not always the case. Sometimes we must choose between obeying the law and living up to our ethical and spiritual values.

The Dalai Lama teaches that the best way to guarantee ethical behavior is to develop spiritual values. While wisdom traditions can be invaluable, we can practice ethical and spiritual behavior whether we embrace one tradition, many traditions, or no tradition at all. No matter which path we choose, a philosophy of life that incorporates both ethics and spirituality will help us to heal ourselves and the world.

Healing

Each of us wants to be healthy—to feel whole and sound—even if we sometimes do things to sabotage this goal. If we aren't healthy, we crave healing, though we may feel confused about how to get it.

Wisdom traditions address healing, either explicitly or implicitly, yet they differ in their explanations of how to live a healthy life.

One approach teaches that we should develop ethical and spiritual values to please an anthropomorphic god. Such teachings often refer to unethical behavior as "sin." If we sin, God will punish us during this lifetime or in the hereafter. If we avoid sin, God will reward us with good health and long life. While some people adhere to this belief, many people reject an ethical, spiritual code that involves sin and punishment.

A second, more secular, approach advocates a social contract based on calculative self-interest. According to this perspective, if everyone behaves ethically and spiritually, we'll create a better, more peaceful world. Then, resources could be used to improve health instead of wage wars. Once the whole world accepts the rule of "You scratch my back, I'll scratch yours," eventually everyone's back will be scratched. Social contract theory, however, doesn't tell us why we should take up ethical and spiritual values if we can live and prosper without the benefit of ethical or spiritual accountability.

A third approach depicts behaving ethically and growing spiritually as the happiest way to live. Good choices lead to a happier, healthier life, while poor ones detract from well-being. This perspective is based on the universal desire to be happy and to avoid suffering. Bad things happen to good people, indeed, and good things happen to bad people. Even so, if we develop ethical and spiritual values, our lives will most often go better than if we don't, and we'll deal more effectively with bad things when they occur.

◆ ◆ ◆

This third approach is evident in daily life. If we resent someone who hurts us, we are hurt twice: first by the person's action, and second by our reaction. Hostility and alienation can lead to high blood pressure, heart problems, emotional dysfunction, and other difficulties. On the other hand, being kind, connected, and peaceful promotes healing of body, mind, and spirit.

The participants in my research studies illustrate this perspective. Some participants had allowed bitterness and hostility to overwhelm them. Drowning in sadness and isolation, they felt alienated from others. As a result, they suffered greatly. Other participants viewed their difficulties as an opportunity for growth. They reached out to help other individuals, and they were rewarded with peace of mind. The more they grew ethically and spiritually, the happier they became and the healthier they felt. Even if their bodies deteriorated, their ethical and spiritual values led to healing of mind and spirit.

The West has developed many proverbs and aphorisms to describe this perspective:

> Virtue is its own reward.
> As you sow, so shall you reap.
> The chickens come home to roost.
> What goes around, comes around.
> Those that live by the sword shall die by the sword.

Tibetans call this phenomenon *karma,* the Sanskrit word for "action." According to the Buddhist Doctrine of Karma, an action always produces a result, which in turn leads to another result. In the West, we often perceive cause and effect as two distinct events. Buddhism, on the other hand, teaches that all things, all actions, are interrelated; thus, happiness and suffering are not accidental—they result from our behavior.

I have come to agree with Tibetans that the Doctrine of Karma offers the basis for a sound philosophy of life. Therefore, this book contends that the way to be happy is to develop ethical and spiritual values. Conducting our lives in this manner will help us to live with meaning and integrity. As a result, we'll be able to bring healing to ourselves and to the world.

Chapter 1

Something Missing

Christianity

"Where will *you* spend eternity?" my father thundered from the pulpit of his rural Midwestern church. He pushed back the sleeves of the black robe that marked him as an ordained minister in the Norwegian Lutheran synod. Then he thumbed through his well-worn Christian Bible to John 3:16. "For God so loved the world that He gave His only son," he read, "that whoever believes in Him should not perish but have eternal life." Looking up, he said earnestly, "God the Father sent His Son, Jesus, to save us from our sins so we'll go to heaven when we die."

About fifty women, men, and children filled the church pews. Their Sunday finery did not hide the callused hands and ruddy cheeks they had acquired from their lives working on the farm. The adults seemed to listen intently, while the children whispered and squirmed until their parents gave them a stern look. I sat in the right front pew, next to the electric organ. The church organist was on maternity leave, and I, only twelve years old, was filling in for her. I wondered what hymn to play after the sermon to inspire the parishioners to hear Jesus' voice.

"Jesus is the only way to heaven," Dad's voice boomed. "In John 14:6, Jesus said, 'I am the way, the truth, and the life; no

one comes to the Father, but by me.' But we must do something, too, for we must be born again." He thumbed through
his Bible. "Let's look at John 3:5. 'Unless one is born of water
and of the Spirit, he cannot enter the kingdom of God.'"
Leaning over the pulpit, he looked directly at the parishioners.
"To be born again, we must confess our sins and ask Jesus into
our hearts. We don't know how long we'll live. Newspapers
carry obituaries of the old and the young. When *you* die, will
you go to heaven?" He paused, gauging the response of the
congregation. "Today's the day to be born again, for tomorrow
may be too late. Let us pray. Ask Jesus into your heart." As all
heads bowed, he prayed: "Lord Jesus Christ, please help each of
us to accept you. In the name of the Father, Son, and Holy
Spirit. Amen."

Dad closed his Bible and sat down behind the pulpit. He
folded his hands and bowed his head in prayer. I quietly slid
onto the organ bench and played the beloved Gospel hymn,
"Blessed Assurance, Jesus Is Mine!" The parishioners sang along
enthusiastically. I glowed with the confidence that I was serving
Jesus—as well as my father's ministry—and that I would go to
heaven when I died.

In high school, though, I questioned whether being a
Christian is the only "right" way to live. I wondered if God
really punishes ethical, spiritual people who follow other
wisdom traditions. That's what the Bible teaches, my father
assured me. He said that my responsibility was to do what Jesus
would do, and to obey the Ten Commandments as they are
written in Exodus 20:2–17:

> I am the Lord your God, who brought you out
> of the land of Egypt, out of the house of
> bondage. You shall have no other gods before
> me. You shall not take the name of the Lord
> your God in vain. Remember the Sabbath day,

to keep it holy. Honor your father and your
mother. You shall not kill. You shall not commit
adultery. You shall not steal. You shall not bear
false witness against your neighbor. You shall
not covet your neighbor's house. You shall not
covet your neighbor's wife, or his manservant,
or his maidservant, or his ox, or his ass, or
anything that is your neighbor's.

After graduating from high school, I went to college and
majored in nursing. My courses focused on developing a
philosophy to guide my nursing practice. *Even more*, I thought,
I *need a philosophy of life that provides wise direction for how to
conduct my life.* But I felt confused about what values to include
in this philosophy.

Once I became a registered nurse, I worked with dying children who belonged to a variety of wisdom traditions. It was
then that ethical problems bombarded me. For example, I felt
conflict about being honest with terminally ill children who
wondered if they were dying, when their hopeful parents had
asked me to say they were getting better. Doing what Jesus
would do and following the Ten Commandments no longer
gave me enough guidance to resolve complicated ethical conflicts. Christianity, my first wisdom tradition, was no longer
sufficient for me.

Judaism

I determined to write a philosophy of life that made sense to me.
To get started, I turned to what was familiar—Jesus' teachings in
the Christian Bible. As I studied the Gospels, Jesus' Jewish roots
began to fascinate me, and I expanded my project to include the
Hebrew Bible and Judaism. Eventually, this work became my
first book, *Hello, I'm God and I'm Here to Help You.*

As I pursued these studies, I concluded that Jesus' teachings were not new, for they were derived from Judaism. Moreover, Jesus described the core of Judaism in Mark 28:12–31:

> And one of the scribes . . . asked him, "Which commandment is the first of all?" Jesus answered, "The first is, 'Hear, O Israel: The Lord our God, the Lord is One; and you shall love the Lord your God with all your heart, and with all your soul, and with all your mind, and with all your strength.' The second is this, 'You shall love your neighbor as yourself.' There are no other commandments greater than these."

Both of these "commandments" are from Judaism. Jesus would certainly have known them well because of his upbringing. The first one, called the *Sh'ma,* lies at the heart of Jewish liturgy and religious practices.

I continued seeking wisdom within the Jewish tradition. As I studied the Hebrew Bible, I noted specific ethical and spiritual guidelines for how best to conduct life. For example, we love God by humbly being God's servant in the world. Moreover, we love our neighbors as ourselves when we forgive, help those less fortunate, tell the truth, treat everyone with respect and caring, and behave responsibly. Humans have been given a great gift— free will—which allows us to act consciously, with intent. We can choose good by adhering to these biblical guidelines, or we can choose evil by not following them. If we make good choices, our lives will go better than if we make poor choices.

Once I had reached this point in my studies, I realized that this was a philosophy that made sense to me and provided guidance for my actions in life. I was eager to learn even more about Judaism.

The most observant branch of the Jewish tradition is Orthodoxy. As my goal was to learn as much as I could, I arranged a meeting with an Orthodox rabbi. When I mentioned my interest in becoming Jewish, he gave me what I knew to be the traditional response: "Stay a Christian," he advised. "Being a Jew is too hard." He told me that the Jews have suffered greatly because of anti-Semitism, most recently and devastatingly in the Holocaust. "You can live a good life as a Christian," he assured me.

Undeterred by the rabbi's response, I looked to other denominations of Judaism. When I attended Sabbath services at a Reform synagogue, the rabbi and cantor greeted me warmly, but I felt momentarily out of place as I sat and observed a completely different service from what I had known—and much of it in Hebrew! As the service proceeded, though, the rabbi, cantor, and congregation chanted words that made me feel right at home: "Hear, O Israel: The Lord is our God, the Lord is One!"

The community that maintained this synagogue welcomed me and taught me about Jewish rituals and holidays. I took classes about Judaism and beginners' courses in Hebrew. Eventually, I went through both Reform and Orthodox ceremonies to convert to Judaism, with my family's blessing. The rabbis helped me to integrate the best of my Christian upbringing with Judaism. I endeavored to be a mensch, a "good person," by not harming others and by doing good.

Yoga

Judaism and its rich philosophy of life might have been sufficient for me, if not for a skiing accident that occurred shortly after my conversion.

While downhill skiing on a snowy winter day, I was suddenly struck from behind by another skier. Having suffered a lower back injury, I was immediately taken to the hospital and placed in pelvic traction. The physicians tried several treatments before recommending back surgery. I confided to a physical therapist my fear that I would end up disabled for life.

"Try yoga," he suggested kindly. "Surgery might cause worse problems. If yoga doesn't work, then have the surgery."

"How can I do yoga when I'm in constant pain and I can't even walk?" I asked tearfully.

"Anyone can benefit from yoga," he replied as he worked on my back, "regardless of physical condition, age, or religious beliefs." He explained that, for centuries, yogis in India have made claims about the health benefits of yoga. Western researchers are now finding that the regular practice of yoga improves body alignment, breathing, circulation, use of the extremities, and mindfulness. The vital organs and endocrine glands begin to work at optimal efficiency. The individual experiences healing and well-being; advanced practitioners achieve a high state of health and self-awareness. The therapist told me about people who have used yoga successfully to heal back injuries and all kinds of other health problems.

I hobbled to a library for information. There I read that yoga, an ancient Indian science, refers to the "union" or "joining together" of the person with the Infinite. Over two thousand years ago, Patanjali systematized yoga into a treatise, *Yoga Sutra,* which is now the authoritative text on this practice. With its unique blend of theoretical knowledge and practical application, yoga consists of eight interconnected limbs—aspects of "the whole"—that lead progressively to higher stages of health, awareness, and spirituality. These limbs are:

1) Universal ethical principles of not stealing, nonviolence, truthfulness, chastity, and noncovetousness.
2) Personal conduct that includes purity, commitment, contentment, self-study, and surrender to the Infinite.
3) Yoga postures.
4) Yoga breathing.
5) Control of the senses.
6) Concentration of the mind.
7) Meditation.
8) Absorption into the Infinite.

What intrigued me most about yoga was the explicit relationship between ethics, spirituality, and healing. According to yoga philosophy, a way to the Infinite can be found through the body; however, we must also behave ethically, or we won't grow spiritually. Our ego lies at the heart of unhappiness, pain, and most diseases, but through the regular practice of yoga, the ego can be made to recede and real healing can take place. The practiced yogi becomes gentle, loving, free from anger, and helpful to others—a state that results in the healing of body, mind, and spirit.

After checking with my physicians, I began a daily regimen of yoga exercises. I ate nutritious foods, slept well, and worked to improve my posture. Eventually, my back healed enough for me to join a yoga class, which was taught by a lively woman. She didn't fit my mental image of a yoga teacher, for she cracked jokes while demonstrating postures, creating a slightly irreverent atmosphere in the class. All the same, she helped me to integrate yoga into my philosophy of life. I soon realized that being a mensch meant more than adhering to the ethical and spiritual guidelines I was learning in Judaism. It required bringing my body, mind, and spirit into harmony—with each other, with other people, and with the Infinite, which is another name for God.

As I practiced yoga, my back pain gradually diminished. My concentration and balance improved, and I became more flexible and relaxed. Even with yoga, though, my back did not recover completely, for my life was too stressful. At a friend's insistence, I turned to the Twelve Steps of Alcoholics Anonymous. Although anonymity is a cornerstone of the Twelve-Step Program, I will break my anonymity here to describe how the Twelve-Step Program became my fourth wisdom tradition.

Twelve-Step Program

My cousin Sara had been descending into alcoholism for several years. As her illness progressed, I discussed her condition with a friend, hoping for advice. "When Sara was two," I confided, "her parents were killed in a car accident, and she moved in with my family. She and I have been like sisters ever since. I think she drinks because she never got over her parents' death. Now, when I try to help her, she pushes me away. She's ruining things for herself, for my parents, and for me!"

"Why don't you come to my support group with me?" my friend asked quietly. "It's for those of us who have family and friends who abuse alcohol and other substances. Our group is based on the Twelve Steps of Alcoholics Anonymous. The meetings are free and convenient."

"I'm not an alcoholic!" I blurted out in shock and anger. "Why should I go to meetings because of *her* problem? It's up to her to fix her own life, and then I'll be fine!"

Several months later, I again sat in my friend's kitchen detailing Sara's latest fiasco. "Tomorrow, I'll pick you up, and you're going with me to a meeting," she said firmly. "Once a week for six weeks in a row. You don't have to say anything at the meetings. If you don't feel better, you can try something else. What do you have to lose?" I didn't want to hurt her feelings, so I agreed, as long as no one would know me there. Having grown up in the preacher's proverbial glass house, I felt ashamed of Sara's behavior and didn't want anyone else to find out she was an alcoholic.

The next day, I followed my friend down a flight of stairs to a well-lit room in the basement of an old hardware store. About a dozen people sat around a large, wooden table laughing and talking excitedly with each other. I forced a smile while trying to hide my shame about being there. *Has my life really come to this?* I wondered resentfully as I sat down at the table.

As it turned out, my friend had signed up to lead the meeting that day. She asked the group to say the Serenity Prayer. All of us stood up and held hands. Then we said in unison:

> God grant me the serenity to accept the things
> I cannot change, courage to change the things
> I can, and wisdom to know the difference.

After we sat down again, she read the Twelve Steps. I noted that the Steps were written in the first person plural, which was comforting, for I no longer felt so alone in my struggle with Sara's alcoholism. "I can only speak for myself," my friend said. "But in my view, the Steps are a prescription for how to become happier and healthier. They don't say how to change anyone else. Most people come here to change another person, but they learn they can only change themselves."

My friend then gave an overview of the Twelve Steps. "Step One asks us to admit our powerlessness over alcohol, or whatever is troubling us, such as a person, emotions, or a job. In Step Two, we admit we aren't behaving sanely, and that we'll only return to sanity by developing harmony with a spiritual Higher Power. We can define Higher Power in any way we want. Step Three asks us to turn our will and life over to this Higher Power.

"Steps Four through Ten," she said, "help us get rid of our guilt, shame, and other negativity. In Steps Four and Five, we take a moral inventory and admit our behavior to our Higher Power, ourselves, and another person. With Steps Six and Seven, we ask our Higher Power to remove our negative behavior. Steps Eight and Nine suggest that we list the individuals we've harmed, including ourselves, and make direct amends without hurting anyone. In Step Ten, we continue to take personal inventory and promptly admit when we're wrong.

"With the last two Steps, we can grow spiritually," she said. "Step Eleven asks us to pray and meditate in order to improve our contact with, and carry out the will of, our Higher Power.

With the help of Step Twelve, we acknowledge the spiritual awakening we're experiencing. We bring this message to others and apply the Steps in our life.

"Each meeting is devoted to a Step," she said. "Today will be Step Eight. It's about making a list of all the persons we've harmed and becoming willing to make amends to them all. When I first came here, I didn't realize how hurtful my actions were. I was preoccupied with what everyone else was doing wrong. This morning, I made a list of people I've harmed, and I'm at the top of the list. That means the first person I'll make amends to is me!"

My friend said she was recovering from codependency, addiction to the alcoholic in her life. She cited the Twelve Step slogans that were most helpful to her: "Easy does it. Take what you can use and leave the rest. Keep it simple. Detach with love. Let go and let God. First things first. Live and let live."

When she finished talking, other members of the group took turns telling their stories. They explained how they were "working the Steps" and creating positive changes in their lives. A newcomer complained bitterly about his alcoholic wife. After allowing him to vent, two "old-timers" helped him to focus on his own behavior, rather than on what his wife was doing wrong.

At first, the Twelve-Step Program seemed simplistic to me. But with time, I came to see that it explicitly addresses the relationship between ethics, spirituality, and healing, though in a different way than yoga does. I could use the Twelve Steps to develop healthy relationships.

This was the element that was missing from, although not in conflict with, my other three wisdom traditions. As I allowed myself to detach, with love, from Sara's behavior and focus on healing my own life, my stress decreased, my serenity increased, and my back recovered.

After I integrated the Twelve Steps into my philosophy of life, my perspective on God began to evolve, too. I no longer viewed

God as a person, but as the Underlying Order or Spirit in the universe. Although I couldn't fully understand, I believed that I was able to experience God personally and to receive guidance. No name did it justice, so for lack of a better term I used words like Infinite, Higher Power, Ultimate Reality, Ultimate Concern, Sacred, and Divine. The way to conduct my life was to live in harmony with this Universal Consciousness, with myself, and with other people.

Bioethics

One evening, not long after my back had healed, I attended a poetry reading for aspiring writers. A handsome, dark-haired man with laughing eyes sat next to me. He introduced himself as Mike. Over the course of the evening he told me he was Jewish, a lawyer, a former philosophy professor, and that he loved music. I was smitten. Afterward, I wrote in my journal, *Tonight I met the love of my life!* Three years later, we were married at my synagogue.

With Mike's encouragement, I fulfilled my dream of attending graduate school to study a fifth wisdom tradition: Western philosophical ethics. I focused on bioethics, which is a branch of ethics involving health. During this time, Mike and I went on long walks together and engaged in lively philosophical discussions. We talked about the three major ethical theories I was learning: principlism, ethical caring, and virtue ethics.

◆　◆　◆

Principlism, which is based on the teachings of Immanuel Kant, John Stuart Mill, and other philosophers, dominates current academic bioethics. This theory states that we should conduct our lives in a manner that is consistent with ethical principles, such as beneficence, justice, autonomy, and truth-telling. For example, beneficence means to avoid inflicting harm or evil, to prevent harm or evil, to remove harm or evil, and to do or promote good. Justice means treating other people as equals in the sense of distributing good and evil equally among them. Autonomy is defined as being self-governing and allowing other people to be self-governing, too. Truth-telling is the same as honesty.

"Here's how we can use principlism to resolve ethical conflict," I said to Mike. "Select the principle we want to use, such as 'always tell the truth,' and apply it to the conflict. Then develop a resolution that not only follows this ethical principle (right action), but also leads to good consequences."

Mike grinned impishly. "If your professor asks whether you like the course, and you don't, should you tell a lie and say that you do?"

"Fortunately, I like the course," I said, chuckling. "But if I didn't, I'd avoid lying about it! I'd find a way to tell the truth that leads to good consequences. That way, I'd take into account the rightness of the action and the goodness of the consequences."

The second major theory I learned was called *ethical caring.* This feminist theory developed, in part, out of a reaction to the abstraction of principlism. We conduct our lives by ethical caring when we act in ways that maintain relationships, and when we affirm and protect the most vulnerable people in our society. From the perspective of ethical caring, the best resolution to ethical conflict accounts for everyone's needs. Behavior is unethical when it breaks bonds among people and sacrifices one person's agenda for another's.

I explained to Mike how ethical caring can be used to resolve ethical conflict. "Consider an ethical problem. Then, think of someone who really cares for you—like me. Let positive emotions flood your mind. Now, try to feel as much as possible what the individuals involved in the ethical problem feel. Work with them to develop a resolution that meets everyone's needs."

"I find that principlism is too objective and impersonal," observed Mike, "and ethical caring is too subjective and personal. If they're combined, though, they can complement each other."

Thanks to the ideas we tossed around in that conversation, I developed my own system of ethics, the "Caring and Justice Ethical Decision-Making Model." This model integrates ethical caring and principlism (justice). To use this model, we analyze ethical conflict first from the perspective of caring, and then from that of justice. Afterward, we develop a resolution that takes into account both perspectives. The combination of the two theories can lead to a better resolution than either theory alone.

Virtue ethics was the third major ethical theory I learned. This theory, developed from the teachings of ancient Greeks—Socrates, Plato, and Aristotle—differs from principlism and ethical caring in its focus on human character. We conduct our lives according to virtue ethics when we develop a virtuous character and we behave virtuously. Virtuous behavior (also called "ethical" or "excellent" behavior) leads to happiness.

Socrates, as described by Plato, asserted that we desire happiness as the ultimate good of everything we do. Aristotle agreed, except to say that we desire happiness as the ultimate good of all our rational behavior. All three philosophers viewed happiness as well-being, or human flourishing, which may not necessarily be the same as pleasure. They believed that if we behave virtuously, we will act with integrity and experience a fulfilled, flourishing, happy life—one that we take to have meaning.

"Principlism, ethical caring, and virtue ethics complement each other," I told Mike. "Combined, they add an essential dimension to my other four wisdom traditions: rationality."

Bolstered by this philosophical background, I conducted two research projects about the experience of ethical problems. The research participants weren't philosophers, and they spoke in everyday language about their conflicts. Their way of resolving conflict was more like virtue ethics than principlism or ethical caring, although they used aspects of both other theories. For example, the participants said they were happier if they behaved ethically than if they didn't.

From the results of these two studies, I developed an ethical decision-making model, "Value, Be, Do: Guidelines for Resolving Ethical Conflict." This model, which brings together principlism, ethical caring, and virtue ethics, is grounded in three questions:

1) What should I value?
2) Who should I be?
3) What should I do?

The first question asks us to identify ethically justifiable values that give life meaning, such as:

- Beneficence (goodness).
- Caring.
- Justice.

The second question focuses on character and integrity by encouraging us to behave in a manner that is consistent with these values.

We would do well to answer the first two questions on an ongoing basis. Then, when we are confronted with ethical conflict, we will have the tools we need to answer the third question. In this way, we can develop a resolution that takes into account our answers to the first two questions and addresses both right action and good consequences.

At this point, I felt I had developed a comprehensive philosophy of life, complete with an ethical decision-making model. I visualized my five wisdom traditions as overlapping circles.

> Christianity gave me the desire for a personal relationship with the Infinite.
>
> Judaism offered detailed ethical and spiritual guidelines.
>
> Yoga reminded me to harmonize my body, mind, and spirit.
>
> The Twelve-Step Program suggested ways to develop healthy relationships.
>
> Bioethics focused on rationality to help me make wise choices.

By conducting my life under the guidance of these wisdom traditions, I could heal, become a mensch, and live with meaning and integrity. This philosophy of life might have been sufficient—if not for a midlife crisis.

Midlife Crisis

While I was finding new balance in my life, Sara kept drinking. As before, she continued to push people away with her addiction. Then she developed cancer, which metastasized despite the latest medical treatments. After a long illness, she died. Her death devastated my family. My parents' health deteriorated. My mother died.

This experience left me depleted—physically, emotionally, and spiritually. Feelings of anger, fear, and loss were overwhelming. As a registered nurse, I was privy to other people's suffering, and now their pain weighed all the more heavily on me. Before, providing nursing care had filled my days with meaning; now I felt an inner void, a vacuum of the spirit. I wanted to listen to my own voice, follow my own vision for how to conduct my life, but all I could hear were audiotapes of my professors' voices, an occupational hazard of graduate school. My comprehensive philosophy of life was no longer sufficient, and I felt confused and dissatisfied. Something important was missing, but I didn't know what.

Psalm 23 in the Bible beckoned me: "The Lord is my shepherd, I shall not want; the Lord makes me lie down in green pastures, leads me beside still waters, and restores my soul."

A still, small voice inside me whispered, *Your academic education, excellent as it was, focused on rationality and knowledge, rather than wisdom. While developing your mind, you've neglected your heart. To be restored, you must go beyond rationality and knowledge and learn about wisdom. Rest, be silent. Look inside, listen, and open your heart.*

I thought of the words of Huston Smith, a philosopher and religious historian. He wrote that Western culture has been nurtured almost exclusively on wisdom traditions arising from Judaism and the ancient Greeks. India's wisdom traditions, he asserted, offer a needed corrective to Western thought.

This analysis described precisely how I felt. I turned to my yoga books for new guidance. They led me to books about Buddhism, Hinduism, Confucianism, and Taoism. Buddhism fascinated me most of all.

"If only we could travel to Tibet and learn about Tibetan Buddhism firsthand," I said to Mike. At the time, we laughed at this pipe dream.

Then, one night, a professor unexpectedly called me from Korea. She invited me to give nine lectures at an international nursing ethics conference in Seoul, and Mike was welcome to accompany me. I accepted without hesitation, and we found ourselves in Asia. During the conference, I became even more painfully aware of the inadequacies in my philosophy of life. My Korean hosts' gracious acceptance of my teaching accentuated my growing recognition of the arrogance of my primarily Western approach. I realized that I needed to incorporate more Eastern wisdom into my philosophy of life and work.

Because we hadn't traveled in the Far East before, we decided to extend our trip beyond Korea. After the conference we flew to Beijing, where we began a month-long tour of China. The tour director turned out to be a Tibetan man named Karma Sakya. Meeting Karma was the first step on my Tibetan odyssey, for his friendship eventually led us on a trip to his homeland. What I would learn from Karma and other Tibetans would bring healing to my life and revitalize my work.

Chapter 2

Buddhism

Karma Sakya

"Next, let's talk about tipping," Karma announced. Mike and I were sitting in a hotel lounge in Beijing, the first city on the itinerary, along with thirty other Americans who were part of the tour group. Karma was telling us about the tour.

Fifty-ish, tall, and muscular, Karma carried himself with dignity. He wore faded blue jeans and a short-sleeved shirt under a sleeveless khaki vest bulging with travel documents. His eyes sparkled when he smiled, which was most of the time. He looked Asian, but he spoke fluent English with a British accent washed with an Indian cadence. I found his accent charming.

"In each city we visit," Karma said, "we'll have a local guide and a bus driver. Tourists—not any of you, of course—often forget to tip them. I suggest we select a treasurer. Then each of us will give that person $3 for every day of the tour. The Honorable Treasurer, in consultation with me, will tip the local guides and drivers." He looked around to see if anyone disagreed with this plan.

"The incentive is the title," Karma continued, and all of us burst out laughing. "Even better, the Honorable Treasurer and partner can sit in the front of the bus behind me all the way through China. The rest of you will rotate seats each day. That way, everyone has the opportunity to sit close to the front. This system has worked well before. Does everyone agree with this plan?" Each of us nodded. "Now, who's willing to be our Honorable Treasurer?"

No one said anything. Karma looked at his notes on a yellow legal pad. Finally, Kathy raised her hand. "I'll do it. Bert and I want to sit in front." The group broke out in applause.

On our previous trips, the tour directors had said little about tipping local guides and bus drivers. "Karma must be an exceptional person," I whispered to Mike, "or else he wants to set a good example so we'll give him a generous tip."

Afterward, Mike and I waited until Karma was alone. "If you don't mind my asking," Mike said to him, "what nationality are you? Chinese?"

Karma looked around to make sure no one was listening, and then spoke softly. "I'm not Chinese. I'm Tibetan. I was born in Tibet. Now I'm an American citizen and live in Michigan."

"Tibet," I said, keeping my voice low. "That's why your name is Karma."

"Yes, Karma is a common Tibetan name," he replied with a grin. "It means the universal law of cause and effect. Good actions lead to happiness, and bad ones to suffering. Evidently, my mother wanted to remind me each day of my life."

Karma chuckled, but then grew serious. "His Holiness, the eleventh Dalai Lama, came from my family. We were part of the aristocracy in Old Tibet. If the Chinese hadn't taken over, I'd have started out as a general in the Tibetan army."

"How did you get from Tibet to the U.S.?" Mike asked.

"My family had to leave Tibet in 1959," Karma said sadly. "That's when the Chinese took over Tibet and His Holiness the Fourteenth Dalai Lama went into exile. I was educated in India. Ten years ago, I moved with my family to the States, where we've been living ever since. The Chinese call their invasion a "liberation," but it was really genocide. Now there are less than six million Tibetans left in the world." He paused to reflect on his words. "I don't blame the Chinese people . . . it's their leaders who are at fault!"

"I've never understood why China annexed Tibet," said Mike.

"Land, mineral resources, power, and strategic position," Karma replied. "Tibet can provide living space for some of China's millions. Beijing makes money from our water, wildlife, minerals, and timber. And by controlling the highest point on earth, China exerts power and intimidates its neighbors."

"But hasn't China modernized Tibet?" I asked.

"Any benefits the Chinese bring aren't worth the terrible price Tibetans pay." He was about to elaborate when a Chinese man in a dark suit edged toward us. Karma noticed him and proclaimed loudly, "It'll be busy tomorrow, so we'd better get some sleep." He shook our hands and hurried to the elevators.

The days that followed were so packed that Mike and I didn't have another opportunity to talk with Karma alone. His disturbing words about Tibet receded in our minds. Despite the authoritarian government officials we encountered, the Chinese people charmed us, and we bought Chinese art to take home.

Throughout these busy days of the tour, we developed admiration and affection for Karma. He treated everyone, Chinese and Caucasian, with compassion—even Lou, a member of our travel group whom we had tried to befriend because he seemed lonely. Lou soon alienated us and everyone else by picking fights, yelling angrily, and then boasting about how successful he was back home. He purchased goods compulsively wherever we stopped, and then demanded that Karma carry them for him. Because he couldn't walk fast, everyone had to wait for him, which put the group consistently behind schedule.

When Karma saw how disruptive Lou was, he began to engage him in conversations, strategically keeping him from arguing with anyone else. He sat by Lou at meals, even though Lou was a messy eater. If Lou bought something, Karma offered to carry it, and he walked beside Lou in order to hurry him along.

In Hong Kong, the final city on the tour, Mike and I invited Karma to an Indian restaurant to thank him for everything he had done on the trip. "You were a lot kinder to Lou than I was," said Mike. "How were you able to do that? He treated you like a pack animal!"

"I'm a Buddhist," said Karma, scooping up dal with a piece of naan bread. "In our religion, we're taught to be compassionate. Lou is about the same age my father would have been, had he lived. I wasn't able to do much for my father, so perhaps I did something for Lou."

"I'd like to learn more about Buddhism and Tibet," I said. "Do you have any suggestions?"

"You and Mike could travel to Tibet with me," Karma replied, his eyes sparkling at the thought. "I'm planning to visit my family in Tibet next year, and I'll take along some of my American friends. His Holiness the Dalai Lama encourages tourists to visit Tibet, even though it brings money to the Chinese government. Tourists may not pick up on everything that's happening politically, but they see enough to go home and tell others. We need you to help us."

I looked at Mike, and he nodded. Karma was offering us an extraordinary opportunity to learn about an ancient culture firsthand, from a member of that culture who spoke English. And we could help his people, too. "Let us know when you go," I told Karma, "so we can travel with you."

A few weeks later, Karma sent us a letter about the trip to Tibet. Our travel group would meet in Bangkok, on the coast of Thailand, then fly to Kathmandu, Nepal, at over 4,000 feet above sea level. We'd board a bus for a spectacular ride through the Himalayan Mountains to Lhasa, Tibet. The road would go near Mount Everest, and the altitude would vary from 12,000 to 17,500 feet. After leaving Lhasa, we'd take a ferry to Samye Monastery and drive by bus to Tsetang. Finally, we'd fly from Tibet's only commercial airport to Chengdu,

China, and then back to the United States via Hong Kong. By traveling in the spring, we'd avoid the summer rainy season and winter snowstorms.

Mike and I called Karma to accept his invitation. He seemed deeply moved by our interest in Tibet. "Thanks for helping Tibetans," he said in a husky voice.

Dorje Rinpoche

"Dorje Rinpoche is in Minneapolis!" Karma announced over the phone a week later. "You still want to learn about Buddhism? Well, Rinpoche is the best teacher, other than His Holiness. He'll only stay in your area long enough to get medical treatment for a kidney disorder. Evidently, he's using a combination of Western medicine and traditional Tibetan medicine. Then he'll go back to India."

In the course of our conversation, I asked what *rinpoche* means. Karma replied, "Literally, it means 'precious one.' It's the respectful title Tibetans use for incarnate lamas and other great teachers. A lama is a highly respected religious teacher or elder, the Tibetan equivalent of a guru."

The next evening, Mike and I drove to a fourplex to attend Rinpoche's teachings. We knocked on the door of the apartment. *"Tashi delek,"* a Tibetan woman said. "That's 'welcome' in Tibetan." She gave each of us a white ceremonial scarf, called a *kata,* and asked us to offer them to Rinpoche as a sign of respect. Following her gesture, we took off our shoes and entered the living room. A brass Buddha dominated the room from a colorful altar, in front of which sat Tibetans and Caucasians on the carpeted floor. Evidently they had been studying with Rinpoche for a while, because they knew each other. I sat down with them, while Mike chose a chair in back.

A few minutes after we arrived, a man wearing the maroon and saffron robes of a Tibetan Buddhist monk walked into the room. The Tibetan woman motioned for me to offer my *kata* to him. He accepted, then draped it across my shoulders and tied an orange cord loosely around my neck "for protection." Mike offered his *kata,* and Rinpoche did the same for him. Rinpoche then sat down cross-legged on the sofa. From my position on the floor, he seemed like a majestic mountain towering above us. He looked around the room with eyes full of sorrow. My heart went out to him, and I wanted to put my arms around him and comfort him as a mother comforts her child.

With the Tibetan woman translating, Rinpoche introduced himself to Mike and me. He said he was born to a poor family in eastern Tibet, a beautiful place with mountains, wild flowers, and peaceful animals. At age four he was declared a *rinpoche*, so he happily left his family and went to study at the local monastery. Before the Chinese could kidnap him in 1956, his teachers sent him to a Lhasa monastery, where he studied with great lamas. In 1959, he followed His Holiness into exile. He continued his Buddhist studies and was granted the Geshe degree, the equivalent of a PhD. Since then, he has been the abbot of a monastery in India. When the Chinese authorities loosened travel restrictions, he traveled to Tibet to see his family. He learned that his parents had died during the Cultural Revolution in the 1960s. Although things are better now, he concluded, life is still hard for his siblings in Tibet.

My eyes clouded with tears. "How do you deal with your anger and grief?" I asked.

He answered slowly, picking his words carefully. "Sadness, yes. Many losses. Anger, no. Root out anger. Anger is negative and destructive. No anger at Chinese. Chinese people aren't bad. Their officials are the destroyers. They treat their own people as harshly as they treat Tibetans. Now tell me, why did the two of you come tonight?"

"I practice family law," Mike said, "and I deal with many angry people. I feel like my spirit is tarnished. How can I purify it?"

Rinpoche chuckled. "Notice when you feel angry," he said. "What is its root? Anger makes us sick. You can figure out how to stop anger." He went on to describe dharma (Buddhist teachings) as medicine for anger and other diseases of the mind. "Slowly you will understand. Then you will be able to transform the way you think and behave as a lawyer."

Rinpoche then turned to me. "I'd like to develop my spiritual practice," I said.

"True understanding of spiritual practice takes a very long time, over many lifetimes." He looked wistfully into my eyes. "Spiritual practice brings about change in your body, your mind, your speech. The most important of these is your mind. Your body and speech are servants of your mind. Buddhism means following the Buddha, not the monks or nuns. It isn't believing in images, nor is it praying at a wonderful altar. The point of Buddhism is to change your thinking to become more compassionate—to transform your mind. It's not easy."

"To whom do Buddhists pray?" I asked.

Rinpoche paused before answering. "The more you engage in spiritual practice, the more you will understand to whom you pray, and how to pray. The more you study, the more value the teachings have."

He turned to the class and said, "Dharma can be taught, but we must be open to it." He recounted the ancient analogy of the "three pots," which describes the faults that keep us from listening. If we are close-minded and confused, our behavior makes us like an upside-down pot, so that we cannot receive dharma. Carelessness and disrespect make us like a leaky pot, so that however earnestly we try, we can't remember dharma as it is taught to us. When we harbor resentment and hurt, we resemble a pot containing poison— we reinterpret dharma to suit our tainted purposes, and this in turn taints dharma.

Rinpoche explained that to make our pots whole, upright, and filled with good—in other words, to make fitting use of dharma—we must develop six recognitions:

1) We are sick because of desire, anger, fear, jealousy, or other negatives.
2) Dharma is the medicine that will heal us.
3) The teacher is the doctor.
4) The members of the *sangha* (the Buddhist community) are nurses.
5) The Buddha's teachings have so far proven to be reliable.
6) It is important that dharma flourishes for a long time.

Someone in the gathering asked if we must take dharma on faith. "Buddhism has nothing to do with blind faith," Rinpoche said. "It's okay to admit that you're full of doubt. Just accept who you are and what you're thinking and feeling. Go ahead and examine the teachings. When they don't make sense, set them aside. At a later time, you can reexamine them. Perhaps then they will make sense to you."

As we drove home after class, Mike appeared uneasy. "I'm uncomfortable with Buddhist deities," he said at last.

"I was thinking the same thing," I said. "How can a person follow Buddhism and still stay true to the biblical commandment to have no other gods before God? Maybe there's an answer in the Twelve-Step slogan, 'Take what you can use and leave the rest.' Learning about Buddhism doesn't mean leaving Judaism behind anymore than studying bioethics or doing yoga does. We're only embracing a larger perspective!"

Mike laughed, but then he grew serious. "There is the problem of assimilation, though. When you integrate wisdom traditions, you may end up diluting the faith you started out with. That's an ethical problem: how to stay true to a tradition, like Judaism, and be open to other traditions at the same time. Jews have survived five thousand years because of their resistance to assimilation. I'd like to find out if there's a way to stay Jewish, but still incorporate ideas from Buddhism."

From then on I viewed Buddhist deities not as gods, but as aspects of the human mind. Some Buddhist deities depict anger, fear, jealousy, and cunning, while others illustrate compassion and wisdom. By meditating on these deities, I could recognize my own negativity and replace it with positive behavior.

The Four Noble Truths

For six months, Mike and I attended Rinpoche's weekly teachings. Rinpoche told about Prince Siddhartha Gautama, who lived in luxury during the sixth century B.C.E. in what is now a border village between India and Nepal. As I listened, I noted that the prince was a contemporary of Socrates, Plato, Aristotle, and the Hebrew prophet Ezekiel. Rejecting his royal position, the prince resolved to find a way out of universal suffering. After six years of wandering around as a holy man, he concluded that asceticism doesn't lead to freedom from suffering. He became enlightened while meditating under a *bodhi* tree. From then on, his followers called him "Sakyamuni Buddha," the Enlightened One. Until his death forty-five years later, he shared his teachings with women and men of all classes. When asked if he was a god, a saint, or an angel, he replied, "No, I am awake."

"The Buddha taught that everyone seeks to be happy and to avoid suffering," Rinpoche said. "I think happiness is the very purpose of life. The Buddha viewed happiness as a lasting, blissful state. That's not the same as temporary pleasure from sensory experience, like eating a good meal. Our mental attitude is the most important factor in developing a happy life."

Rinpoche explained that suffering doesn't just result from natural disasters and physical pain, but also from mental dissatisfaction and agitation. We bring suffering upon ourselves when we
engage in negative thinking. This, in turn, can lead to behaviors
that are harmful and unethical. The more negative we become, the
more we suffer, for we fail to understand the effects of our actions
on other people and ourselves. We may try to hurt someone who
has hurt us, thinking that this will bring satisfaction and relieve
our pain; later, though, a feeling of unease comes, producing more
negative behavior and taking away our peace of mind.

"Because each of us is a composite whole," said Rinpoche,
"happiness results from a healthy body, mind, and spirit. We can
aspire to more than just health, however, for we have the potential to experience an advanced level of health and to become
enlightened, a state called nirvana. An enlightened person is
happy, wise, compassionate, and completely conscious of being
interconnected with all sentient beings. Through his Four Noble
Truths, the Buddha explained how we can escape suffering and
develop this kind of lasting happiness and enlightenment.

"The First Noble Truth states that life inevitably consists of
suffering, called *dukkha,*" said Rinpoche. "No matter who we
are, we feel pervasive dissatisfaction and unrest. Illness, loss,
aging, disappointment, and death clash with our fantasies of
self-sufficiency, freedom, and immortality. The hard fact is, we
can't get what we think we want, and we're stuck with what we
don't want. Estranged from our happy, enlightened buddha
nature, we don't know who we are. The First Noble Truth asks
us to acknowledge our experience of *dukkha,* the pangs of life we
try to ignore by covering them up with distractions.

"The Second Noble Truth asserts that suffering arises from
our craving or attachment," Rinpoche continued. "Attachment
to ourselves, to other people, and to material things, all of
which are, by nature, impermanent." We try to make our
world, our possessions, all the things we love, concrete and

substantial—but they are only temporary. Defining ourselves by our fleeting feelings and attitudes, we spend precious energy defending this self that doesn't actually exist. Because we see everything through the prism of the self, we crave sensual pleasures that ultimately become addictive, thereby perpetuating the dissatisfaction that we want these addictions to cure.

"The Second Noble Truth recognizes our frustration," said Rinpoche. "We have an insatiable desire for certainty and permanence. We are like a man who has been wounded by an arrow, but who nevertheless craves concrete answers. When people ask to remove the arrow and treat his wound, the man first demands to know who shot the arrow and what kind of bow and arrow were used. He won't let anyone help him until all his questions are answered. Because he delays treatment, he dies from his wound.

"The Third Noble Truth teaches how we can release ourselves from *dukkha* by developing an enlightened mind. In this way, we become fully awake and unhampered by confused subjectivity. We realize that the world, as interpreted by our senses, is devoid of any intrinsic reality, and that ideas and decisions resulting from our senses lack real meaning or a solid foundation. By acknowledging our cravings, we stop attributing a false solidity to anyone or anything, and our fleeting emotions no longer comprise our reality.

"The Fourth Noble Truth explains that by following the Buddha's Middle Way, we can liberate ourselves from suffering and develop an enlightened mind." This middle road avoids the extremes of self-indulgence and self-mortification. Rinpoche elaborated further: "Meditation and ethics are the means to help us. The mind is like a wild horse that needs training. An untamed mind leaves the path and indulges in negative action. Meditation and ethics restrain the mind so it becomes virtuous and thereby follows a virtuous path.

"Through meditation," he said, "we transform our mind. We decrease our cravings—all of our negative emotions—and in their place we promote the positive. As our compassion grows, turmoil disappears. Wisdom replaces confusion. Equanimity takes the place of jealousy. We develop mindfulness, the ability to attend to the moment-by-moment nature of the mind. Mindfulness leads to selflessness, or emptiness.

"We can also transform the mind by behaving ethically. Ethical behavior protects us from the craziness surrounding unethical actions. Again, it is through proper education and training that we learn to live ethically, and thanks to this education we are more likely to stay the course . . . if we surround ourselves with virtuous people."

The Buddha's method of ethical behavior can be broken down even further into what Rinpoche called the Eightfold Path of Ethics, a system that helps us come to the virtuous path leading toward enlightenment. This path consists of:

1) Right knowledge—We realize that we suffer, and that the cure is contained in the Four Noble Truths.
2) Right aspiration—We stop behaving in ways that cause suffering for other people and ourselves, and we single-mindedly seek liberation.
3) Right speech—We speak truthfully and with compassion, and we avoid false witness, idle chatter, gossip, slander, and abuse.
4) Right behavior—We shun violence, and we do not steal, lie, behave in an unchaste manner, take drugs, or drink intoxicants.
5) Right livelihood—We work in occupations that promote, not hinder, our ethical, spiritual progress.
6) Right effort—We persevere according to the tenets of Buddhism.
7) Right mindfulness—We become fully awake and see things as they really are.
8) Right absorption—We devote ourselves to spiritual practice and ethical living.

When we live by the Four Noble Truths, Rinpoche said, we see more clearly, and we stop taking ourselves so seriously. We find a safe home, a refuge, in the Three Jewels: Buddha, dharma, and *sangha* (the Buddhist community). As we transform our thinking, we uncover the peace and goodness of our buddha nature, and we feel at one with the cosmos. Because our mind is balanced, we don't experience conflicts within or between our outer, inner, and secret levels. We are open to whatever happens; we do not withdraw into ourselves or isolate ourselves. Our suffering diminishes. Radiating compassion and wisdom, we devote our lives to helping free all living beings from *dukkha*.

"The term *buddha*," Rinpoche said, "refers to the historical Indian prince, a human being. Buddhists are individuals who follow his teachings. *Buddha* has a deeper meaning, though. It refers to any person who has completely awakened from ignorance, has opened to the vast potential of wisdom. A buddha has brought a final end to her or his suffering and has discovered lasting happiness."

Karma and Ethics

"Are you ready to hear about the Doctrine of Karma?" Rinpoche asked the class one evening. He was beaming, and I figured his health was improving and he was feeling better. I moved to sit closer so I could feel the kindness emanating from him.

"The Doctrine of Karma underlies the Four Noble Truths," he said. "*Karma* is a term from Sanskrit. What does it mean? Predestination? Fate? No, karma means that an action always produces a result, which in turn leads to another result. There is cause and effect in everything we do, for all matter in the universe is interrelated. Karma is not independent energy that predestines the course of our life. It isn't similar to the notion of 'fate.' We aren't powerless over what happens to us. No, we create our own karma by what we think, say, and do . . . and also by what we fail to do."

Rinpoche explained that we develop good or bad karma depending on how we behave. To produce good karma, we must behave in a manner that is positive, compassionate, right, virtuous, and ethical—all of which are synonyms. In short, we are bidden to help one another. And if we can't help, we at least must avoid doing harm. Bad karma results from actions that are wrong, negative, or lacking in compassion, virtue, or ethics. When we engage in bad action, we behave hurtfully. An obvious corollary to this idea is that positive thoughts and emotions lead to positive behavior, while negative ones cause us to hurt each other and ourselves.

"Good karma produces happiness," he continued, "but bad karma leads to suffering. Happiness and suffering aren't accidental. They result from the choices we make about how to behave. Because of karma, my every thought, word, and deed affect not only me, but you as well. That's why my interest and your interest are intimately and inextricably connected."

He explained that the way to be happy is to purify the bad karma in our lives by replacing it with good karma. This means looking deep within, connecting with our ethical and spiritual values, and filling our lives with the by-products of happiness— love, kindness, compassion, altruism, joy, patience, tolerance, forgiveness, humility, contentment, responsibility, and peace of mind. Through discipline, we habituate ourselves to these behaviors; our relationships become smooth and we feel valued. We experience a sense of tranquillity that's unaffected by adverse circumstances. We are, in fact, happy.

"But how can Tibetans believe in karma?" I asked. "You've lost your country, your culture is under the threat of being wiped out. I can't accept that Tibetans are suffering because of behaving unethically!"

"Tibetans have come close to losing everything," said Rinpoche, "but we have endured. The thirteenth Dalai Lama told us to follow Buddhism. We ignored his advice, and Tibet has become a land of beggars. Now we follow the Buddhist path again, and our faith is strengthened. We place our hope in Buddhism and in the guidance of His Holiness the Fourteenth Dalai Lama. Perhaps China invaded Tibet and we have been dispersed so that we can bring Buddhism to the world."

"After all," I said, "if it weren't for the Tibetan Diaspora, you wouldn't be here to teach us about Buddhism. I'm still sorry about your suffering, all the same."

"Tibetans look at the big picture," he replied, a smile starting to cross his face. "If we develop good karma, we will experience a good rebirth. The Buddha taught that we are born again and again in an endless, wearying cycle called samsara. We are affected by the karma we have developed over many lifetimes. That's why I am the accumulation of all my behavior, and you are the accumulation of all your behavior. Because of reincarnation, you and I have met and exchanged ideas many times. We'll go on interacting for many more lifetimes. Consequentially, our responsibility to each other has no end and no beginning.

"If we view life in this way," he continued, "the world can become a better place through our determination to make it so. Then the kind of atrocities that are occurring in Tibet won't take place anymore. Each of us endeavors to become a bodhisattva, a highly accomplished spiritual practitioner who has attained enlightenment. Bodhisattvas can liberate the world from suffering, for such persons are gentle and not abusive. They lack deceit and fraudulent thoughts, and are full of love toward all living beings.

"Let's each take responsibility for how our behavior affects ourselves, others, and society," Rinpoche said, looking around the class with affection. "Individuals who lack faith in karmic actions will not behave ethically, even if society imposes rigid laws and strict enforcement. If more people believed in karma, police and prisons wouldn't be needed. The way to produce a happier world is if each of us develops an internal code of ethics and practices universal compassion."

With these words, Rinpoche concluded the lesson. The class dispersed into the night.

When we got home, Mike said to me, "I liked what Rinpoche said until he started talking about reincarnation. Then he lost me."

"Reincarnation makes more sense to me than the heaven and hell I learned about as a child," I said. "When a leaf dies, its energy becomes something else. Maybe our energy turns into something else when we die, too. Reincarnation may mean our energy or consciousness lives on after death, not that we as specific individuals are born repeatedly."

"Reincarnation is too big a leap for me," protested Mike.

"British philosopher John Locke wrote about the problem of choosing 'the right beliefs,'" I said. "Because no one knows for sure what truth is, we might as well select beliefs that comfort us. I'm not sure if I believe in reincarnation, but it's comforting for me. The idea that Sara and Mom don't exist anymore seems depressing, or that you and I will cease to exist after we die. I like to think of us as ocean waves—a wave rises for a moment, breaks on the shore, and then it's gone. In a sense, we could say that a single, identifiable wave has run its course. But the wave is part of the ocean, and when the wave disappears, the ocean remains. In the same way, each of us has a separate identity, but we're part of something larger."

"That's fine for you if you want, but I'm having trouble," said Mike. "Fortunately, it seems I don't need to believe in reincarnation to benefit from Buddhism."

Other Buddhist Teachings

"This is our last class," Rinpoche said one warm spring evening. "I am going back to India tomorrow. If you come visit me, we'll continue the teachings there. Tonight I will cover a variety of topics we haven't discussed yet. I'll only have time to 'scratch the

surface,' as you say in America. That means you'll need to keep
studying after I leave." He laughed cheerily, and the rest of us
did, too. I felt sad about him leaving, but I was pleased that he
was healthy enough to return to his monastery.

"Buddhism does not advocate belief in an external
creator-god," Rinpoche said. "The mind creates itself according
to the Doctrine of Karma. The essence of the mind—what makes
it and what sustains it—is its interconnection with all living
beings in the universe. Because of this perspective, many people
don't see Buddhism as a formal religion at all. They think of it
as a philosophy, as psychology, or as an ethical, spiritual discipline. Buddhism can be followed by itself, or it can be combined
with other wisdom traditions."

Even if it is not strictly a religion, Buddhism has developed
extensive teachings about dying and what happens after death.
Buddhism encourages being mindful and conscious while dying.
To die well, we must live well. If we meditate and behave ethically, we will be able to face death with peace, confidence, and
even joy, rather than with fear and remorse. An accomplished
meditator views death as an opportunity to gain spiritual realization and a good rebirth.

Another aspect of Buddhism's flexibility is the number of
interpretations that exist simultaneously. Two major branches are
Theravada Buddhism, found mostly in Southeast Asia, and
Mahayana Buddhism, which spread throughout Tibet, Korea,
China, and Japan over the past millennia. Theravada may be
closest to the Buddha's actual teachings, while Mahayana has sev-
eral schools, some of which are familiar to westerners: *Ch'an,* or
Zen, developed in China and Japan, and Vajrayana, or Tantric
Buddhism, developed in Tibet.

Tibetan Buddhism encourages intensive spiritual practice to
produce a clear mind, good heart, and enlightenment in one
lifetime. Tibetan lamas have identified several hundred thousand operations of the mind, and they have developed methods

for understanding the nature of being. When a great spiritual practitioner dies, Tibetans use meditation, dreams, and portents to locate a gifted child who is believed to be the lama's next incarnation. They groom the child to resume the deceased person's duties. In Old Tibet, the search for a new Dalai Lama, the highest lama, used to take on political ramifications, for he was both the spiritual and secular head of state.

"Recently, Buddhism has been moving to, and becoming influenced by, the West," he said. "I think you westerners turn to Buddhism for several reasons. You view Western healthcare and wisdom traditions as being incomplete. You hope to use Buddhist thought to open your heart, to experience beauty, to still the mind. You want to become replenished, control pain, heal yourselves, and face death."

The Sixth Wisdom Tradition

After bidding Rinpoche an emotional farewell, Mike and I drove home. "I'm amazed at the similarities between Buddhism and my other wisdom traditions," I said. "Each tradition has an ethical, spiritual basis and offers a way for us to conduct our lives well."

"Aren't you glossing over their major differences?" asked Mike.

"Maybe I am," I answered, "but aren't you intrigued by their shared vision?"

We talked about how Buddhism helped us to clarify Aristotle's two kinds of thinking: contemplative reasoning (which Buddhism calls *meditation*) and calculative reasoning (rationality). Both the Buddha and Aristotle advocate contemplative reasoning when pieces of information are missing, which is most of the time. In this case, we need to access our internal wisdom to figure out what to do about the situation. In contrast, calculative reasoning helps us when we have all the pieces of the puzzle and we'd like to figure out a way to put them together. Without contemplative reasoning, our calculative reasoning may be blind.

When we're in a contemplative frame of mind, we live happily in the moment. Constant thoughts may be going through our mind, but we give them little attention. If we are engaged in calculative reasoning, though, we are thinking about the past or future and paying close attention to our thoughts.

Buddhism teaches that we're happier if we maintain a mindset of contemplative reasoning and only revert to calculative reasoning when necessary. Aristotle wrote little about how to engage in contemplative reasoning, whereas Buddhism has developed extensive knowledge regarding meditation.

◆ ◆ ◆

That night, I lay in bed thinking about Rinpoche's teachings. Buddhism offered a comprehensive philosophy and psychology about ethics, spirituality, and healing. The Four Noble Truths shed light on how to deal with negativity and turn suffering into happiness. The Doctrine of Karma provided a compelling reason to behave ethically.

Buddhism was opening my heart and counteracting my excessive reliance on rationality. Through Buddhism, I might even come to appreciate death. These strengths made up for what seemed to be missing in my other wisdom traditions. Buddhism, I realized, was becoming my sixth wisdom tradition. As author Jack Kornfield would put it, Buddhism was a path with heart.

My interest in Buddhism grew, though now we had no formal classes to attend. Mike and I both missed Rinpoche's teachings. A few weeks after his departure, some friends from the class told us that a Tibetan Buddhist monk would speak at a local college, so we went to hear him. But instead of providing more insight into my new wisdom tradition, his lecture raised ethical problems.

Chapter 3

Ethical Problems

Should We Put Ourselves in Danger?

Mike and I walked into the lecture hall where the monk was to give his talk.

"Tashi delek," said a Tibetan man clad in a fur hat and leather boots as he greeted us with a handshake. "I'm Lobsang."

He wore a beige robe belted at the waist. Several women in the room behind him were wearing a female version of this attire, which consisted of a long, sleeveless dress over a silk or cotton blouse. Later we learned the dress was called a *chupa* and that women who wore an apron were married. Each apron's design indicated the region in Tibet from which the woman came.

As the room filled with people, we slipped past monks in maroon and saffron robes to seats near the front.

Lobsang stepped to the microphone at the front of the room. "Tibetans are becoming American citizens. We are bringing our families here from refugee camps in India and Nepal. To those of you who are helping us, thanks." Then he introduced the speaker. A thin, gaunt monk with a twisted back and sorrowful eyes came up to the microphone. He spoke in Tibetan, and Lobsang translated into English.

"My name is Jampa Topgyal," the monk said. "I became a Buddhist monk when I was ten. When the Chinese invaded Tibet in 1959, I was twenty-nine years old. The Chinese arrested me for putting up posters saying that Tibet is an independent country. Because of this crime, I spent thirty-three years in Chinese prisons and labor camps in Tibet."

Jampa Topgyal shared some of the details of his life in prison. He said that the Chinese guards wanted to see who would survive and who would die. In the name of this "curiosity," they repeatedly tortured and humiliated the prisoners. They would tie rope around the prisoners' necks and pull back their arms, dislocating shoulders and elbows. The guards would lash the prisoners to beams and beat them with metal pipes and wooden boards studded with nails, until the prisoners could no longer control their bodily functions. In the summer's heat, the guards dangled the prisoners above a fire, or they dripped boiling water onto the prisoners' naked bodies in the cold of winter. The prisoners were yoked to plows and forced to till prison lands. Because they were given only a cup of soup a day, they stayed alive by eating leather, grass, bones, mice, worms, insects, and, on rare and fortunate occasions, food that was meant for pigs.

Jampa Topgyal told how the guards knocked out all his teeth and beat his head so he became deaf in one ear. They split his tongue with a cattle prod, broke his nose with metal pipes, and tried to rip out his eyes. He showed us scars on his wrists from self-tightening handcuffs and rope burns on his neck and arms. His arms could no longer extend. When he was released from prison in 1992, he bribed the guards to give him some of their instruments of torture. Then he fled to India, taking these instruments with him. He held them up for us to see, but I could only look away in disgust.

"One thing they could not take from me," he said. "My belief in human rights. As my experience shows, some people still don't understand the importance of human rights, the honor of being a human being." He put his hand over his heart. "It's a pain I can never forget, even if I wanted to. I received no medical treatment. I cry every day when I think about it. The memory of what I witnessed will burn inside me forever." His eyes brimmed with tears, and so did mine.

When Jampa Topgyal sat down, Lobsang told us that about three hundred thousand Chinese soldiers are stationed in Tibet, and that they use many excuses to arrest and imprison Tibetans. For example, Chinese officials ordered that all photos of the Dalai Lama be removed from every public place and private home. Recently, Chinese work teams raided Chamdo Monastery to look for such photos. When they found pro-independence leaflets during the raid, they arrested three monks. One of them died after severe beatings and torture with electric shock; the other two are in prison. More than five hundred monks were expelled from the monastery after the discovery of the leaflets.

After the lecture, we asked Lobsang and Jampa Topgyal if traveling in Tibet would be dangerous for us. Jampa Topgyal said Tibetans might seek us out to tell their story, an act that could be very dangerous for them. It probably wouldn't be dangerous for us, though, because the Chinese want tourist dollars and would be careful not to scare away visitors. If the Chinese found us carrying photos of the Dalai Lama, or if we gave a picture of the Dalai Lama to a Tibetan, that person could end up in prison . . . and so could we.

"An American couple visiting Tashilhunpo Monastery asked a monk about religious discrimination in Tibet," said Lobsang. "The monk said there wasn't any, so the couple felt safe and placed a photo of His Holiness on an altar. The monk wasn't really a monk, but a spy. He removed his monk's robe and arrested them."

"We won't carry pictures of the Dalai Lama," Mike assured them.

"If you talk politics with Tibetans," warned Lobsang, "they can get twenty years in prison for mentioning Tibetan independence.

It's a 'counter-revolutionary crime.' You may think that if you participate in political protests, this will keep Tibetans from being arrested, but they'll be arrested anyway, and you will, too, in all likelihood. There are regular protests in Lhasa, but they usually consist of a few monks or nuns waving flags, and the police quickly round them up. There were larger protests in the late 1980s. At one of these, Chinese soldiers fired live bullets into the crowd and hit a tourist. She thought her presence would keep the soldiers from shooting the demonstrators."

"Maybe a trip to Tibet is too dangerous," I said, feeling increasingly alarmed.

"No, go. Enjoy," said Lobsang. "Regulations are posted in Lhasa. They forbid anyone from joining in or even watching protests. As long as you keep alert, you probably won't be in any danger. The Chinese don't want tourists to go home and speak ill of them, and Tibetans don't want to harm their only witnesses. Foreign journalists aren't allowed in Tibet, so only tourists can bear witness to what is actually happening."

Back home, we called Karma to ask if our trip to his home country would be dangerous. He said the Chinese government controlled Tibet so tightly that we probably wouldn't see any violence, and besides, he'd take good care of us.

Should We Criticize China?

As we were preparing for the trip, Mike and I drove to a park for a celebration of the fourteenth Dalai Lama's birthday on July 6. We walked into the pavilion carrying a salad for the potluck dinner. A smiling Tibetan woman in a *chupa* said *"Tashi delek"* and put the salad on a table crowded with food. She motioned for us to go back outside where Tibetans were already gathering.

Local monks from a newly established Tibetan Buddhist monastery sat down on the grass and began chanting and burning incense. Everyone else sat down near them and picked up the chant. Someone passed around a dish of *tsampa* (roasted barley flour) and each person took a pinch. Everyone stood up and, with laughter, threw the *tsampa* into the air. "For good luck," a woman told me.

Then everyone walked into the pavilion to an altar decorated with a Buddhist scroll painting, called a *thangka,* and a photo of the Dalai Lama. They took turns placing a *kata* on the altar and prostrating themselves three times. Afterward, everyone sat down on Tibetan rugs on the floor, and a man put a *kata* around the neck of each newly elected local Tibetan leader. Women and men passed out bowls of sweetened rice with raisins, meant to be eaten with the fingers, and cups of *chai,* tea infused with sugar, milk, and spices.

After this ceremonial, Tibetan dancers, each wearing a *chupa* and a traditional mask, formed a circle that rotated clockwise as they and the audience sang. A man beat a Tibetan drum, while two men played Tibetan instruments that looked like a flute and a guitar. The meditative music, drumbeat, and dance steps reminded me of a Native American powwow, and I felt mesmerized. "Our American friends eat first," a man announced. "Thanks for helping Tibetans." Tables were laden with Tibetan, Indian, Nepalese, and American food.

When we returned home, we discovered a journal sent to us in the mail by Mike's mother. She is an "old-style leftist" and an unshakable admirer of Chairman Mao. The journal, published by the Chinese government, included an article declaring that the Tibetans are grateful to China for liberating them from the Dalai Lama's human rights abuses and feudal system.

"Unbelievable!" I said, angry on behalf of the Tibetans we had just met. "How can the Chinese government get away with publishing this rubbish? Who believes this?"

"We could try writing the journal to protest," Mike said, "but do we know enough about Tibet?"

"Probably not," I said, slowly cooling down. "This isn't anything new, really. Conquerors have always imposed their values on the people they conquer. So in the name of what the victors call 'progress,' indigenous people disappear. Is it right for us to criticize China when the United States and other countries have mistreated native people, too? Can we honestly say that our country isn't still mistreating native people?"

"I'm bothered about spending money in Tibet when it's only going to benefit the Chinese," said Mike. "But, Karma did tell us that we'll use Tibetan facilities as much as possible. And the Dalai Lama teaches that Tibetans' struggle is not anti-Chinese, but pro-justice. Let's focus on justice, not on criticizing China."

Why Help Tibetans, or Anyone Else?

As we became acquainted with Tibetans and their Caucasian friends, we wondered if we should take an active role in working for the Tibetans' cause. This came up one day when I was having lunch with a friend. "I want to help Tibetans," I told her, "but I don't make policies for the United States, and I have limited resources. I can't devote all of my time, energy, or money to this cause. The more I give to others, the less I have for my own family, friends, career. Why should I take responsibility for Tibetans, or anyone else?"

"I don't help anyone I don't know!" my friend burst out. "I do my best to make a good living. I care for my husband and daughter, and I'm there for my friends when they need me. But I don't have time or energy for anyone else. Most of my family died in the Holocaust, so I rely on friends to be my family. If I need something, my friends help me, and I help them when they're in need. Will Tibetans be there for you? Probably not!"

"I don't help other people to get something from them," I said, shocked at her reaction. Perhaps the bitterness of losing her family to the Nazis' destruction had colored her views.

She went on. "I used to volunteer, but I got burned when someone cheated me out of money," she explained. "Now I don't do any volunteer work at all. If something's worthwhile, someone will pay me to do it!"

"I'm learning a lot from Tibetans," I replied, trying to present a more positive picture of altruism. "That's worth more than money to me."

"Will Tibetans visit you if you have surgery or you're in a car accident?" she demanded to know. "Only your closest friends will do that. But if you're so busy helping Tibetans that you don't have time for your friends, you won't have anyone left to help you when you need it."

The next day, as Mike and I hiked around Cedar Lake in Minneapolis, I wondered out loud, "Does the Doctrine of Karma really require that we help Tibetans? Why not focus on our own lives? Don't we have enough problems of our own without taking on theirs, too?"

"Remember when you were choosing a research topic for your PhD?" Mike asked. "After you heard about Le Chambon, you decided to study people with AIDS."

He was referring to a French village where, during World War II, the villagers risked their lives to save six thousand people, mostly Jews, from the Nazis. When someone asked them why they did it, they replied, "There was nothing else to do." To them, it was natural to help human beings who were in desperate need, as natural as breathing or eating. In the ethical climate they had created, their actions weren't praiseworthy, but necessary. "Don't Tibetans deserve the same help as the Jews of Le Chambon, or people with AIDS?" Mike asked.

"Yes," I said. "For the sake of acting ethically, we should assist the Tibetans, even if it might seem easier to turn away from them." When I did my research, it was meant as a way to help persons with AIDS, but they gave me much more than I ever gave to them. In much the same way, Tibetans could teach us a great deal, even as we reached out to help them.

"Okay," said Mike, "so we're going to help the Tibetans. But how can we be sure we're helping and not hurting?"

"Maybe that's where the concept of treating people justly comes into play," I said. "We help them by treating them justly. But what's justice?"

To a philosopher trained in the West, that sort of question ultimately leads to Plato's *Republic*. In that dialogue, one definition of justice is "returning to another what's owed." Socrates questioned that definition by asking if it would be just to return a spear to a man who could hurt himself or someone else with it. He argued that justice involves more than returning material goods to their owner. Justice also entails a benefit for the recipient of justice. But if that's true, who gets to decide what is just or helpful to another? The person doing the helping, or the one being helped?

"I feel conflict about how to help people who are sick," I said. "Health professionals need sick people as job security. With that in mind, how much do we unintentionally encourage illness in order to hold on to our jobs? Is the appearance of altruism only a mask for self-interest? If that's the case, then are we helping, or are we hurting?"

"As a lawyer," Mike responded, "is it okay for me to adopt a losing legal strategy because I think that my client will benefit by losing the case? Can I benefit my client at the expense of someone else? Should I help my client, or focus on making a living? Or think of this: If two people are in conflict, should I take the side of the individual I'm trying to help and turn against the other person? With the Tibetans, are we called on ethically to be their allies, and, if so, do we declare our own personal war on the Chinese?"

"All I know is that simply *wanting* to do good isn't sufficient," I said. "If we love human beings in general but don't help individuals, we're hypocrites. To really help, we have to take a person's illness, injury, or complaint seriously, based on the understanding that each person will experience life in a particular manner. Now that we are getting to know individual Tibetans, we may be more helpful to them on that level."

Why Behave Ethically?

We left the shore of Cedar Lake and walked over to nearby Lake of the Isles. Far ahead of us a woman was walking alone. In an instant, she stumbled and fell. Two joggers stopped running, helped her to her feet, and then continued on their way.

As Mike and I watched from a distance, I asked, "Why did the joggers help her? They could have run by her." I thought for a moment. "Actually, there's a more pressing ethical problem than whether or not to help. We should be asking, 'Why behave ethically?' The rationale of 'If you scratch my back, I'll scratch yours' doesn't work in this situation. If it's to my advantage, and I can get away with it, why not act unethically? Does ethical behavior come from wisdom and discipline, or from fear and stupidity?"

Mike brought up Plato's myth about the magic ring found by Gyges, a peasant. When Gyges twisted the ring on his finger toward the inside of his hand, he became invisible, but if he turned it outward, he became visible again. Using the ring to make him invisible, Gyges committed adultery with the king's wife, murdered the king, and took over rule of the country as a tyrant.

"If you could be invisible, what would you do?" I asked.

"Hide on airplanes and travel free," Mike laughed. "I hope I'd behave ethically. I might accumulate more material goods if I got away with sneaking around, but I'd be less of a person. And I'd probably hurt a whole lot of people. But since I can't be invisible, I suspect much of my decency results from the fear that other people will see me behaving badly, unethically. I don't want to have to live with those consequences."

We left the lake and walked to an Italian restaurant. "The Buddha, Aristotle, Plato, and other sages taught that to be happy, we must behave ethically," I noted. "Moses' final admonition to the Israelites in Deuteronomy is a cornerstone of Judaism, Christianity, and Islam: 'You shall walk in all the ways which the Lord your God has commanded you that you may live, and that it may go well with you.' We are expected to act with integrity by consistently doing the right thing. That's the way to live a happy, flourishing, meaningful life."

"Deciding to behave ethically isn't the same as actually doing it, though," said Mike while we ate our meal of fresh pasta. Our conversation turned to the subject of *akrasia,* an ancient Greek word for weakness of the will. *Akrasia* means to behave in ways that we say are wrong, or to act against our own best judgment.

"Plato and Aristotle wrote that *akrasia* is impossible, for right knowledge leads to right action," I said. "If we know in our heart what is right, we will act accordingly."

"My smoking habit was an example of that," Mike said. "When I really knew in my heart that smoking was wrong for me, I stopped smoking."

"That's one interpretation of Aristotle," I said. "Another interpretation is that we act wrongly because we lack the motivation to do what's right. Let's say that we *do* know which behaviors lead to happiness, but we let our desires and passions get in the way. To act ethically, we must not only know the right thing to do, but we have to be motivated enough to do it."

"Makes sense," Mike said. "You could argue that I didn't stop smoking until I knew in my heart that smoking was bad for me—*and* I was motivated enough to quit."

"By the way," he went on, "that dinner was so fattening, I figure it's about time for us to go on a diet. Of course, considering the famous chocolate torte on the menu, I say we start the diet *after* dessert."

What Is the Right Thing to Do?

As Mike and I walked back to Lake of the Isles, it struck me that wisdom traditions agree on a key guideline for determining right action: Do not harm, and, if at all possible, help those around you.

Of course, this guideline isn't always sufficient. That's why Aristotle, Buddha, Confucius, the Jewish sage Maimonides, and other wise people have offered another way to determine right action: Choose a middle road between too much and too little. For example, just as both overeating and undereating will lead to poor health, even a noble cause, when carried too far, becomes harmful.

"A middle path will take both an action and its results into account," I said, thinking of the classic split between deontology and consequentialism.

In the debate over "ethical action," followers of deontology, such as Immanuel Kant, focus on the rightness of an action as opposed to the action's consequences. Is it ever right to lie? A deontologist might say that lying is wrong by its very nature; the lie's consequences matter not at all, for the action itself is flawed. This follows even if lying leads to a better outcome than honesty does.

In contrast to the deontologists' position, consequentialists such as John Stuart Mill focus on the consequences of an action. For them, the rightness lies in the value of the consequences, which is independent of the rightness or wrongness of the action that produces them. A consequentialist might say that lying is justifiable if it leads to better consequences than honesty does.

Throughout history, atrocities have been committed using rationalizations based either on deontology or consequentialism gone awry. For example, deontologists who believe that their own values are right may insist that it is justifiable to impose those values on others, even if the results are harmful. Extreme consequentialists might hurt individuals in order to bring about a greater utilitarian good; in other words, the ends justify the means by providing the greatest good for the greatest number of people. An ethical middle road, however, avoids the pitfalls of both excessive deontology and excessive consequentialism.

Mike mulled this idea over a bit. "Behaving ethically calls for an evaluation both of the rightness of the action and the goodness of the consequences. But aren't there times when lying is simply and obviously the right thing to do?" We turned away from Lake of the Isles and walked back toward Cedar Lake.

"If Nazis ask me if I'm hiding Jews," I said, "and I am, I'd better lie! But that kind of situation doesn't happen often. Most of the time, lying isn't justifiable, I don't think. Moreover, if I persist in lying, I may no longer realize when I'm lying, and this will take a heavy toll on me."

At Cedar Lake, we sat on a bench to watch the setting sun send pink, blue, and yellow shimmers across the water. The beauty of the evening contrasted sharply with our conversation, and we grew silent. The downtown skyline framed the lake, with skyscrapers sparkling in the fading light. A full moon rose behind the trees on the far side of the water. A jogger stopped to pick up trash and put it in a garbage can.

"Now that's doing the right thing!" I declared in the twilight.

How Should We Live
with Meaning and Integrity?

"Everyone has options when dealing with ethical problems," I mused, as we continued walking along Cedar Lake. "We can deny that these problems exist, we can lash out in anger, or we can get depressed. But then, as we experience life's troubles, we might become bitter and resentful and turn into worse people as a result. The sages teach that the best choice is to acknowledge an ethical conflict, determine the right thing to do, and then do it. Of course, that's much easier said than done!"

"Aristotle, as well as the Buddha, taught that we must educate ourselves to be ethical," said Mike. "We become virtuous by habitually behaving virtuously, and we behave virtuously by first doing what a virtuous person would do. Once ethical, virtuous behavior becomes a habit, we become autonomous ethical agents who are mindful of the world around us. We are able to distinguish between right and wrong, good and bad, ethical and unethical."

"Why not pursue excellence!" I blurted out. "Then we'll become sages as we age, rather than just get older. That's something Rabbi Zalman Schachter-Shalomi teaches. Ethical conflicts aren't necessarily bad—they can show us how to live with meaning and integrity. That's the way to be happy."

Our conversation turned to Viktor Frankl, who wrote that the primary force motivating each person is the search for meaning. He determined that everyone is free to choose her or his own values in any circumstance. As a prisoner in a Nazi death camp, he saw how some prisoners found meaning in their lives, if only by helping others. This meaning gave them the will and strength to endure. After the war, he saw his task as a psychiatrist to assist people in finding meaning in their lives no matter how dismal the circumstances. From his perspective, nothing so effectively helps one to survive, even in the worst conditions, as the belief that life has meaning.

"Frankl gives a good answer to our question about whether to help Tibetans or anyone else," I said. "He'd probably tell us to reach out and help, because that brings meaning to life. By using our lives to make a contribution, we'll follow the Doctrine of Karma and live with meaning and integrity as a result."

"Aristotle taught that we are political, social beings," said Mike, as we climbed into our car for the drive home from Cedar

Lake. "Helping other people is essential to our full humanity and happiness. That includes helping people we don't know personally, even people who live on the other side of the planet."

"Don't harm, do good, choose a middle road, and live with meaning and integrity," I said, attempting to summarize all that we'd discussed on our walk. "That's the way to develop good karma and be happy. Let's go to Tibet with these values in mind."

Mike continued the thought. "We're doing what the Dalai Lama has suggested will help the Tibetans: reminding Tibetans that their plight isn't forgotten, supporting Tibetan organizations, and visiting Tibet so we can see the situation and tell others back home."

"If we're really going to be helpful, though, we still need to know more about the Tibetan situation," I said. "We've been hearing what Tibetans think about the conflict with China. Before we get too self-righteous, let's talk to someone who's Chinese. I'll call Lu Ying tomorrow. She's a friend from graduate school. I'll ask her out for lunch and find out what she thinks of all this."

Chapter 4

Who's Right: Tibetans or Chinese?

A Chinese Perspective

"I don't agree with China's treatment of Tibet," Lu Ying said, as she and I slurped noodles in a Chinese restaurant. "After all, I'm from Hong Kong. I was taught that there's no justification for torturing, imprisoning, and killing peaceful protesters, for taking Tibetans' land, for destroying their culture and religion. At the same time, I feel confused about Tibet because we Chinese have always thought that Tibet is part of China. What would Americans do if Minnesota tried to secede from the U.S.?"

Lu Ying explained that many westerners imagine Old Tibet as a timeless preserve of untainted Buddhist wisdom. In this idyllic nation, a peasant boy could grow up to become a great lama, and a police force wasn't needed because Tibetans voluntarily observed the Doctrine of Karma.

In contrast, many Chinese view Old Tibet as backward and medieval. They think that Tibetans were always fighting among themselves, and that the clergy and aristocratic class monopolized power. The old feudal system oppressed women, non-Buddhists, and laypeople who weren't members of the aristocracy.

"The truth about Tibet lies somewhere between the idealized national image and the harsh Chinese stereotypes," Lu Ying explained.

"Corporations in the West eagerly do business with China," I said. "The world community has done little to pressure the Chinese government about its human rights record."

"The Chinese leaders don't like other countries meddling in their affairs," said Lu Ying. They punish dissidents because they're afraid of chaos and fragmentation. While westerners emphasize personal freedom, the Chinese value a stable government and unified nation. For their part, the Chinese can't understand how Americans can be so insensitive to the homeless and starving people in the United States. To the Chinese government, "human rights" means a decent income, decent housing, and a decent life for China's 1.25 billion people. To achieve this daunting task, government policies rest on a Confucian principle: People live in groups, therefore one's life will improve as the group improves.

China is spending huge amounts of money to build roads, bridges, hospitals, schools, and other projects to improve living standards and the country's infrastructure. Tibet is not being left out; electricity and telephones are being installed even in rural Tibet. According to Lu Ying, Tibetans are better off now than before, and an emerging middle class of Tibetans agrees. Ideas and technology brought by China will create new Tibetans who can compete in the world. Although Chinese policies are causing anguish among some Tibetans, Lu Ying said that this is the price they must pay for modernization.

"What about the argument that any so-called advances primarily benefit China?" I asked. "Rich pickings are to be had for your people, but for Tibetans, the Chinese immigrants spell disaster."

"Tibetans may be edged out of their land," agreed Lu Ying, "but Tibet has a lot of land with little population. Chinese cities are crowded. As for China exploiting Tibet's resources, Tibet's government wasn't developing them anyway. On human rights, the Chinese government doesn't even grant basic human rights to Chinese people. Prosperity and openness might eventually lead China to reassess its Tibetan policy. In any event, significant changes are taking place there: Quality of life and human rights are improving. A new generation in China is growing up more sensitive to Tibet and its needs."

That evening, I told Mike about my lunch with Lu Ying. "I'm trying to behave ethically by following the Doctrine of Karma," I said, "but what does that mean in terms of Tibet? Who's right: the Tibetans or the Chinese? I thought I'd have more clarity about this issue by now, but I'm just getting increasingly confused."

"I don't know," said Mike. "I still need more information before I can form an opinion."

It just so happened that the day's newspaper announced a series of lectures on Tibet, beginning that evening. They would be given by Dr. David Kahn, a professor at a local university. We needed more perspective on this complicated topic, so we decided to attend the talks.

Geography of Tibet

Dr. Kahn, a professor of history, began his first lecture with a breakdown of what he would discuss. "The history of Tibet isn't an easy one. I can tell you about the geography and early history of Tibet, the period after 1949, and the experience of the Tibetan Diaspora. By the very shortness of our time together, I can only give a brief overview of dates, events, and important figures. I warn you, you won't find much objectivity in what I have to say. You may think I'm pro-Tibetan, but I would prefer to say that

I'm not anti-Chinese. I have visited China and I admire the Chinese people. The best I can do here is to present my perspective and hope that you will keep an open mind."

He began his account by describing the mysterious Tibet that has exercised a unique hold on the world's imagination. It has been called Shangri-la, Land of Snows, the Roof of the World, and Holy Land. Images come to mind of an ancient country in Central Asia, locked behind impenetrable Himalayan Mountains. Its incredible slopes and valleys are guarded by maroon-robed monks imbued with mystic wisdom and living in monasteries jutting from high cliffs. Tibet's lofty perch above the hurly-burly of the lowlands and its traditional resistance to outside influences has produced otherworldly attitudes in its native population, which has become known for its piety, independence, and austerity. Other qualities that early visitors associated with Tibetans included shyness, tenacity, nonviolence, and family cohesiveness. Adventurers and traders considered Tibet to be a land of riches, but the indigenous people allowed few foreigners to enter their kingdom to visit Lhasa, their holy city.

"An ocean once covered what is now Tibet," Dr. Khan said. "Then the Indian tectonic plate collided with the Asian mainland and pushed Tibet to its present, dizzying heights. Tibet's average elevation is fifteen thousand feet. Gifted with the earth's loftiest mountains and highest, largest plateau, the country also holds the headwaters of Asia's great rivers: the Ganges, Indus, Sutlej, Brahmaputra, and Mekong. Nearly half of the world's population lives downstream from Tibet."

Tibet's mountains, high plains, and forests form a unique ecosystem and serve as home to an array of rare wildlife, such as the snow leopard, blue sheep, and Tibetan wild ass. Recent deforestation, agricultural practices, and mass killings of wildlife are threatening this ecosystem; the plateau is becoming a desert. Rivers are developing high sediment rates, leading to floods in the lowlands.

"Two Tibets exist," he said. "Historical Tibet was a vast nation, about the size of Western Europe. It included regions such as Kham and Amdo, which Communist China absorbed into present-day Sichuan and Qinghai. Political Tibet, in contrast, exists as the area now called the "Tibet Autonomous Region" (TAR). It consists of three traditional Tibetan provinces: U and the region around Lhasa; Tsang and the area near Shigatse; and Ngari, or western Tibet."

History of Tibet

Dr. Kahn then turned to Tibet's history before 1949. According to Tibetan legends, he said, the birthplace of the Tibetan people was in central Tibet's Yarlung Valley, near present-day Lhasa. For thousands of years they had no written language. They lived mostly as farmers, bandits, and nomads. The first Yarlung king ruled around 127 B.C.E. Probably, the Yarlung kings were local chieftains whose rule did not extend beyond the Yarlung Valley. Legend has it that in the third century, the twenty-eighth Yarlung king received Tibet's first Buddhist scriptures, which literally fell from the heavens onto the roof of Yumbulagang, Tibet's first fortress. In the six century, by the time historical records emerged about the Yarlung dynasty, the Yarlung kings had made significant headway in unifying much of central Tibet through conquests and alliances.

Songtsen Gampo (618–649), the thirty-third Yarlung king, expanded Tibet's borders. He traded with China, India, Nepal, and lands to the west. China and Nepal reluctantly agreed to an alliance with Tibet and sent brides for the king. When Princess Wencheng from China and Princess Bhrikuti from Nepal joined the king's three Tibetan wives, they brought Buddhism, the major religion of the surrounding countries. Until then Tibetans had followed Bon, a shamanistic religion, but with these new alliances Buddhism gained royal patronage and a foothold in

Tibet. The king moved his court to Lhasa and erected a small palace on Red Hill, where the Potala Palace now stands. To house the Buddha images of his two foreign queens, he built the Jokhang and the Ramoche temples. He introduced a written script (developed from Indian sources) for the Tibetan language.

King Trisong Detsen (755–797) brought well-known Indian Buddhist teachers to Tibet, in particular Padmasambhava and Santarakshita. They founded Samye, Tibet's first Buddhist monastery. The king ordered noble families to support Samye despite the resistance of Bon worshippers. Under the king's leadership, Tibetan armies conquered Chinese Gansu and Sichuan. In 783, Tibet took the Chinese capital, Chang'an (Xi'an), and forced China to sign a treaty accepting the new borders. Tibet became nearly double the size it is today, and its influence extended all across Asia. In 821, during the reign of King Tritsug Detsen Ralpachen, Tibet and China signed another treaty. The two countries immortalized the treaty on three stone pillars in Chang'an, along the Tibetan-Chinese border, and outside the Jokhang in Lhasa. Only the Lhasa pillar still stands. The words that were carved into it state that there will be no more warfare, hostile invasions, or seizure of property between Tibet and China.

"By this time," said Dr. Kahn, "Buddhism was an integral part of Tibet. However, Bon worshippers reacted to their loss of status. Internal fighting reduced the Tibetan Empire to feudal states by 842, and Tibet entered a dark age that lasted until the eleventh century. By the time the Chinese Tang dynasty ended in 907, China had recovered most of the territory it had lost to Tibet in the previous centuries. During the Chinese Song dynasty (960–1279), Tibet and China maintained little contact."

In the eleventh century, Atisha, Marpa, Milarepa, and other Indian Buddhist teachers traveled to Tibet. Their teachings led to a revival of Tibetan Buddhism. Tibetans traveled to India to study and returned home with ideas that revitalized Tibetan thought.

Eventually, four main orders of Tibetan Buddhism developed: Nyingmapa, Kagyupa, Sakyapa, and Gelugpa. The belief emerged that the abbot of a monastery was the reincarnation of its founder. Lineages based on reincarnation maintained continuous spiritual authority that substituted for hereditary power, an important point since many of the clergy were celibate.

In 1206, Genghis Khan created a vast Mongol empire in Central Asia, and his forces invaded Tibet in 1239. A priest-patron relationship developed between the Tibetans and the Mongols. The Mongols made Tibetan Buddhism the empire's state religion. The head Sakyapa lama became its spiritual leader, with temporal authority over Tibet. Some contemporary Chinese scholars argue that when the Mongols subjugated Tibet, it became part of China. Nationalistic Tibetans counter that the Mongols also subjugated China, and Tibet didn't become a part of China anymore than China became part of Tibet.

In the fourteenth century, Tsongkhapa (1357–1419) founded Gelugpa, the order that came to dominate the other, earlier orders. Tsongkhapa's disciples began monasteries at Chamdo, Drepung, Ganden, Sera, and Tashilhunpo, which became vital centers of art, learning, and culture. Gelugpa is called "the Yellow Hat sect" because of the yellow headgear worn by its followers. Although Tibet did not have a caste system per se, the nobility occupied a privileged position that was perpetuated through heredity. With the rise of great monasteries, religious leaders also held an increasingly important role. Through talent and hard work, even a man from a poor background could rise high within a religious order.

The Mongols gave to Sonam Gyatso (1543–1588), third reincarnated abbot of Drepung, the title *Ta-Le,* meaning "Ocean" or "Ocean of Wisdom." Because the Mongols bestowed the title retroactively on his previous two incarnations, technically he became the third Dalai Lama, the "Lama who is an Ocean of Wisdom." He was given authority over Tibet, with central Tibet around Lhasa his center of government.

In 1640, the Mongols intervened on behalf of Gelugpa and executed the Tsang king, a rival of the Buddhist monasteries. This helped the fifth Dalai Lama (1617–1682), a Gelugpa abbot, become spiritual and temporal head of a unified Tibet, although regional rivalries persisted. The borders ranged from Mount Kailash in the west to Kham in the east. The fifth Dalai Lama invited Indian scholars into Tibet, and he also renovated and expanded temples and monasteries. Work began on the Potala Palace, which was to serve as his residence.

The Manchus ousted the Mongols and became the new Chinese power in the form of the Qing dynasty (1644–1911). The fifth Dalai Lama visited Beijing in 1656 to meet the new rulers of China. During the visit, the Chinese emperor treated him with respect, giving no indication that Tibet was politically subordinate to China. When the fifth Dalai Lama died in 1682, China still accepted its neighbor's independence. Taking no chances, Tibet's regent was canny enough to keep the death of the spiritual leader a secret for twelve years, an act that held Tibet in one piece. When the secret finally leaked out, the regent enthroned a boy he had chosen as the sixth Dalai Lama.

In 1705, the Mongols still held sway in much of Asia. That year, it is alleged, they murdered the sixth Dalai Lama and replaced him. This action aroused hostility in Tibet and created enemies for the Mongols, since the Mongols had murdered the figure whom many viewed as a spiritual leader.

In 1720, Emperor Kang Xi sent Chinese troops to Lhasa. When they reached the city, the Tibetans treated them as liberators. Declaring Tibet a protectorate of China, the emperor installed Chinese representatives and troops in Tibet. These events led to two centuries of Manchu overlordship and served as a justification for the Communist takeover nearly 250 years later, just a few decades after the Qing dynasty fell in 1911.

By this time, the world had noticed Tibet's strategic location as a buffer zone between Russia, China, and India. Britain, in particular, was concerned that Russia would create an alliance with Tibet and gain control of Central Asia, thus threatening British interests in India. In 1904, unable to accept this potential alliance, the British marched troops into Tibet and killed seven hundred Tibetans. They then forced the thirteenth Dalai Lama to sign a treaty granting Tibetans autonomy under Chinese rule. The thirteenth Dalai Lama wanted to modernize Tibet, but monks opposed his innovations as contrary to the Tibetan theocracy. Conflict arose between him and the Panchen Lama, who later fled to China. The issue was put on hold when the thirteenth Dalai Lama died in 1933.

In the midst of growing unrest, and with no spiritual leader in place, Tibet once again seemed on the brink of turmoil. Then, on June 6, 1935, a boy, Lhamo Dhondup, was born to Tibetan peasants in Takster, a village in Amdo. At age two he was identified as the next Dalai Lama, and in 1940 he was installed. A regent ruled for him until he was given full political power. At that point, Lhamo Dhondup forfeited his name, in accordance with ancient custom, and adopted the name Tenzin Gyatso, the Fourteenth Dalai Lama. Tibetans call him Kundun, "Presence of the Buddha."

During World War II, Britain, the United States, and China pressured Tibet to allow passage of military supplies from India to China. Still unstable, and fearing more from China than from Japan, Tibet remained neutral throughout the conflict. It was to be one of the last decisions Tibet would make as an independent nation.

Liberation or Occupation?

For his second lecture about Tibet's past and present, Dr. Kahn walked to the podium and said, "My address tonight will be more controversial than the previous week's. I will discuss my perspective on the conflict between Tibet and China. Historians disagree about whether China has liberated Tibet or is, in fact, occupying that country. I encourage you to draw your own conclusions."

He drew a deep breath, took a sip of water, and began. "Chairman Mao Zedong's Communists took over China in 1949. Mao announced that Tibet had always been part of China and that he wanted to liberate Tibetans from feudalism. The Tibetans replied that they had been independent for three thousand years and they did not want China to rule them. They asserted that Tibet was never part of China, for their language, religion, government, culture, and history were distinct from China's."

In October of 1950, thirty thousand Chinese soldiers attacked Tibet from six directions. The Tibetan army, a poorly equipped force of four thousand troops, stood little chance. To strengthen its position, Tibet's government gave the teenage Dalai Lama full political power, an action that brought dancing in the streets but offered little protection against the advancing soldiers. Tibet appealed to the United Nations, and only El Salvador sponsored a motion to condemn China. Britain and India, Tibet's supposed friends, convinced the United Nations not to debate the issue for fear of incurring Chinese wrath.

The Dalai Lama sent a mission to Beijing, where Chinese leaders drafted a seventeen-point document called the "Agreement on Measures for the Peaceful Liberation of Tibet." Under pressure, Tibetan diplomats signed the document, and the Chinese forged the Dalai Lama's seal. Fearing for his life, the Dalai Lama fled from Lhasa but soon returned. He reluctantly approved the agreement, and Tibet officially became part of the People's Republic of China. In 1951, the Chinese government granted Tibet autonomy in its domestic affairs, but at the same time, it garrisoned troops within the country's borders. Soldiers ate up food stores, which led to inflation, and confrontations escalated between Chinese and Tibetans. In 1954, the Dalai Lama accepted an invitation to Beijing, where Mao shocked him with an announcement that "religion is poison."

Despite fierce Tibetan resistance, Chinese officials in Kham and Amdo imposed huge taxes, seized private property, and tried to indoctrinate Tibetans against Buddhism. The authorities stirred up mobs consisting of Chinese and dissatisfied Tibetans, who desecrated monasteries and carried off or destroyed sacred images and books. The mobs tortured, raped, and killed nuns and monks, often barbarously and in public. Some children were kidnapped for education in China, and those left behind were incited to abuse their parents. The government deported men and boys or forced them to do labor in harsh conditions.

"As in other years," said Dr. Kahn, "the Tibetan New Year of 1959 attracted large crowds to Lhasa. Chinese officials invited the Dalai Lama—without his bodyguards—to attend a Chinese dance performance at their military headquarters in Lhasa. He and his advisors suspected that he would be put under house arrest, so the family entourage fled to India. Lhasa exploded in revolt, which the Chinese viciously suppressed. After three days of fighting, over thirteen thousand Tibetans lay dead in the streets."

With this, the Chinese officials abolished the Tibetan government and restructured Tibetan society according to Maoist Communism. They banned Tibetan folk festivals and traditional dances, art, and songs. Many Tibetans were forced to change their names to Chinese equivalents. Educated Tibetans worked in menial jobs and became victims of *thamzing,* class struggle sessions, during which they were spat at, humiliated, beaten, and kicked to make them confess reactionary thoughts and behavior. The Panchen Lama, the highest-ranking spiritual leader remaining in Tibet, was imprisoned for requesting better treatment for Tibetans.

The Chinese government instructed farmers to grow wheat and rice instead of barley, the Tibetan staple. Tibetans protested that these crops were unsuited to the altitude of their country, but to no avail. In Old Tibet starvation was unknown, but by 1961 seventy thousand Tibetans had died or were dying of starvation. In 1965, China established the Tibet Autonomous

Region, with Beijing as its central authority. The government carved out two-thirds of Tibet to create the Chinese province of Xizang and augment existing provinces.

"There is no question that the Cultural Revolution, from 1966 to 1976, was difficult for the Chinese people," said Dr. Kahn. "It was even more brutal and long-lasting in Tibet. Tibetans were told to replace their mantras with 'thoughts of Chairman Mao.' Red Guards set out to destroy 'old thinking, old culture, old habits, and old customs.' By 1969, no practicing monks or nuns remained. Tibetans were forced to denounce the Dalai Lama as a parasite, traitor, and abuser of human rights."

The Chinese government was fervent in its elimination of Buddhism as the opiate of the masses. Mobs destroyed prayer flags and tore down stupas. Monks and nuns were forced to discard their robes and marry. Scriptures were burned or used as toilet paper. Tibetans were not allowed to donate food to monasteries and nunneries. Priceless images were melted down or sold in Hong Kong.

Throughout their history, Tibetans have followed Buddhist teachings about Right Livelihood. These teachings stress contentment and discourage over-consumption and over-exploitation of the earth's natural resources. Back in 1642, the fifth Dalai Lama had even issued a "Decree for Protection of Animals and Environment." Now, the Chinese officials were cutting down Tibet's vast forests. They slaughtered wildlife and livestock for sport, hides, and meat. Much of Tibet's abundant wildlife soon vanished.

"In 1975," Dr. Kahn said, "China invited foreign journalists to Tibet. Rather than praise the liberated Tibetans they expected to see, the journalists painted a picture of a people battered to their knees. The Dalai Lama and over one hundred thousand Tibetans had fled. Over a million Tibetans had died. One in ten Tibetans had disappeared in prison, and one hundred thousand were in labor camps. Only a few of Tibet's 6,254 monasteries and nunneries remained, and 60 percent of Tibet's sacred literature was gone. Much of Tibet's heritage had been rapidly and irretrievably destroyed."

Tibet Today

"Today," said Dr. Kahn, "about 2.5 million Tibetans live in the Tibetan Autonomous Region. An additional 2.5 million live in formerly Tibetan areas that have been incorporated into China. Of the 150,000 Tibetans in exile, about 5,000 have moved to Europe and over 3,000 reside in the United States."

Tibet still sees the traditional lifestyles of nomad, farmer, and clergy within its borders. Nomads tend yaks, sheep, and other animals. In farming communities, which consist of a few homes surrounded by fields, farmers plant and harvest crops by hand, with a mule, or with a *dzo* (a cross between a cow and yak). Nuns and monks are at the forefront of the "Free Tibet" movement; the government views them with suspicion and frequently interrogates, harasses, and tortures them. Even so, nuns and monks are again donning vestments and rising early to read scriptures and chant prayers.

"Chinese officials acknowledge past excesses," Dr. Kahn said, "and they have relaxed some regulations. They are restoring a few monasteries. However, they imprison, torture, and even execute protesters, and they continue to conduct crackdowns and reeducation sessions. They search businesses, nunneries, monasteries, and homes for pictures of the Dalai Lama."

Despite Tibet's sparse population, the Chinese government carries out a strict birth control policy. Officials dispense contraceptive pills and engage in forced abortion, sterilization, and infanticide. Refugees describe the sterilization of entire regions in Tibet. After these procedures, women often develop health problems; some even die. Each woman is forced to pay the expenses for birth control measures the government imposes on her.

Because of disastrous agricultural practices, starvation is widespread, and many children suffer from malnutrition. These children are less likely to live through childhood and are prone to die from infectious diseases.

Dr. Kahn went on to describe what sounded like the looting of Tibet. He explained that the Chinese government has uncovered Tibet's rich deposits of gold, coal, borax, zinc, copper, silver, iron, chromium, lithium, tungsten, lead, salt, and oil. Mining operations remove these resources, which account for one-third of Tibet's industrial output. Environmental safeguards are nearly nonexistent, leading to slope destabilization, land degradation, and hazards to the health of humans and wildlife. Officials build, test, and stockpile nuclear weapons near villages. They dump radioactive waste into shallow, unlined landfills, and soldiers keep civilians away. Although Tibet's vast forests and abundant wildlife are gone, hunting tours are conducted for wealthy clients from China, Europe, and the United States. As a result, many rare animals and birds have become extinct or are on the verge of extinction.

Since 1983, thousands of Chinese have flooded into Tibet. The government offers them good salaries, interest-free loans, housing, and other perks. Before 1959, Tibet was almost totally populated by Tibetans; now, Lhasa's Chinatown dwarfs the Tibetan quarter. To accommodate the settlers, the government is building and improving schools, mostly in urban areas where Chinese live. Schools offer little education in Tibetan culture and history. Teachers mainly speak Chinese, and at higher levels of education Chinese is the only language of instruction. Only Tibetans who have a Chinese education are allowed to conduct business, develop economic power, and exert political influence; yet, about one-third of Tibetan children don't go to school at all, for they live in remote areas. Those who do attend must pay high fees. Even if families can afford the expense, many Tibetan parents are afraid of losing their children to a foreign, Chinese education.

"Today, Tibet is a remarkable place to visit," said Dr. Kahn. "The high plateau offers picturesque monasteries, stunning mountain views, and ancient pilgrimages. Despite their resiliency, however, Tibetans have many scars. In my view, their country is under direct Chinese occupation, and visitors are never far from this reality. Travel in Tibet is fascinating, moving, and memorable, but also a deeply disturbing experience."

Tibetan Diaspora

When he arrived to give his final lecture, Dr. Kahn began with several questions. "What do you think? Is China liberating Tibet, or occupying it? Yes, China is modernizing Tibet, but are the Tibetans paying too heavy a price? Is there a better way to bring a developing country into the twenty-first century?"

When the Dalai Lama fled to India, he said, the Indian government gave him asylum. He set up the Tibetan Government in Exile in Dharamsala, an abandoned British hill station in the northern *pradesh* (state) of Himachel, which is near Kashmir and Punjab. After reestablishing governmental departments, he and the Kashag (his cabinet) drafted a democratic constitution calling for election of the National Assembly of People's Deputies. He insisted on a clause stating that a two-thirds majority can remove him as head of state, asserting that unless Tibetans view him as dispensable they cannot be truly democratic. When they are once again free in Tibet, he will stop participating in government.

"Tibetans are recreating their world," said Dr. Kahn, "but it's a different world in many ways from Old Tibet." In Dharamsala, the Tibetan Government in Exile runs small hotels, guesthouses, restaurants, travel agencies, handicraft centers, and an import-export business. It builds schools and children's villages to educate youth and care for orphans. The Tibetan Youth Congress encourages young people to participate in government. "When I visited Upper Tibetan Children's Village in Dharamsala," Dr. Kahn said, "I saw babies, toddlers, school-age children, and adolescents. One of the teachers told me that some parents couldn't leave Tibet, so they gave their children to fleeing adults who took them across the border."

Tibetans have recreated other institutions outside of Tibet as well. They have reestablished most major nunneries and monasteries in India. Tibetan clergy travel around the world to give teachings and establish Buddhist centers. In Dharamsala, the Men-Tsee-Khang (the Tibetan Medical and Astrological Institute) offers traditional Tibetan medicine, while Delek Hospital provides Western care. The Library of Tibetan Works and Archives, Tibetan Institute of Performing Arts, and Center for Tibetan Arts and Crafts are all located in Dharamsala. Elsewhere, the Tibet House is in New Delhi, and the Institute of Tibetan Higher Studies resides in Sarnath.

Dr. Kahn said that hundreds of refugees continue to leave Tibet each year, withstanding dangerous mountain passes, frostbite, and brutal border guards who conspire against them. If they reach Kathmandu, Nepal, the Tibetan community and United Nations High Commission for Refugees offer them protection. Reception centers in Kathmandu, Dharamsala, and Delhi give them food, healthcare, and temporary housing.

In 1989, as Tibetan exile communities grew increasingly crowded, the United States Congress passed a bill granting one thousand immigrant visas. The Immigration and Naturalization Service allowed persons with these visas to become citizens and to bring their families to the United States. Since then, Tibetans have been settling all over America.

"Most Tibetan exiles set up a successful, self-sufficient life," said Dr. Kahn. "They bring with them a colorful heritage of dance, music, literature, and art. However, some exiles, especially those without family nearby, have trouble healing from their psychological and physical scars. They don't feel safe enough to trust anyone, and many experience depression, loss of concentration, alcoholism, insomnia, bad dreams, and fear. Away from Tibet, they lack purpose in life."

The single figure to whom most Tibetans look for guidance is still the Dalai Lama. Dr. Kahn returned to this leader's life story, describing his continued studies in Buddhism as an exile. At age twenty-three, he was awarded the Geshe Lharampa degree, the equivalent of a PhD and the monastic system's most advanced degree. Since then, he has become a prominent international leader, a lama to the world. On September 21, 1987, he presented his Five-Point Peace Plan to the United States Congressional Human Rights Caucus. The Five Points are:

1) Transformation of Tibet into a zone of peace.
2) Abandonment of China's population transfer policy.
3) Respect for Tibetans' fundamental human rights and democratic freedoms.
4) Restoration and protection of Tibet's natural environment, and abandonment of China's use of Tibet for production of nuclear weapons and dumping of nuclear waste.
5) Commencement of earnest negotiations on the future status of Tibet and relations between Tibetans and Chinese.

The U.S. Congress drafted a letter supporting this plan.

Continuing his efforts for the Tibetan cause, the Dalai Lama told the European Parliament in Strasbourg on June 15, 1988, that he was willing to abandon his claims for full Tibetan independence and leave foreign policy and defense to China, if the Chinese would accept his other requests. The fallout from Strasbourg was enormous, and shock waves caused by his words are still reverberating today.

The Chinese government denounced the Dalai Lama's statement as "splittist," since they wanted him to say that Tibet is

part of China. But their reaction was nothing compared with the
fury of many Tibetan exiles who felt he was selling out to China.
They asserted that Tibetans in Dharamsala didn't have the right
to hand over independence, for which Tibetans in Tibet were
daily paying with their lives.

"The Dalai Lama was awarded the Nobel Peace Prize on
October 1, 1989, soon after his statement at Strasbourg," said
Dr. Kahn. "In his acceptance speech, he asked the world to
adopt values of nonviolence, understanding, love, peace, compassion, patience, and respect. He insisted that these values are
the best way to create a better place to live, where all of us work
together to overcome problems. Reiterating his fervent prayer,
he hoped Tibet might again serve as a sanctuary of peace and
spiritual inspiration."

Chinese government officials continue to protest the Dalai
Lama's international activities, and they have not relented in
their view that Tibet is part of China. India discourages the Dalai
Lama from speaking out against China, and foreign governments
avoid recognizing him as head of an exiled government for fear of
disturbing their relationship with China.

The Dalai Lama responds to this scant support with declara-
tions that Tibetans' culture, peacefulness, perspective on
healing, and environmental concern can benefit the world. He
holds dialogues with political and religious leaders worldwide,
maintaining that his purpose is not to criticize China, but to
promote peace, religious harmony, and reconciliation, and to tell
the world about Tibetans' desperate plight.

Most Tibetans long for the Dalai Lama to return to Tibet.
At Passover, Jews traditionally say, "Next year in Jerusalem!"
Similarly, Tibetans pray at their festivals, "Next year, His
Holiness in Lhasa." To this end, some Tibetans advocate vio-
lence against China, an option the Dalai Lama strictly opposes.
His work tries to forge a middle road between two divergent
perspectives, each represented by one of his older brothers.

The Dalai Lama's brother Gyalo Thondup asserts that the conflict is between two opposing rights: the right of a people (Tibetans) to self-determination and independence, and the right of a multiethnic state (China) to maintain what it views as its historic territorial integrity. Thus the conflict is about who controls the land, who lives there, and who decides what goes on. The Dalai Lama must acknowledge China's control, Gyalo Thondup says, for the Chinese are counting the days until he dies and Tibet will be theirs once and for all. His brother should make the best deal he can while he's alive. If he encourages Tibetans to give up their claim to independence and return to Tibet, they can work to improve the low standard of living there.

Thubten Jigme Norbu, the Dalai Lama's oldest brother, sees things differently. He claims that if Tibetans and Chinese talk, they must view themselves as equals, rather than allow China to dictate terms. Tibetans shouldn't yield to the Chinese, for the Chinese are notorious for breaking promises. Instead, the Tibetans should fight for justice—with compassion in their hearts—using political, legal, and economic weapons, not military weapons. The struggle might be long, and contemporary Tibetans may not live to see the outcome. However, they must hope that Tibet will be free again and strive for that end.

"To conclude," said Dr. Kahn, "I met the Dalai Lama a few months ago when I was in Dharamsala. He told me that he might be the last Dalai Lama. Even if the institution remains, the method of choosing the next Dalai Lama may change. However, he's optimistic about a peaceful resolution to the Tibetan situation, and he thinks China's totalitarian system can't last much longer. He believes that he and other Tibetans will soon return to Tibet, as long as Tibetans behave according to Buddhist values and the world becomes a more compassionate place."

There was applause, and then Dr. Kahn put his notes away and walked out of the room. For a few moments, everyone was quiet. Then the room burst with conversation. "My heart breaks for the Tibetan people," I whispered to Mike.

"I feel bad for them, too," he replied, "but Dr. Kahn's lectures trouble me. He didn't mention Tibetans who were glad to get rid of the feudal system, or Tibetans who are doing well under the Chinese government."

"We're getting more confused all the time about the Tibetan situation, aren't we?" I said. "Next week we'll start on our trip, meet Karma and our travel group in Bangkok, and then finally see Tibet for ourselves. I hope that witnessing the situation first-hand will make it all clearer."

Chapter 5

Mindfulness

Tashi Delek

"Tashi delek," Karma said affectionately to our group. Mike and I sat with ten other Americans in the hospitality room of a five-star hotel in Bangkok. Fresh orchids decorated the room. "While we're in Thailand, we'll get over our jet lag. Then we fly to Kathmandu and begin our Tibetan adventure. Are you ready?" Everyone clapped enthusiastically.

Karma demonstrated an easy familiarity with the group. Each person seemed as fond of him as Mike and I were. "Before we go any further, let's introduce ourselves," he continued. "All of you know me, so, Karen, you start." He turned to a friendly looking woman sitting next to him.

"My husband, Jack, and I have been friends with Lisa and Marge for years," said Karen, gesturing to two women on her left. "We all live in San Francisco. I just retired after thirty years. Jack still works—he has his own company and travels a lot." Then, Jack told us about the United States military sending him to Vietnam in the 1970s, and how he spent time in Thailand for rest and relaxation. Now that he had returned, both good and bad memories were coming back to him.

"Karen, Marge, and I follow the 'Shop 'til you drop' philosophy when traveling," joked Lisa. "I almost backed out of this trip, but now I'm glad I came. We've found some great bargains in Bangkok." In lieu of introducing herself, Marge mumbled that she had an upset stomach because of something she ate at a Thai buffet, but that she'd feel better soon.

Another fellow traveler, Ken, introduced himself and his partner, Trudi. They were middle-aged newlyweds from Florida, and Ken had taken an early retirement. "I'm a nurse," said Trudi, "but Ken wants me to retire. I can relate to Marge's problem, 'cause I have an upset stomach, too. That's a change from last year when I traveled in India—I didn't get sick once."

Next, Alice introduced her husband, Bernie, and herself as college professors from North Carolina. Bernie interrupted Alice to tell a long, complicated joke that included a pun about *Kat-man-do* and *Kat-women-don't*. Alice laughed, while everyone else groaned.

"Lorna and I haven't met before," said June, another woman in our group, "but we're going to be roommates. That is, if Lorna doesn't poison me with her cigarettes. Maybe all of us can help Lorna to quit smoking on this trip. I'm from Utah. After my husband died, I retired." Lorna puffed on a cigarette and coughed. She said she was seventy-two years old and lived in Oregon. Her major interest was archaeology, and she boasted that she wouldn't stop traveling until she dropped dead. At that, all of us chuckled.

With all of the travelers introduced, Karma turned the conversation to the trip before us. "Let's talk about Tibet," he said. "This trip won't be like traveling in the United States, or even China. Everyone will have two or three bad days. We'll know a lot about each other before this is over. That's why it's best to expect nothing and accept whatever happens."

Jack mentioned some of the well-known disasters on Mount Everest, reminding us that 150 climbers had died there. "Our bus driver will do all the work," Karma assured us. "We won't climb the mountain on foot. Now, we have one more piece of business." He explained the position of Honorable Treasurer. Bernie raised his hand and said that he would do it, and everyone applauded.

Later, as all of us ate dinner together, we shared scraps of our life stories. Our reasons for going to Tibet were similar. Having traveled extensively, we looked forward to a new adventure. We wanted to experience the people, culture, religion, and political situation of Tibet. Karen asked Karma if he had any suggestions for how we could get the most out of the trip.

"Mindfulness," replied Karma, with a grin. "Be fully present, in the moment, not stuck in the past or future. Be mindful of your body, feelings, and thoughts—of everything in and around you. Mindfulness helps us to look into the heart of things so we can understand their true nature and develop wisdom. If we stay mindful, we'll get a lot out of this trip."

Buddhism's Hindu Roots

After several days in Thailand, our group flew from Bangkok, at sea level, to 4,368-foot-high Kathmandu, the capital of Nepal. The Himalayas, the highest mountains in the world, outlined the frozen boundary between Nepal and Tibet. I was eager to visit Nepal, the world's only Hindu kingdom; after all, Buddhism had emerged from Hinduism, just as Christianity rose out of Judaism. From my study of yoga, I knew something about Hinduism, but now I wanted to learn about its connection to Buddhism.

Karma led us out of Kathmandu's airport, luggage in tow. *"Namaste,"* said adults and children who crowded around us begging for money. Karma gave some of them money and told them in Nepalese to put the luggage on a flatbed truck. Then he instructed us to squeeze into a tiny old bus.

As the bus wound through busy Kathmandu, Karma told us that many Tibetans lived in Nepal, especially in the north. He mentioned ethnic groups inhabiting the border region: The people of Mustang were Tibetan, and Tamangs were mostly descended from Tibetan cavalry or the grooms of Tibetan invaders. Sherpas had migrated from Kham to Nepal. Because most Tibetans were Buddhist, Buddhism was more prevalent in northern Nepal, while Hinduism was prominent in the south. In Kathmandu Valley, Hinduism and Buddhism shared the same festivals and shrines, and by and large lived in harmony.

The bus crossed the Bagmati River into Patan and stopped in front of a large hotel. This one was a couple of stars away from the one in Bangkok, but it had bathrooms with hot and cold running water. After checking into our room, Mike and I went for a walk. The air was badly polluted and dirt covered everything, but we were still fascinated. We walked back across the bridge over the Bagmati, a sacred river for Hindus. Debris floated in its dirty water. The decaying carcass of a cow lay half-submerged, giving off a stench that filled the air along the banks. Nearby, two women washed clothes in a basin and a girl bathed a baby. A man and woman took water from the river to a fire on the ground where they were cooking meat. A woman lay sleeping on a mat with holes in it.

Kathmandu was even more polluted than Patan, and the smell of traffic, cooking fires, and decay made breathing difficult. We walked along streets crowded with cars, trucks, rickshaws, bicycles, scooters, and pedestrians dressed in both traditional and Western garb. In every direction were small shops in which people cooked, ate, made goods, welded, butchered meat, and conducted business. A barber cut a man's hair on the sidewalk. Women in colorful saris waved from an ancient Hindu temple, while children and monkeys played nearby. At a well, women pumped water to fill large brass jugs; when they were done, they carried the jugs away on their heads.

Back at the hotel, Karma introduced our group to Shamvu, our local guide while we stayed in Nepal. Shamvu said this was the poorest country in Asia, with a per capita income of $220 a year. The literacy rate was 40 percent, but that figure was only 13 percent for women. In about 1700 B.C.E., when the first so-called Aryan invaders settled in northern India, they recorded the Vedas, a collection of over one thousand hymns defining their religion. From the Vedas grew Brahminism, which evolved into modern Hinduism.

Shamvu explained that Hinduism has no formal creed or governing principle. It comprises many views, some of which contradict other tenets within the tradition. Individual Hindus can select beliefs that make sense to them. While this allows for free choice among the devotees, most Hindus believe in the trinity of Brahma, Vishnu, and Shiva. Ancient stories tell about Rama and Krishna, both of whom are incarnations of Vishnu.

Different Hindu cultures emphasize different aspects of the trinity. Shiva enjoys a prime position in Nepalese religious practice, having taken on the role of protector of animals and special guardian of Kathmandu Valley. One of Shiva's sons by his consort Parvati is Ganesh, the elephant-headed god who decides between success and failure, whether to remove obstacles or to create new ones. Hindus worship Shiva because all things end, and from endings come new beginnings. They believe that karma rules the universe, that rewards or punishments for our actions in previous lives will be meted out in this one, and that our behavior in this life will determine our next life.

"How do Buddhism and Hinduism differ?" I asked our guide.

"The two are hard to distinguish," he said. "Both religions teach mindfulness, or stopping and looking deeply. You do this through conscious breathing. If you are a Hindu, and you become a follower of the Buddha, you don't stop being a Hindu. Buddhists give Brahma, Shiva, and Vishnu an important place. In fact, Hindus regard the Buddha as an incarnation of Vishnu. Religious tolerance is important in Nepal, so proselytism is unlawful. Converter and convert both might get a lengthy jail term!"

Shamvu led us on a walking tour of Pashupatinath, Nepal's holiest Hindu site. Children walked beside us, and we gave them money. We passed men in turbans and loincloths who played flutes and wound live snakes around their bodies. King cobras undulated in time to the haunting music.

Pointing out stone gods, Shamvu explained that Shiva is worshiped at Pashupatinath as a phallic symbol. A bearded ascetic, wearing only a loincloth, called out, "I carry 60 kilos on male organ for ten dollar." I was curious, but Shamvu hurried him away.

We reached the Bagmati River. On the opposite riverbank stood the temple complex, a mixture of corrugated iron roofs clustered around the gilded triple roof of the temple. Shamvu said we would watch from this side of the river because only Hindus were allowed to enter the temple. "Before dawn, Hindus come here and to other temples to wake up the gods," he explained. "They carry metal plates piled with ritual offerings—called *puja*—of rice, red powder, and flower petals. They mix these offerings with clay and apply some to their forehead, between the eyes. This is called *tika,* a symbol of the divine presence."

As we watched the captivating temple scene, holy men contorted themselves into unimaginable positions. Pilgrims washed in the river or crowded into buildings to talk and pray, competing for space with lively monkeys that climbed everywhere. A priest burned human corpses on a funeral pyre and dumped the ashes into the river. Shamvu pointed out individuals who were sick and disabled, explaining that the temple also served as a hospice where they can receive care and engage someone to pray for them. Some people presented flowers, money, milk, and river water to a statue. "They ask Shiva for blessings," Shamvu explained.

Noting individuals by a smoky fire, he went on: "Hindus conduct ritual sacrifices of chickens, goats, buffalo—always male—for weddings, initiation rites, religious festivals, and blessings when building a house. They kill the animal in the presence of the god. An unfortunate brother is released from imprisonment as an animal and given the opportunity to be reborn as a man."

Shamvu told us that the most important festival of the year at Pashupatinath is Shivaratri, the birthday of Shiva. Thousands of pilgrims come from all over the subcontinent, and many walk from India. They take ritual baths and offer prayers to Shiva in his form as Lord Pashupati. Keeping votive oil lamps burning all night long, they sing and beat drums until dawn.

After a Nepalese meal of basmati rice, lentils, chicken, fish, wild boar, spinach, and "fire water," we walked through the center of Kathmandu. Children begged for money and peddlers accosted us. Pedestrians stepped over a sick woman who lay on the ground. Flies buzzed around fresh meat on a table. "Butcher shop," said Shamvu. "Butchers are from the lowest caste."

Shamvu pointed to a building with intricate woodcarvings of deities, peacocks, and doves. "Here lives the Kumari, the living goddess," he said. "She embodies the harmony of Hinduism and Buddhism. Everyone, including the king, pays her homage on the third day of the Indrajatra Festival. She is painted like a hummingbird and rides in a special chariot. Two boys, who represent Ganesh and Bhairav, accompany her." Shamvu gave a donation. The Kumari, an unsmiling girl wearing a colorful headdress and makeup, appeared briefly at an upstairs window.

Shamvu said the Kumari is chosen from a group of four- to five-year-old girls. Men wearing demon masks try to scare the girls by placing bloody buffalo heads around them in the dark. The girl who remains calm and selects belongings of the previous Kumari is considered to be the goddess. Once she reaches puberty, her term ends and she leaves the temple. She can marry, but men hesitate to marry her because an ex-goddess is powerful and may bring bad luck to her husband.

Om Mani Padme Hum

"We've been visiting Hindu sites," Karma said excitedly one morning, "but today we'll go to Bodhnath—a famous Tibetan Buddhist site!" He delighted in anything Tibetan, and so did the rest of us. "Bodhnath is the largest stupa in Nepal. It lies on the ancient trade route from Lhasa. Its design is like a mandala. Also, this is a copy of the stupa that we'll see in Gyantse, in Tibet."

Karma explained that a mandala is basically an image that is painted, carved, or "drawn" with colored sand. In ancient times, monks constructed mandalas with precious gems. Road maps of the universe, mandalas depict the interrelationship of heavenly bodies, the human body, and the mind. They are used for meditation and increased mindfulness.

Buddhist texts contain thousands of mandalas, each of which embodies a deity representing an aspect of buddha nature. Sand mandalas are created as part of an empowerment or initiation ceremony given by a ritual master such as the Dalai Lama.

"Doesn't a monk dismantle a sand mandala by wiping his arm across it?" asked Trudi.

"Yes," said Karma. "That's how monks deconsecrate a sand mandala. The ritual master removes the sand representing the deity. Then he thanks the deity for its great compassion in benefiting students, and he visualizes the deity leaving the mandala. Finally, the monks sweep up the sand and put it in a local body of water. In that way, they share the blessing with all other beings."

Karma led us past pastel, antique buildings staffed with shopkeepers wearing *chupas*. They urged us to purchase fur hats, turquoise and coral jewelry, felt boots, and *chupas* ranging from black wool to teal silk. Also for sale were Buddhist rosaries, prayer wheels, prayer flags, and butter lamps, which Tibetans set next to religious images just as Christians might place candles by icons.

"This is 'Little Tibet.'" Karma said. "When Tibetans escape to Nepal, many of them settle here. In some ways, Little Tibet is more Tibetan than Lhasa. The buildings here are the way things used to look in Lhasa before the Chinese leveled the Tibetan Quarter around the Potala and Jokhang."

Ahead loomed Bodhnath, a gigantic dome-shaped structure with a spike on top. Rising from the whitewashed base stood a four-sided gold pyramid. Each side was painted with a pair of red, white, and blue, droopy-lidded, all-seeing eyes beneath heavy black eyebrows. The compassionate gaze of the eyes followed us everywhere. "They are the Buddha's eyes," said Karma. "The left eye is the sun, and the right eye is the moon. The dot between the eyebrows is the third eye, representing wisdom. Bodhnath is one of the largest stupas in the world. Because it's made of solid rock, we can't go inside. Some people say that a bone from the Buddha is inside."

Rainbows of blue, white, red, green, and yellow prayer flags streamed in all directions from the spire and buildings around Bodhnath. Tibetans with radiant faces walked clockwise around the stupa base, spinning hand-held prayer wheels and large wheels embedded in the stupa's lower walls. Their fingers counted prayer beads, and their lips moved as they chanted silently. When we joined them, they smiled at us. Two women used rags to clean the stupa's prayer wheels.

"The turning motion of the prayer wheels shows that creation and destruction are connected," Karma said. "Tibetans believe that prayers ascend from the heart of the worshiper, from paper scrolls wound up inside spinning prayer wheels, and from writings on prayer flags fluttering in the wind. In Tibet we'll see prayer flags in fields, on rooftops, on roads, and at monasteries. They put prayer into the very air we breathe." He said that when Tibetans converted to Buddhism, they kept beliefs from their ancient Bon religion, vestiges of which still survive in Tibet and Nepal. Bon practices include circumambulating counterclockwise (the opposite of

Buddhist practice), placing stone cairns on hilltops, hanging prayer flags, sending children to be monks or nuns, accumulating merit, going on pilgrimages, and respecting the sanctity of natural places.

"Mani stones," Karma said, pointing to stones with writing painted on them. "We'll see them all over Tibet. The writing spells the Sanskrit mantra, *'Om Mani Padme Hum.'* That's the mantra of Avalokiteshvara, the Buddha of Compassion. He's the patron deity of Tibet. The mantra means 'All hail to the Jewel in the Lotus.' We are like a lotus rising out of mud—compassion blooms in our hearts if we open ourselves to it."

Long ago, Karma explained, a thousand princes wanted to become buddhas. Avalokiteshvara (called Chenrezi by Tibetans) vowed not to attain enlightenment until each of them had become a buddha and all sentient beings had been liberated from suffering. The Buddha granted him the special, noble task of assisting every being toward buddhahood. At that moment, the gods rained flowers on him, the earth shook, and the air rang with the sound, *"Om Mani Padme Hum."* By reciting this mantra, Buddhists protect themselves from negative influences. They purify themselves of the six poisonous emotions of pride, jealousy, desire, ignorance, greed, and anger, transforming them into generosity, harmonious conduct, endurance, enthusiasm, concentration, and insight. Uncovering their true, good, buddha nature, they develop wisdom and compassion, and ultimately attain enlightenment.

Karma led us to a building near the stupa, then into a dark room that was dominated by a massive gold statue of the Buddha smiling serenely and looking into the distance. "This is Sakya Gompa, the monastery of my root lama," he said. "A root lama is one's most important spiritual guru." The air was difficult to breathe because of burning incense and butter lamps, but at the same time the atmosphere felt peaceful and meditative. A monk smiled warmly at me. Tears came to my eyes as I felt close to God—the Nameless, the Infinite.

Outside, Karma said, "People come to Little Tibet from all over the world to celebrate Losar, the Tibetan lunar New Year. Lamas blow copper horns. Masked dancers perform. There is laughter. We drink *chang*, Tibetan barley beer. Everyone throws *tsampa* into the air."

As he spoke, a white cow ambled by, reminding us that we were in Hindu Nepal.

Tibetan Music

"Now we'll visit Swayambhunath," Karma announced, "another important Buddhist stupa. By 1234, Swayambhunath had become an important center for Buddhist learning, and it was closely linked with Lhasa." An ancient structure loomed on top of a green hill west of Kathmandu. Karma said the stupa's base was a white hemispherical mound that represented the four elements of earth, fire, air, and water. The Buddha's all-seeing eyes were painted on four sides. Above the eyes, thirteen gilded rings symbolized the thirteen degrees of knowledge leading to nirvana, which was represented by an umbrella at the top of the structure. Four niches each sheltered a Buddha in a posture of meditation, and a fifth niche contained a Buddha facing the steps to the parking area below. Believers walked clockwise around the building, turning prayer wheels.

Accompanied by children and monkeys, we climbed the three hundred flagstone steps up the steep hill to the terrace on which the stupa was built. In the distance, smoggy Kathmandu looked like a scene in a hazy Buddhist painting. At the top of the hill, hawkers tried to steer us toward Buddhist ritual items laid out on blankets. A statue of a Hindu god stood nearby. Young Tibetan Buddhist monks strolled past, and when Karma stopped them to ask their ages, their leader said they were between eight and fourteen years old.

Karma led us into a monastery filled with burning incense. Butter lamps flickered in front of sacred images. In a dark, smoky room, monks sat in two rows facing each other. They chanted from pages of scripture lying on wooden tables. One monk beat a large frame drum while two others blew into trumpet-like instruments. The atmosphere felt electric in spite of the room's putrid air.

As we emerged from the monastery, Karma explained the role of music in all aspects of Tibetan life, whether plowing fields, harvesting crops, playing games, or even begging. Tibetans sing and dance at weddings and other festive occasions, and when entertaining guests with *chang*. Traditionally, music has not only expressed their love of Buddhism, their sages, and their land, but also criticized political and social ills. Most Tibetan music has never been written down or translated.

Karma explained that sacred Tibetan music consists of chanting and playing wind and percussion instruments, whereas secular music is made up of folksongs *(lu/shye)*, aristocratic music *(nang-ma)*, music from the Dalai Lama's court *(gar)*, and opera *(lha-mo)*. Musicians sometimes play string instruments, though folksongs may be sung without instruments. Opera, which dates back to the twelfth century, is performed outdoors or in large tents during the summer. Opera performers act, recite, dance, and sing, while someone plays cymbals *(rol-mo)* and another person beats a frame drum *(nga)*. Traditionally, dozens of troupes traveled around Tibet to give opera performances that would last for days. Today, Tibetans in exile keep alive this and other forms of music.

An Animated Discussion

After sightseeing, our group was ready for a Tibetan feast. "Meet Dondup, the owner of this restaurant," Karma said excitedly, as his cousin welcomed us to a cold, damp, dimly lit room. "Dondup lives in Kathmandu because he isn't safe in Tibet. His parents went into exile before he was born, so he's never even been to Tibet." A look of sadness crossed Dondup's face for a moment, but soon he was jovial again. He was delighted that we would visit Tibet and witness his country for the world.

Dondup brought platter after platter of steaming *momos*, stir-fried meats and vegetables, curries, rice, and noodles, which we washed down with *chang* or Sprite. In front of every third person, he placed a hotpot with noodles, green beans, and meat. After the meal, he served Tibetan liquor.

As the conversation grew louder, Karen asked about the Tibetan language. "It's Tibeto-Burman," Karma said, "although Tibet shares few cultural traits with Burma. Tibetan has thirty letters based on a form of Sanskrit. It isn't related to Chinese."

"Is exiles' Tibetan changing from the Tibetan used in Tibet?" Karen wanted to know.

"Yes," said Karma. "The Tibetan language has no words for modern concepts like 'computer.' I use the English word, but Tibetans in Tibet use the Chinese word. At times I don't understand what Tibetans say because of this split in the language. Also, in English-speaking countries, we add 's' to Tibetan nouns to make them plural, as in the word *momos*. These changes contribute to the communication problems among Tibetans. And if we Tibetans can't communicate well enough among ourselves, how can we force the Chinese out of Tibet? This is a problem that the Chinese are exploiting."

"Do you think we should boycott Chinese goods?" Ken asked.

"I avoid buying anything Chinese," Karma answered.

"But doesn't that hurt the Chinese people?" Marge asked.

"I only buy Chinese if other goods aren't available," said June.

"But shouldn't we show concern for poverty-stricken Chinese?" I asked.

"By buying Chinese goods, we make China strong," Lorna said.

"China won't give up Tibet on its own," Mike said. "The U.S. and world community need to put pressure on the Chinese government about its human rights record and treatment of Tibet."

"Chinese leaders are afraid of disintegration," said Karma. "They remember when China was vulnerable to foreign attack, to government by warlords, to the opium trade. Separatism is their worst nightmare. That's their motivation for getting back Hong Kong and fighting for Taiwan, or making sure nothing happens to Tibet. Outsiders don't understand how important these 'escaped' territories are to China."

Jack cut in, "In that case, the United States needs to help the Chinese leaders develop a different perspective. Then they may feel more confident about doing the right thing about Tibet."

"The Chinese view the United States as a paper tiger when it comes to Tibet," replied Karma. "The American government speaks loudly, but it doesn't do anything to back up what it says."

Ken disagreed with this view. "The United States hasn't been just a paper tiger. In the early 60s, the CIA organized Tibetan operations against the Chinese. Of course, the CIA didn't do this to defend Tibetans' human rights, much less to support Buddhism. It was part of the Cold War strategy of containment."

Tibetan Refugee Camp

The next morning, our group visited Jawalakhel, the largest Tibetan refugee camp in Kathmandu Valley. The welcome sign at the entrance informed us that the "Tibetan Refugee Camp and Handicraft Center" was established in 1960 with the help of the International Red Cross, Swiss Confederation, and Nepal. The Center employs more than one thousand refugees, many of whom weave traditional carpets from sheep wool. Proceeds from carpet sales "go to the workers to maintain their livelihood, to educate their children, and to support the aged and handicapped."

Karma led us into a cold, damp room filled with Tibetan women wearing *chupas*. I zipped up my jacket against the chill. Poor lighting and rank air filled with floating debris made it difficult to see and breathe. The women sat on stools or on the cement floor, spinning wool by hand. They looked up with soulful eyes. A flood of sorrow overwhelmed me, and my eyes filled with tears. I thought of their struggle, of how they risked their lives to flee Tibet. Now, poverty-stricken, they were trying to build a new life. I walked outside to force back my tears. Karen and Lisa joined me; they, too, were crying.

Don't go back inside, a voice in my head whispered. *Protect yourself from their pain. You didn't cause their problems. Why suffer with them?* Then I thought of my nursing students who were afraid to talk with sick people. I had tried, unsuccessfully, to help them improve their communication skills. Finally, I suggested that they simply be kind; if they saw that others were like themselves—"of their own kind"—perhaps they would have an easier time talking with them as human beings. Almost immediately, the students developed better communication skills. Like my students, I had to steel myself against feeling self-conscious when I went back into the room. I would not focus on the difference between me and these refugees—instead, I would be kind.

A Buddhist phrase came to mind: "Breathe in suffering, and breathe out compassion." Pema Chödrön, an American Buddhist nun, describes this phrase as "*tonglen* practice." She suggests that on the in-breath, we acknowledge our own suffering and the suffering of others. With every out-breath, we open up and feel joy, well-being, satisfaction, tenderheartedness, and anything else that is fresh, clean, wholesome, and good. With this breathing technique, we become increasingly awake to all that the world has to offer—the pain and the joy—rather than hide in a hole that gets continually smaller.

I walked mindfully back into the room of women. On my in-breath, I breathed in their suffering, and on the out-breath, I breathed out compassion. As I circled the room, I stopped by each woman, smiled, bent down, shook her hand gently, and said, *"Tashi delek."*

"Tashi delek," each woman replied, smiling back brightly. My intention was to be kind to them, but they breathed in my suffering and returned kindness to me.

A woman spoke to Karma in Tibetan. "She wants us to sing for them," he said, chuckling. June started a rendition of "Old McDonald Had a Farm," and the rest of our group joined her. After several verses, everyone—Caucasians and Tibetans—burst out laughing.

In other rooms, women were dying wool and weaving rugs. A young woman called out to me in broken English, "Give coins from America . . . I collect . . . help me come to America." When I gave her money, she told me that her name was Tashi. She was twenty-six years old, married, and had two children. Two toddlers with sparkling eyes appeared from behind a carpet and hugged me.

The carpet shop had hundreds, perhaps thousands, of Tibetan carpets for sale. They ranged from two-foot squares to carpets that could cover the floor of an entire room, all with traditional designs in blue, red, yellow, green, brown, and black. In one room stood an altar with a picture of the fourteenth Dalai Lama. Buddhist paintings and portraits of the King and Queen of Nepal hung on a wall.

After Mike and I bought two carpets, the sales clerk urged us to support the "Free Tibet" movement. She hugged me and choked up as she said, "God loves you because you have a compassionate heart. God bless you." I wondered what god she meant: the Buddha, or the God of Western religions? What difference did it make? The Infinite can be described by many names. Most important, we were connecting. "Thank you," I said through tears. "You have a compassionate heart. God bless you."

Back at the hotel, I sat in bed and meditated on mindfulness. I thought of the Tibetan teacher Sogyal Rinpoche, who wrote that through mindfulness we can "bring home" our scattered, fragmented mind. Mindfulness helps us to dissolve negativity and unveil our essential good heart. As we remain open and mindful, we begin to feel well-being, a profound sense of ease.

I began an entry in my journal. *I feel guilty because several families could live for a year on the money Mike and I are spending on this trip. My heart goes out to everyone we've met, but I feel most deeply moved by the Tibetans, the people of the Dalai Lama. Is there a way to help them? What does this experience mean? Tomorrow we'll enter Tibet, and answers may become clearer.*

Chapter 6

Suffering

A Disturbing Dream

On our last evening in Nepal before leaving for Tibet, Mike and I sat with Karma at dinner. We wondered how he was able to treat everyone with compassion. "Ever since we traveled with you in China," Mike said, "we've been wanting to ask about Lou. Do you remember him? He was a real jerk! We were angry about how he treated you, but you were kind to him."

"Lou wasn't the easiest person to like," Karma said with a twinkle in his eyes. "If I remember right, he gave me a generous tip. That wasn't what motivated me, though. As a Buddhist, I believe in karma, not just because it's my name, but because it's a good way to live. I think the purpose of life is to become a better, more compassionate person, and to help anyone I come in contact with to become a better, more compassionate person. That's what I was trying to do."

"Your life is meaningful," I said. "By taking us to Tibet, you put money in the pockets of Tibetans, you educate us about Tibet, and you inspire us to help Tibetans. Being around you encourages me to live up to my best values. If everyone in our group does that, the group will function smoothly."

Karma's face lit up. "This is the best way to use my life." Then the smile left his face, and he looked distressed. "It's not easy for me to see how things have deteriorated in Tibet. Each time I go back, the situation is worse. You'll find out what I mean tomorrow when we enter Tibet."

That night I had a disturbing dream. Mike and I were in our living room with a man and woman who were offering me a job that I wanted. A child walked into the room and introduced herself as our daughter. We were surprised to learn we were parents, but soon she charmed all of us. When we turned back to our guests, however, she didn't think she was getting enough attention, so she ran around the room. We ignored her, and she screamed and rolled on the floor. She disappeared into the kitchen and returned with knives, which she threw into the wooden floor. I put my arms around her to calm her as our guests made a hasty exit. Distraught, I asked Mike, "How can I take a demanding job when our daughter needs attention?" He told me she was adopted, her problems might be genetic, and maybe we should try medication to settle her down. "I don't want to give her pills!" I protested. "I thought things were going well, but now they're falling apart."

I woke up frightened. When I calmed down, I realized my dream was reminding me of the child within who felt scared about going to Tibet. My dream was advising me to stop ignoring her and denying that she was part of me. If I comforted her, she could represent new growth. I visualized cuddling her. "I'll take good care of you," I promised. "I love you." Eventually, I went back to sleep. The dream was prophetic, for we were about to experience suffering in Tibet.

Pain

"All aboard for Tibet," Karma said excitedly after breakfast. "Lhasa is only six hundred miles and five days away. "We'll drive seventy-one miles to the Tibet-Nepal border. Dondup will carry our luggage in a truck. On the way, we'll see some of the world's most spectacular scenery. After going through customs, we'll have five more miles to Zhangmu. That's where we will stay overnight. Are you ready?" Our travel group enthusiastically climbed into the Nepalese bus. Finally, we were on the road to Tibet.

The streets of Kathmandu turned into a narrow gravel road twisting through green fields and villages. Villagers waved as we passed. The weather was warm and sunny, and on either side of us verdant gorges dripped with water and flowers sparkled in the sun. The Himalayan Mountains rose ahead. "We're going across them," Karma announced, as the road became steeper and more winding. When we stopped to take photos of Kathmandu Valley below, children with dirt-caked hair and clothes appeared from nowhere and pointed to their mouths. A girl carried on her back a toddler dressed only in a T-shirt. Karma talked with them kindly and several of us handed out candy.

As the altitude increased, the landscape turned from subtropical green to golden and then brown. Flowers, fields, and grass became scarce. In their place, stones and sand appeared. The temperature dropped, and I put on a sweater. The road became steeper. Hairpin turns made visibility near zero. Every time we met a colorful Nepalese truck, our bus stopped so the truck could inch around us. The road barely hung onto the mountain, with no guardrails to protect us should the driver make a wrong move. He downshifted for the turns, and the old bus engine groaned.

Trudi's face turned white as she looked over the side and saw a rusty vehicle far below. Evidently it had slid down the cliff. "Oh lord, I hope the brakes don't fail!" Karen responded with a laugh that was contagious, and soon the rest of us were joking, too. Later, she told me, "In traveling, I've found it's important to turn negatives into positives."

As the bus rattled into the village of Karichour, Nepal, Karma made a welcome announcement: "We'll stretch our legs at the truck stop. There's even a bathroom. That's something we won't see much of in Tibet. I'll treat you to a beer or soda." The truck stop consisted of a room with a few tables and chairs and one wall open to the narrow dirt road. A woman and man behind the counter offered soft drinks, beer, bottled water, and clothing. I carefully climbed the steep, dark, dirty wooden steps to the bathroom below, where the tiny space was only large enough for a hole in the floor. I held my breath because of the stench and tried to keep from stepping in excrement.

Back upstairs, Mike and I watched people walking by with large packs on their backs. Aside from the truck stop, the village consisted of one street with a handful of small shops on either side. The shops displayed dry goods, clothes, food, and beverages. Nepalese trucks rumbled through, revving their motors and spewing exhaust. The street was so narrow that when two trucks met, a traffic jam occurred. A jovial crowd gathered, and, amid the crowd's instructions, the two drivers slowly maneuvered their trucks around each other.

The bus continued on its bumpy way. Each day, everyone (except Karma, Bernie, and Alice) rotated seats so that we'd all have the opportunity to sit in front. Karma sat behind the bus driver on the left, and because Bernie was "Honorable Treasurer," he and Alice were assigned to the seat behind Karma. Today Alice sat alone in that seat, for Bernie had taken over the right front seat. Mike and I sat in the back seat, which seemed to jump up and down with every bump in the road. We held on to each other and to the seat in front of us so we wouldn't slide onto the floor or hit the roof of the bus.

As the road worsened, the jarring increased. I developed abdominal pain and nausea, probably from food I had eaten in Kathmandu. I felt like someone was throwing knives into me, just as the girl threw knives into the floor during my dream the previous night. Mike and Jack urged me to go up front where the seats weren't so bumpy. "Since all the seats are filled," Jack suggested, "ask Bernie if you can sit with him. Alice and Bernie don't have a right to both front seats."

Anger

I struggled to the front, grabbing seats so I wouldn't fall down. "I have abdominal pain," I yelled to Bernie and Alice over the roar of the engine. "Sitting in back makes it worse. Could I sit with one of you for a while?" Alice stared ahead grimly, but Bernie yelled back, "It's bumpy up here, too." Neither of them invited me to sit down. I persisted, "It's much better up here. Please, I need to sit up here." With obvious irritation, Bernie curtly motioned for me to take the window seat by him. I sat down, trying not to disturb him, and I leaned against the wall of the bus to reduce the jarring.

June, who sat alone in the seat behind Alice, looked at Mike by himself in the back seat. She yelled to him, "Mike, why don't you and I change places so you and Mim can sit together." I yelled to June, "You're wonderful. Thank you." June and Mike changed places, and I joined Mike. I held the backpack firmly on my abdomen and leaned against the side of the bus. Mike leaned against me. The ride was still bumpy, but I no longer felt like I had knives in my abdomen.

Until now, our group had gotten along well. Now we were angry with each other, exhausted, oxygen-depleted, headachy, and queasy. By monopolizing both front seats, Bernie and Alice had become scapegoats for the others' irritation. On previous tours, Mike and I noticed that someone who behaved badly became a scapegoat; the more dysfunctional the group, the more the members got locked into harmful roles. In China, Lou performed the scapegoat's role admirably. But the more we ostracized Lou, the worse he acted. On this trip, the group was turning against Bernie and Alice. If our group became dysfunctional, we would end up with suffering on emotional, spiritual, and even physical levels.

I thought about karma, and how the impact of our positive and negative behavior registers deep within. Unless we recognize the destructive potential of our negative emotions and thoughts, we'll nurture them until they grow and lead to negative actions. If we act unkindly, we may at first feel justified, but eventually we develop a sense of unease and alienation, leading to more negative behavior. As the cycle continues, we become oblivious to the impact that our actions have on others and on ourselves, which results in suffering and interferes with happiness.

I endeavored to put myself in the mindset of Buddhism's Eightfold Path: right knowledge, aspiration, speech, behavior, livelihood, effort, mindfulness, and absorption. Rather than resent Bernie and Alice, I'd try to be compassionate toward them. I leaned forward and asked Alice how she was doing. "I don't feel well," she said. "My stomach has been upset for two days."

"I'm sorry," I said as kindly as I could, given my anger at her and Bernie. "This drive must be hard." Alice nodded tearfully. I leaned back in my seat, feeling better about her. Perhaps she and Bernie were monopolizing the front seats because they were sick. They deserved our sympathy, not our hostility.

The bus stopped abruptly at a log blocking the road. "Checkpoint," Karma announced. Since leaving Kathmandu, we had gone through several checkpoints. Each time, Karma had paid a fee, and men standing on the roadside had lifted the log. This time, men at the checkpoint took our passports into a shed by the road. Karma tried to soothe us, realizing how vulnerable we felt without our passports.

Once we had our passports back, he warned, "Now that we are about to enter Tibet, the oppressiveness of autocracy will become all too clear! In Tibet, be careful what you say about the Chinese. If we are alone on the bus, you can ask questions. But when we are out of the bus, Chinese spies dressed as monks, tourists, businessmen, beggars—anybody—may try to follow us.

Best to avoid political topics. Don't talk about 'Free Tibet.' If they don't like what we say, they may kick us out of the country, or keep me from going back to Tibet again. They could make life miserable for our Tibetan staff."

Disappointment

The bus rumbled into Kodari, the border town and last checkpoint. "Well, folks, this is it," said Karma. "I never know if the Chinese will let me back into Tibet."

He told us to walk to the Nepalese side of Friendship Bridge, the bridge separating Nepal and Tibet. The Chinese officials would most likely go through his luggage, he said, but probably not ours, unless they were suspicious of something. When porters brought back our luggage, we needed to make sure everything was there. The porters were from the Tingri region at the foot of Mount Everest, a hundred or so miles to the east. We could identify them by the coiled ropes they used in their work. Because they were desperately poor, they would beg us for money, but Karma would pay them on our behalf.

Jack asked Karma why he had so much luggage. "Our travel documents are in this bag," replied Karma, lifting a brown duffel. "In one suitcase, I put my clothes. The other suitcase is full of gifts from Tibetans in the States for Tibetans in Lhasa. I'm just a boy going home, bringing makeup and other things they can't get in Tibet. Then I'll carry back what the people in Tibet want to send to their relatives in the States. Dried yak meat and yak cheese and other things you can't get in the United States."

We got out of the bus and started walking up the steep road to Friendship Bridge. Sloshing through mud and puddles, we confided our excitement and anxiety about entering Tibet. "I wrote a letter for Amnesty International," Bernie whispered. "I hope that won't be a problem."

I whispered back, "Mike and I are members of a Tibetan organization. June, did you hide your 'Free Tibet' T-shirts?"

"You bet I did," she said. "They'll never find them."

As we waited on the Nepalese side of Friendship Bridge, the sun came out and then disappeared again. The temperature dropped, and a cold rain began to fall. The Nyanang River cascaded down the mountain far below the bridge. Zhangmu, on the Tibet side, sat precariously in the middle of a sheer cliff high above. "That's spectacular! Just what I thought we'd see in Tibet," Mike gushed.

"We're supposed to stay in Zhangmu tonight," noted Jack, "but I don't see a road to get up there."

On the Nepalese side of the bridge, Nepal's blue and maroon flag blew in the wind. Beneath it, Nepalese soldiers joked over cups of tea by a customs house. A People's Liberation Army (PLA) guardhouse stood on the Tibetan side of the bridge. The Chinese flag, deep red with five stars, flew beside a single sentry standing rigidly at attention with other Chinese soldiers nearby.

The porters, many of whom were boys, struggled up the muddy road with our luggage. Some bags looked larger than the boys who were dragging them. One porter exclaimed, "Those damn Americans! Why do they have so much luggage?" Their poverty contrasted sharply with the wealth of our group.

After a long wait, Karma and Dondup appeared. They looked stressed from dealing with the Chinese officials. "We've cleared customs," Karma said with a sigh, "and we're ready to cross over into Tibet. I told them that we're paying guests, so they'd better let us in. Unfortunately, we have to say goodbye to Dondup now. It's not safe for him to go across the border." Dondup gave Karma an emotional handshake. Then he put a *kata* around each of us and shook our hands. *"Tashi delek,"* he said with deep emotion. *"Tashi delek,"* we replied solemnly.

Karma led the way across Friendship Bridge, and we walked gingerly into a land where we felt vulnerable. The porters followed with our luggage. Pointing to an old flatbed truck, Karma said, "This truck will carry our luggage. If our bus gets stalled, it can bring us help." Exhausted, we climbed onto an old bus. Bernie and Alice once again took both front seats. Mike and I sat on the seat behind Alice. The Chinese bus was larger than the Nepalese bus, and there were plenty of seats for everyone.

Karma turned on an ancient, crackling microphone to introduce us to a Tibetan woman and man who entered the bus. "Tara will be our guide in Tibet, and Ngawang will drive the bus. I just met them now myself, but I know we're in good hands."

Tara was about five feet tall and couldn't have weighed more than 100 pounds. Her large brown eyes were full of humor and compassion, but also suffering. Each day of the trip, she wore the same faded blue jeans and sweatshirt. Her hair was pulled into a ponytail. Ngawang had a jolly look, although sadness periodically came into his eyes. Because he couldn't speak English, he didn't say much, but he was quick to help when needed. Tara placed a *kata* around each traveler's neck. She welcomed us to Tibet in limited, broken English. Tears flooded my eyes, and I stared out the window. She announced that we had been scheduled to stay in Zhangmu, but the hotel had been torn down. This meant that we'd eat a late lunch in Zhangmu and then continue on to Nyalam, where we would spend the night.

Most likely, Karma was disappointed about Tara's poor English, but he repeatedly went out of his way to draw on her expertise throughout the trip and to keep her from feeling insecure about her language skills. Moved by his example, we gradually developed affection for her, and then we had an easier time comprehending what she was saying.

I wondered how often I treat people with compassion when they disappoint me. Before I left home, a Tibetan Buddhist nun had told me that compassion means "doing the right thing at the right time in the right place," which, of course, is also a definition of ethics. Ethics and compassion are interchangeable, because to act ethically means to be compassionate, and vice versa.

Anxiety

After several tries, the old bus engine struggled to life. We were off, with the luggage truck behind us. "Zhangmu is 7,541 feet high!" Karma yelled. "That's 2,300 meters!" I could barely hear him over the roar of the engine and the tires on the dirt road. "Twenty years ago, Zhangmu didn't exist. Then the Chinese built Friendship Highway, the highway between Friendship Bridge and Lhasa. Of course, it's not a highway, but a dirt road." He laughed, and so did everyone else, an expression of our anxiety. "Chengdu, the capital of the Chinese province of Sichuan on the other side of Tibet, is about a ten-day hard drive on this highway. Trucks come to this border town carrying cheap Chinese goods or wool and animal skins from Tibet. When they get to Friendship Bridge, the porters who carried our luggage put the goods from the Chinese trucks into Nepalese trucks, which take them to Kathmandu."

Ngawang slowly maneuvered the bus along the steep switchback ascent to Zhangmu. The mountains surrounding us were more than a landscape. They were awe-inspiring monuments for which the word "beautiful" would be far too pallid. They resembled rows of gigantic temples, each with individual galleries, ledges, balconies, cornices, and recesses, crowned with spires, domes, and pinnacles.

The cold rain was turning to sleet.

"Spend night in Nyalam," Tara shouted over the microphone. "Altitude 12,500 feet—3,750 meters." In one day of traveling from Kathmandu to Nyalam, we would climb about 8,000 feet. According to the guidebooks, we were only supposed to ascend 1,000 feet per day to avoid altitude sickness, or "acute mountain sickness" (AMS).

Mike and I had consulted a travel physician before leaving home. He couldn't predict if we would get AMS. There was no way to train to avoid it, he said, but we could eventually become acclimated to the altitude. Symptoms of AMS include headache, nausea, vomiting, dizziness, confusion from cerebral edema (swelling of the brain), wheezing, coughing, shortness of breath, a gurgling sound in the lungs, and chest pains indicating pulmonary edema (fluid in the lungs). Altitude sickness can be life threatening. The only cure is to go to a lower altitude and breathe more oxygen as fast as possible. Individuals with AMS may refuse to believe how ill they are, so their companions must insist they go to a lower altitude. Diamox can be administered to lessen symptoms of AMS if it is taken before going up high, but a side effect of this drug is tingling in the hands and feet, which worsens as the altitude increases.

Because of Mike's allergy to sulfa, the physician advised Mike not to take Diamox, but he gave me a prescription. Considering the side effects, Karma suggested that I not start it unless I really needed it. Now that we were climbing fast, I wondered if I needed Diamox after all. Ordinary breathing was a whole new ball game. With each breath I felt thirsty for more oxygen. Mike's skin color was becoming darker, indicating a lack of oxygen. Both of us worried about what was happening to our bodies.

Ngawang drove into Zhangmu, a near vertical zigzag of shacks, where everyone was from somewhere else, drawn by the possibility of making money. Tibetans, Chinese, and Nepalese walked in and out of shops. Picturesque Tibetan buildings mingled with Chinese cement structures. Chinese music blared from karaoke bars. "We'll eat lunch here," Karma said, as our group climbed off the bus and entered a bleak, unheated room. Windows with broken glass provided a breezy view of the mountains. I zipped my winter jacket and put up my hood.

A woman seated us at round tables covered with soiled oilcloths. The floor was muddy and chairs were broken. In the center of each table stood a Chinese-style glass turntable, known as a "lazy Susan" back in the United States. The woman put bowls of steaming Chinese cabbage soup on the turntables and gave each of us a small dirty plate, bowl, and spoon. Karma and Tara passed out box lunches from Kathmandu. They had not been refrigerated. Mine contained a still-warm piece of cooked chicken, condiments, two hard-boiled eggs, and sponge cake. The eggs looked unappetizing, but the chicken smelled good. My abdominal pain and nausea had subsided, and I felt hungry. I ate the chicken and sipped Sprite.

Fear

Karma announced that we could either use Zhangmu's public restroom or wait for the bus to stop along the way. I decided to wait after Mike reported that the restroom was no more than a five-foot-high wall facing the gorge below, though it had excellent ventilation and views.

On the road again, Ngawang brought the bus to a halt. Karma called out, "Men to the front, and women to the rear behind the rocks."

"We're taking a rock stop," Karen laughed, as we women disappeared behind some rocks. We came to prefer rock stops to most toilets in Tibet: The scenery and smell were better, by far. However, we had to do our business quickly, or Tibetans would almost magically appear from nowhere and stand watching us. They didn't seem embarrassed, so we learned not to be, either.

The narrow gravel road zigzagged up a gorge scored into the steep cliffs. As the altitude increased the sleet turned into snow, which came down hard. The road changed from slush to ice. Visibility, never good because of the hairpin turns, became almost zero. When Mike learned that the bus had no defroster for its windshield, he offered his charge card, which Karma used to scrape ice off the front window. Conversation stopped. Everyone seemed focused on the driver. "Please help him," I prayed, my hand at my throat.

To calm my fear, I thought about the Buddhist perspective on the preciousness of human life. Buddhism teaches that each person, even those who behave badly, accomplished something incredible in a previous life in order to be born as a human in this life. Many Buddhist writers claim that this perspective leads to self-esteem and compassion, compared with the belief that individuals are born in original sin and have a propensity toward aggression.

While I was trying to distract myself with Buddhist philosophy, the slippery, steep climb became more arduous as the road snaked round and round, higher and higher. Suddenly, the road disappeared. Ngawang slammed on the brakes and the bus slid to a halt—ten feet short of a sixty-foot drop. There was no road or bridge in sight. Ngawang took a deep breath and then calmly backed up the bus. I quieted my pounding heart. Eventually, he found another route up the mountain, and we continued on our way.

"This road was built in 1969," Karma shouted, trying to comfort us. "It's called 'Highway to Hell.' The pass ahead is 'the Gates of Hell.' We're traveling in the spring because the road washes out during the summer rainy season. In winter, snow makes the road impassable, and frequent avalanches make it easy to tumble off the edge of the cliff. But I promise you, that won't happen to us."

Jack cut the tension by cracking a joke. "Hey, Karen," he shouted, "did you pay our insurance premium?" She joked back that "insurance won't help us in hell."

As the sun set, the temperature dropped well below freezing. I shivered despite my two pairs of long johns, warm socks, gloves, and a winter jacket—an outfit that would be my uniform both day and night in Tibet. Pulling up my hood, I huddled with Mike to stay warm.

With all the jarring, my abdominal pain and nausea returned. I regretted eating the chicken in Zhangmu. Mike's skin color was turning brownish and his nails were becoming blue from lack of oxygen. I was frightened. We were on a dangerous, life-threatening ride from which we could not escape.

To calm myself, I meditated using an exercise taught by Thich Nhat Hanh, a Vietnamese Buddhist monk. "In, out . . . deep, slow . . . calm, ease . . . smile, release . . . present moment, wonderful moment," I said as I breathed in, out, in, out. Hanh wrote that the purpose of meditation is to heal and transform. In this frightening situation, I needed both healing and transformation.

Rather than avoid my fear of dying, I followed Buddhist teachings and meditated on death. I visualized my fears coming to the surface and flying away. Soon I no longer worried so much about what could happen. Instead, I felt mindful of the present. My breathing grew lighter, gentler, slower, and deeper. I entered a more relaxed, peaceful state, bringing some harmony to my body, mind, and spirit. My abdominal pain and nausea lessened. I squeezed Mike's hand to reassure him.

No Way Out

It was dark by the time the bus reached Nyalam. Cold and exhausted, we looked forward to the comfort of our hotel . . . but it wasn't to be. Ngawang stopped in front of a cement building. "Only rooms available," Tara announced. We waded through deep snow, climbed steps, and entered a dirty, cold lobby. Tara led us up a dark stairway to a small room with two holes in the floor and excrement everywhere. "Toilets," Tara said. "Just cleaned. No running water. No toilet paper."

In the dim light of our bleak, unheated room, Mike and I saw two broken chairs, two twin beds covered with dirty pink spreads over thick quilts, two basins on a stand, and a dresser with a thermos of hot water for tea. Acrid smoke hung in the air from cooking fires made with spruce boughs. Dirty towels lay on the window ledge. I tried to pull shut the torn curtains, which hung at large windows overlooking a nearby building, but they would not budge. Someone outside was singing off-key to loud Chinese music, which would blare all night long. "I hope we don't get asphyxiated," I said. "How can we sleep here in this cold? The room is too dirty to open our luggage!"

Eager for warmth, Mike and I walked to a tiny restaurant where our group was gathering. It, too, was unheated. We sat on a bench in a dimly lit room below street level, huddling around a table covered by a dirty oilcloth. In a back room, a woman and man cooked over the fire of a blowtorch. Smoke made breathing difficult. The man brought small plates, bowls, spoons, and chopsticks, and then he served steaming rice, vegetables, and meat. The food smelled good, but most of us felt too sick and tired to eat anything.

"Including tonight, we have only four nights of winter camping until we reach Lhasa," Karen said, trying to be positive.

"We didn't bring equipment for winter camping," Trudi grumbled. "We're not prepared for these conditions."

Back in our room, I put the quilts from both twin beds onto one bed so we could snuggle together and keep each other warm. We took off our shoes, but nothing else, and climbed under the covers. The bed was icy cold and too small for both of us. The quilts slid to the floor. I stood up in my stocking feet on the dirty, frigid floor and alternated the quilts crosswise and lengthwise. The covers stayed in place, but now I was too chilled and sick to sleep. All night long I was up and down with vomiting and diarrhea. Each time I got up, I became even more chilled. Mike, usually like a hot furnace, was too cold to warm me.

This experience was turning ghastly. We wondered why we'd come. No one could airlift us out. We didn't want to drive back to Kathmandu *or* stay in Nyalam. There wasn't a way out. We had no choice but to continue to Lhasa, four days away, during which the altitude would range from 12,500 to 17,500 feet. Tibet's only airport was in Lhasa. When we got there, we could decide whether to fly home early.

Physical challenges are supposed to sharpen the mind and focus one's thoughts. That has seldom been true for me, especially when I'm sick and cold. As Mike dozed, ideas bounced around in my head like stones kicked loose on the mountainside.

More than at any time in my life, I felt homesick. I desperately wanted to be lying in my own warm, comfortable bed at home. Yet, I didn't want to miss the rest of the trip. I told myself we were fortunate to experience Tibet before it becomes westernized. Tibet felt like a holy land to me, though what it offered its pilgrims was different from what I had expected. Perhaps we were on this pilgrimage to Lhasa to learn more about suffering.

Like the frightened child in my dream, I needed comfort. The only comfort here was spiritual. I remembered reading about the late Dr. Tenzin Choedrak, the Dalai Lama's senior personal physician, and what he did to survive seventeen years in a Chinese prison. He accepted his fate by viewing what was positive and negative as his karma. Every day he visualized a purifying white light suffusing his body. The light ascended through his tantric energy centers and washed away all of his suffering, replacing it with ineffable joy. This technique was similar to a Jewish meditation, so I decided to try it.

I visualized a point of light above my head where, according to the Kabbalah, the Infinite's vast energy connects to one's spiritual being. The light surrounded me, and I breathed it in. I imagined that the light became bluish and washed away all my negativity before leaving through my feet. Then the beam faded until only the point of light remained above my head.

As my body relaxed, I visualized sitting in a rocking chair and cuddling my inner child. Soon I felt like the Infinite was embracing me. I recited the Tibetan Buddhist mantra, *"Om Mani Padme Hum."* Then I repeated the Jewish mantra in Hebrew and in English, *"Sh'ma Yisrael: Adonai Eloheinu, Adonai Echad!* Hear O Israel, Adonai is our God, Adonai is One!" I felt strengthened, cleansed, and connected to the Infinite. Despite illness and the cold, I finally dozed off.

◆ ◆ ◆

Mike and I awoke feeling stiff, cold, and tired. Because we still were wearing our clothes from the day before, we didn't need to dress. Vanity about our appearance was no longer a priority; all our energies were focused on survival. We walked into the hall where everyone except June looked haggard and complained about it being "the worst night of my life."

"The temperature in our room is thirty-four degrees," announced Jack. "That's inside!"

"I slept like a log," said June cheerily. "Must be from taking Diamox."

A foot of snow had fallen. It was still dark outside, but Mike's brown skin and blue nails were even more apparent than the night before. Tara suggested that Mike breathe from an oxygen pillow, but Mike insisted weakly that he was fine and did not need oxygen.

When we returned to the grimy restaurant for breakfast, we felt somewhat comforted as the man from the night before served hot dumplings, scrambled eggs, and congee, Chinese cereal. I sampled the congee, but Mike didn't eat anything. "At least we didn't have to sleep outside or in a yak-skin tent," I said, trying to lighten everyone's mood. "Some Tibetans might view this hotel as luxurious."

"If it were summer," said June brightly, "the temperature would be warmer, but monsoons might wash away the road. I heard that a group of Americans who traveled here last summer had to rebuild the road in order to get to Lhasa. We don't have to do that!"

Karma walked into the restaurant. Lorna complained that he hadn't warned us about the difficult conditions in Tibet. "I didn't know it would be so cold," Karma said wearily, "or I would have told you ahead of time." He seemed exasperated with our grumbling. "Now, let's finish our breakfast so we can get on the road. You'll feel better once you adjust to the altitude."

As we walked to the bus, Mike pulled his jacket sleeves down over his cold, oxygen-starved fingers. "Suffering in Tibet is giving me a new appreciation for the power of nature," he said to me. "On the way to Lhasa, we'll have time to think about what's really important. This will give us a chance to reflect on the preciousness and fragility of human life!"

Chapter 7

The Nature of Reality

Dependent Origination

As our group waited to get on the bus, I overheard Karen whisper to Karma, "Please ask Bernie and Alice not to take both front seats. Other people don't feel well and need to sit up there."

Karma acted immediately. "Whoever is sick can sit in front," he announced. "Honorable Treasurer Bernie, you and Alice sit in your seat on the left. Lorna and Mike are suffering from altitude sickness. Lorna, you sit in the right front seat. Mike, you and Mim sit behind Bernie and Alice. Trudi, you aren't feeling well, so you and Ken sit behind Lorna. The rest of you, sit where you wish. Is that all right?" Everyone but Bernie and Alice called out, "Yes!" Karen made an ironic crack about how much she liked sitting in back. Using humor, she helped to defuse a tense situation.

Ngawang cranked up the old bus engine and off we went. The town didn't look as bleak as it had the night before. Snow was melting, turning the street to mud. It was nine in the morning and the sun was just rising over the mountain peaks.

The late appearance of the dawn reminded me of the curious way China had taken care of its regions' time zones: All functioned under Beijing time. Even though Tibet is far to the west of Beijing, Tibet and the rest of China are, administratively, in

119

the same time zone as Beijing. I yelled up to Karma, "How do Tibetans like being on Beijing time?"

"They don't like it, but they can't do anything about it. They adjust. Offices and shops don't open 'til 9:30 or 10:00 A.M. At midday people take a break, then they open up again at 7:00 or so at night."

During a rock stop, Mike complimented Karma. "You handled the seating situation well back there. How are you able to deal so effectively with difficult people? As an attorney, I'd like to have your skills."

"Buddhism teaches that we are interdependent," said Karma with a grin. "I'm affected by other people, and they're affected by me. I think everyone wants to behave well. If I approach difficult people in a way they can accept, they behave better than if I don't. It's up to me to find out how to approach each person. I try to deal with people in a manner that brings out their best."

On the bus, I thought of how interdependent we are with each other and with the environment. The Dalai Lama teaches that because of karma, we suffer if there's a gap between reality and how we view things. When we don't understand what's really going on, we're more likely to behave in harmful ways. We need to learn about the nature of reality—that everything and everyone arises from and is dependent on a complex web of interrelated factors. "Dependent origination" is the name given to the concept that no person, thing, or event comes into existence or remains by itself.

A tree, for example, seems like a distinct object. If we look at it closely, though, we realize it has no independent existence. Rain and snow water it, wind blows off leaves and branches, soil and sun give it nourishment. Everything in the universe helps to make the tree what it is; therefore, we can't isolate the tree from anything else. Human beings also illustrate the concept of dependent origination. The person I am today is a result of all my behavior up to this point, as well as my parents, friends, genes, education, work, diet, lifestyle, and multiple other factors. To perceive individual objects within the world is a kind of blindness, since everything exists in relationship to everything else.

Because of this principle, the Dalai Lama teaches, we are mutually dependent. We can't separate a phenomenon from its context anymore than individuals can be distinguished from the factors that created them. Each person's well-being is intimately connected with everyone else's, and with the environment. Every thought, word, and deed—no matter how inconsequential—has implications not only for the individual, but for all people. Therefore, it's in everyone's interest to do what promotes happiness and to avoid what results in suffering.

While I was thinking about this, the bus bumped, bounced, and swerved over a rocky dirt track. The drive was punctuated with sudden stops, diversions, and washouts. I thought of how jarring the ride was for everyone, including Bernie and Alice. One person's anger about the trip influenced everyone else, and so did one person's humor, as Karen had demonstrated. Despite my illness, I wanted to rise up to my best behavior and encourage the others to do the same. Accepting that "we are all in this together," whether on the bus or anywhere else, would make the trip more enjoyable for everyone.

As we drove along, the vast, treeless wilderness almost defied words. There were no electric or telephone wires. No airplanes flew overhead. Our noisy bus was the only traffic, except for the occasional Tibetan walking along the road and a Chinese army truck that passed us. Now and then, colorful Buddhist paintings appeared on large rocks. In the bright light the mountaintops seemed closer than they were. Pointing to the clear sky, Karma said, "No pollution here. But we'll see other places in Tibet where Chinese factories and mining are causing pollution."

Enormous landscapes opened up, seemingly devoid of life. Wildlife and forests were noticeably absent. "This part of Tibet has always been barren," said Karma. "Other areas had large forests, but the Chinese cut them down and sent the lumber to China. The PLA machine-gunned most of Tibet's deer, antelope, and wild asses, just for fun. That's caused much hardship for Tibetans." Just then, a nomad settlement came into view, and he pointed to yaks standing by tents that were pitched in deep snow on the steep side of a mountain. "We still have yaks, and nomads, though."

Tibetans and yaks are interdependent, he said. Nomads use yaks for shelter, food, and transportation. A yak-skin tent has one room where the whole family lives; inside, huge pots simmer over an open fire of yak dung and juniper branches. From *dri* (female yak) milk Tibetans make cheese, which hangs from the ceiling, and butter to put in candles and drink in tea. When used for transportation, yaks are sure-footed on steep, snowy mountain paths, and extreme cold and low oxygen don't bother them.

Tara pointed in the distance. "Famous cave where Milarepa meditated. Tibet's greatest songwriter and poet. In eleventh century. Disciple of Marpa. Chose ascetic path, not monastery. Founded Kagyupa sect. Good karma. Attained enlightenment in one lifetime. Monastery built there in reign of fifth Dalai Lama. Monastery being renovated. Tibetans go there on pilgrimage."

As she finished her description, the bus screeched to a stop. All of us got out to view the unusual spectacle of a traffic accident in the middle of the vast, desolate snowscape. A jeep driven by two Caucasian men had come around a cliff and collided with the Chinese army truck that had passed us earlier. Both vehicles blocked the narrow road cutting into the mountainside. Chinese soldiers stood in the snow trying to figure out what to do. They looked like boys in men's uniforms that were too big for them, but their unsmiling faces told us to stay away. The jeep was too badly damaged to start, and the only way to get around the vehicles was to drive on the outside of the road, on a patch of snow and ice.

Thupten, the driver of our luggage truck, offered to go first. He started to drive forward, knowing full well that if the truck slid on the ice, it would tumble to the bottom of the mountain far below, taking him and our luggage with it. To ease my fear, I whispered to Mike, "Time to meditate on interdependence. This is where we can really see how all of us—Chinese, Tibetans, and Caucasians—are mutually dependent."

Thupten was able to inch the luggage truck around the bus, the army truck, and finally the jeep. The Tibetans didn't seem alarmed, since they were joking in Tibetan, but the other members of our group were worried. When Thupten reached the other side, the soldiers didn't crack a smile, but everyone else clapped. Now it was Ngawang's turn to drive the bus around the stalled vehicles. Halfway through, the bus got stuck in the snow, forcing Tara and Thupten to take out rusty shovels and dig out around the tires. Swaying precariously from side to side, the top-heavy bus crept along the truck tracks. When Ngawang finally made it to the other side, we piled back in and prepared to continue along the road. Even though the Caucasian men might have been spies for China, Karma let them ride with Thupten in the luggage truck until they could find a place to call for help. I felt sorry for the forlorn soldiers we left behind next to their smashed truck.

Being the Dalai Lama

Not much farther down the road, the bus passed an old flatbed truck crowded with Tibetans who were laughing and chattering. They wore soiled, heavy jackets, wool socks as gloves, and scarves wound around their heads. They smiled and waved when they saw the sign on our bus indicating that we were Americans, and Tara yelled into the microphone, "Being hospitable builds good karma. His Holiness say, treat foreigners nice. He have international fame. We proud. We follow his activities."

Karma explained that the Dalai Lama isn't like the Pope, who defines Catholic church doctrine. Foreigners call the Dalai Lama "God-King," but that's misleading: Tibetans believe he is an incarnation of Chenrezi, the Bodhisattva of Compassion, also known as Avalokiteshvara in India, Kwan-yin or the Goddess of Mercy in China, and Kannon in Japan. In Tibetan lore, Chenrezi has reincarnated himself thirteen times; thus, this Dalai Lama represents the most recent incarnation, the fourteenth. No one knows if Chenrezi will reincarnate himself again. The current Dalai Lama—like others before him—was born to peasants, Karma explained, and he credits his lowly birth for his ability to understand his downtrodden people. He feels strongly for them and has tried his best to improve their lot in life.

The landscape changed from snow to a high desert plateau. Rocks and sand were everywhere. Suddenly, Ngawang brought the bus to a skidding halt: The right rear tire was flat. As Ngawang and Tara replaced the tire, the rest of us sat on the ground with our box lunches. Mike and I felt too ill to eat, but we continued talking with Karma about the Dalai Lama. "If Tibetans take the Dalai Lama's teachings about interdependence seriously," I asked, "why not invite the Chinese to move to Tibet? Tibetans have a great deal of land with a sparse population. The Chinese who come to Tibet would help reduce overcrowding in their own cities."

"Tibetans might have done that if the Chinese hadn't been so aggressive and hostile," Karma said. "From the beginning, the Chinese thought they were better than us. They tried to take what was ours and impose their system . . . but they didn't destroy Tibet in the hearts of the people!"

"Then how can Tibetans' bitter resistance to the Chinese be compatible with the Dalai Lama's teachings about nonviolence?"

asked Mike. "Tibet must be a ticking time bomb. Are Tibetans going to let China run Tibet without resorting to terrorism?"

Karma replied, "His Holiness can't control the violent feelings indefinitely. But if violence happens in the future, the Chinese government will crack down even more than they do now. That's a major deterrent to terrorism."

"A common threat—China—might help Tibetans to develop a sense of nationalism," I said.

"Before the 1950s," said Karma, "Tibetan nationalism was not well developed. Now His Holiness represents Tibetan nationalism. For us, he isn't just the ruler of Tibet; he *is* Tibet. If harm comes to him, Tibet is finished. His Holiness hopes that powerful nations will persuade Beijing to grant Tibet concessions, but he knows that they may inadvertently push China into a more hard-line strategy."

Just then, a girl ran toward us and held out her hands for food. Like most Tibetan children we would meet, she wasn't dressed warmly enough; her nose ran profusely. "Her name is Jigme," Karma said. "She's twelve years old and doesn't attend school. Let's give her whatever we don't want. The people in her village may be starving. Her future is bleak. She'll get married in a few years, have a baby, and live pretty much the way her ancestors lived." We piled our box lunches into Jigme's open arms, and she ran back to her village. "Before the Chinese invasion," Karma said quietly so that the men from the jeep wouldn't hear, "malnutrition was unheard of. Then, China imposed disastrous agricultural policies that led to widespread starvation, especially here in rural Tibet."

Interdependence

The road started climbing to Lalungla Pass. The scenery was spectacular, with snowy peaks all around. But Mike's nails were turning an even darker blue as we ascended; his face flushed,

and he began gasping for air. "Drink some water," I urged. I
had been sipping Sprite to control my own nausea. When
I sat up I felt fairly well, but if I bent over, my head felt like it
would explode.

When it's too cold, you can put on clothes or move to a
warmer place; if it's too hot, you can take off clothes or find
someplace cooler. But with altitude sickness, there's nothing you
can do to get away from the lack of oxygen . . . except descend to
a lower altitude. Since reaching Zhangmu, even the smallest
exertion caused us breathlessness and a pounding heart. At this
stage, I couldn't walk and talk at the same time. Even my backpack felt too heavy to carry.

The Tibetans didn't seem troubled by the increasing altitude.
Ngawang focused on driving, while Karma and Tara joked in
Tibetan. But when Ngawang shifted to a low gear and the engine
groaned, Karma and Tara grew silent. Fear churned in my
abdomen, and my nausea increased. Mike looked scared, too,
which frightened me even more. What if the motor or brakes
failed? What if we slid over the cliff? What if we got sicker and
died? I wanted to rescue us, but there was nothing to do except
meditate and have faith in the bus and Ngawang's driving.

The engine roared on the last steep incline. With a final
thrust, the bus reached the top of the pass and stopped. "Thank
you," I prayed. With a pounding heart I climbed off the bus,
gasping for oxygen and resting after every step. Mike, who ordinarily relished new sights, was too weak to leave his seat.

The air was cold and thin and the sky overcast, with snowy
peaks jutting up from far below. The Himalayas are to other
mountains what wild animals are to those in a zoo. These
mountains felt vast and solid, yet they had the ability to lose
themselves behind clouds, to appear and then disappear again
in a matter of seconds. Awestruck, I watched the changing
scene. Hundreds of faded prayer flags attached to wooden
posts whipped in the wind. At this pass—and at every other

pass we crossed—Karma, Tara, and Karen tied new prayer flags to posts for a safe journey.

The luggage truck chugged to the top of the pass and stopped behind the bus. I noticed that the men from the jeep were no longer riding with Thupten. Tara explained that they had gotten out at the last checkpoint to fetch help for their mangled vehicle.

The road downward was more treacherous than the road up, but I forgot my fear when Karma announced, "Get your cameras ready for the north side of Mount Everest. Tibetans call it 'Chomolungma.'" A gigantic cone of snow-capped rock appeared from behind the clouds. Towering high above the other peaks, the mountain looked serene and majestically foreboding, yet reclusive. A ring of snow-tipped peaks protected it, like courtiers and servants waiting on a queen.

At a lower altitude, the bus stopped at yet another checkpoint. When Karma returned to the bus, he asked Ngawang to drive on quickly before something else could detain us. "I never know if the Chinese will let us continue," he explained. "They always demand a bribe above the usual fee. I brought along plenty of extra money, but the bribes have been more than I expected this time." When I asked if he wanted us to help pay for the bribes, he said with a smile, "No, I promised you beforehand how much the trip would cost, so we'll stick with that."

As the sun set, we reached the ruins of Shegar Dzong, an ancient fortress consisting of an enormous rock encircled by a crumbling wall with watchtowers. Below stood the village of Shegar, or New Tingri, the capital of Tingri. "We'll stay in Shegar," said Karma. "It's 13,300 feet, 4,050 meters up. That means we'll be sleeping at a higher altitude than in Nyalam. Try not to become dependent on oxygen pillows. Soon your body will adjust to the altitude, and you'll feel better."

In Shegar Hotel, as in every other hotel, registration included filling out a mandatory government form that asked us to explain the purpose of our trip. "Pleasure isn't the right word," quipped Lorna. "We're paying a lot of money to suffer."

Mike and I were delighted to find a bathroom with a sink, Western-style toilet, and bathtub in our unheated room. No matter that the faucets didn't work and the toilet didn't flush. Tara dropped by to show Mike how to breathe from an oxygen pillow, which is a pillow-sized rubber bag with a tube in one corner. She untied the tube and bent it between her thumb and forefinger to keep air from escaping. Then she placed the tube into one of Mike's nostrils, closing his other nostril with his finger. Slowly, she unbent the tube to let out a small stream of air.

Mike felt cold, weak, and listless. I tucked his comforter around him and lay on top of him to warm him up. "I'm afraid that if I go to sleep, I'll stop breathing," he said hoarsely. "Try to relax," I said as bravely as I could, "and you'll need less oxygen. I'm too sick to sleep, so I'll hear if you have trouble. We'll be in Lhasa soon."

I lay shivering in bed, disappointed that survival had become the focus of our trip. As Lorna put it, "Tibet is a somatic experience." I wanted to be on a spiritual journey, not a test of physical endurance. Then I thought of how yoga teaches that one way to the Infinite is through the body. Perhaps life-threatening challenges push out other thoughts and purify the mind. This kind of purification may be what individuals seek when they climb Mount Everest or engage in other dangerous pursuits. As a nurse, I knew many people who said that having a heart attack, AIDS, or cancer transformed them. I could view this physical adventure as more than a threat; it was an opportunity for spiritual growth. Being on the Roof of the World lent itself to esoteric thinking: Spiritual energy was stored in these mountains and in the thin air that clung to them. I felt invited to a higher state of consciousness.

A dog howled mournfully outside the window. "That dog sounds like we feel," Mike joked weakly. "At least we're inside. Here's a Buddhist insight: We're having a better night than the dog."

The next morning, Karma handed Mike and me four small brown glass vials containing a liquid. "This is a Tibetan herb made from the root of a bush," he said. "It decreases the body's need for oxygen. Tibetans use it for altitude sickness. Russian astronauts take it when they go into space. Do you want to try it?" He twisted the metal top off two of the vials.

Mike and I gulped down the bitter liquid. "Take one twice a day," Karma said. "We'll buy more in Shigatse." A few hours later I didn't feel as nauseated, but Mike had developed a low-grade fever. "Mike might be too sick," said Karma. "A person has to take the herb before symptoms get serious. Mike had better try aspirin for his fever, but I suggest that you drink another vial later today." At dinner I was able to eat some rice and soup broth. The only side effect of the herb was insomnia if I took it at bedtime. From then on, I drank two vials each day, one when I woke up in the morning and another after lunch.

We left Shegar and the bus crossed Gyatsola Pass, the highest point on our trip. Because Mike and I knew what to expect, we didn't feel as anxious as we had at Lalungla Pass. After that, the road wound through desolate terrain where the mountains looked like sheets of shale with jagged pinnacles pointing to the sky. Then we passed over a painted desert, striated in pastel hues. The mantra *"Om Mani Padme Hum"* was written on the cliffs.

The sun was setting as we reached Shigatse. "Second largest town in Tibet," Tara said. "Capital of Tsang, trading and administrative center." A dusty boulevard cut through Chinatown's low, rectangular concrete buildings. In the

Tibetan quarter, buildings made of yak dung, stones, and peat roofs clustered along the narrow streets. Prayer flags were everywhere. "Stay at Shigatse Hotel," Tara said. "Three-star, not like American three-star."

While waiting to check into our rooms, June and I paged through an English-language booklet published by a Chinese press. The author wrote that because the Tibet Autonomous Region gives autonomy to Tibetans, new life and vigor are transforming traditional Tibetan culture. Since the peaceful liberation of Tibet in 1951, the booklet stated, China has placed great importance on training Tibetans and making foreign scholars and friends correctly understand the past, present, and future of Tibet. "Who believes this stuff?" June said, throwing the booklet in a basket.

In the hotel, I bought more of the Tibetan herb, as well as a T-shirt that had a face with a serene side and an angry side. "Nice Buddha, angry Buddha," the Chinese clerk told me.

"It symbolizes the trip," said Mike. "Being in Tibet is profound, but we're too sick to enjoy it." Despite—or perhaps because of— our suffering, Mike and I felt summoned to Lhasa, the East's holy city, just as we previously had felt summoned to Jerusalem, the West's holy city. Tibetans believe that anyone who completes the thirty-four-mile *kora,* or circuit, around Lhasa will erase their bad karma. For more than one thousand years, pilgrims have walked or prostrated themselves in and around the city. We, too, looked forward to purification of body, mind, and spirit.

The Panchen Lama

The following day, Karma announced, "We'll visit Tashilhunpo Monastery, the seat of the Panchen Lama. The word *panchen* means 'great scholar.' Tibetans consider the Panchen Lama to be second only to the Dalai Lama. For us, the Panchen Lama is a manifestation of Manjushri, the Bodhisattva of Insight."

On the bus, Tara said, "Panchen Lama connected to Chinese, so Tashilhunpo not destroyed in Cultural Revolution. Before Chinese invasion, over six thousand monks. Now six hundred. Tashilhunpo one of six great Gelugpa monasteries. Others are Drepung, Sera, and Ganden in Lhasa, Kumbum and Labrang in Amdo." She explained that the monastery had become the seat of the Panchen Lamas when the fifth Dalai Lama declared his teacher, the abbot of Tashilhunpo, to be a manifestation of Amitabha, a deification of the Buddha's faculty of perfected cognition and perception. Rivalry between the Dalai Lama and Panchen Lama was encouraged by the Chinese, and, by the 1920s, the thirteenth Dalai Lama and the ninth Panchen Lama fell into disagreement about Tashilhunpo's right to self-rule. The Panchen Lama fled to China and never returned to Tibet. The Chinese government kept the tenth Panchen Lama in Beijing, allowing occasional visits to Tashilhunpo.

After the 1959 uprising in Lhasa, Tara explained, the tenth Panchen Lama had a change of heart about his Chinese benefactors. He presented Chairman Mao with a seventy-thousand-character petition about Chinese-orchestrated famines, executions, and mass beatings of Tibetans. The petition appealed for increased freedoms for the Tibetan people. In response, the Chinese government demanded that the Panchen Lama denounce the Dalai Lama. Instead, at the Monlam festival in 1964, he announced to Tibetans in Lhasa that Tibet would regain independence and the Dalai Lama would return as leader. Soon after, the Chinese authorities arrested him, torturing and imprisoning him somewhere in China. He was released fourteen years later, less defiant but still determined to advocate for Tibet. In 1989, he died at Tashilhunpo of poisoning—or, some say, of a broken heart.

With the death of the tenth Panchen Lama, Chadrel Rinpoche, the abbot of Tashilhunpo Monastery, organized a search committee to find his replacement. It was a long search.

On May 14, 1995, the Dalai Lama announced that six-year-old
Gendun Choekyi Nyima was the reincarnation. Chinese authorities held meetings with Tibet's religious leaders, calling on
them to denounce the Dalai Lama's choice. In November of
1995, the Chinese chose another six-year-old boy, Gyaltsen
Norbu, as the eleventh Panchen Lama and installed him in an
elaborate ceremony at Tashilhunpo Monastery. Then they
arrested Gendun Choekyi Nyima and his family and took them
to Beijing, claiming that they were being held to prevent
Tibetan separatists from kidnapping them. At the same time,
the authorities arrested Chadrel Rinpoche, along with at least
fifty other monks and laypersons, and held him in solitary con-
finement. The charges against him were "conspiring to split the
country" and "leaking state secrets," because he had communi-
cated with the Dalai Lama regarding the search for the Panchen
Lama's reincarnation.

"We afraid eleventh Panchen Lama and family dead," Tara
said sadly.

At the entrance to the monastery, beggars surrounded us
while Chinese spies in black suits watched nearby. Beyond the
gate was a cluster of white, one-story buildings with black paint
around the windows and doors, "to keep out devils," Tara said.
Up the ridge were ocher-colored buildings topped with golden
roofs and spires. High above stood a wall where a massive
thangka normally hung during Buddhist festivals. Pilgrims
chanted and turned prayer wheels, staring at us as if they hadn't
seen Caucasians before. Women and men wore colorful strips of
cloth braided into their hair and full-length robes with sleeves
long enough to cover their hands. Men with gold caps on their
teeth carried long swords or knives. One man used his sword to
peel an apple in one long corkscrew.

Tara pointed to a colorful mandala called "the Wheel of Life."
It illustrated the Six Realms of Existence through which all of us
cycle endlessly unless we become enlightened. In the Human

Realm, we lack insight about who we really are, and we experience vague, disturbing feelings of alienation. If we harm others, we enter the Hell Realm, in which we burn with rage or are tortured by anxiety. Indulging our instinctual passions, such as eating, drinking, and sex, puts us in the Animal Realm. Those of us in the Hungry Ghost Realm search for gratification of old, unfulfilled needs whose time has passed. We are in the God Realm if we constantly strive for an unsustainable state of sensual bliss. When we use relentless competitive force to pursue satisfaction, we are in the Realm of Jealous Gods.

At the center of the Wheel of Life were a pig, a snake, and a rooster trying to devour each other. They represented attachment, hatred, and confusion. When these negative emotions drive us, Tara explained, we suffer, for we are afraid to experience ourselves directly. Ignorant of our buddha nature, we struggle adrift in samsara, the dimension of endless rebirths.

Inset into each realm of the Wheel of Life sat a tiny Bodhisattva of Compassion, indicating that the cause of suffering is also the means of release. Tara said that our perspective determines whether a given realm is a vehicle for awakening or for bondage. Freedom from negativity comes through nonjudgmental awareness of our emotions. We gain release from suffering by changing our perception.

Mike and other sick members of our group watched monks selling rosaries, prayer wheels, *thangkas, katas,* plastic spoons, and plastic bags of butter. Tara led the rest of us, including the Chinese spies, up and down treacherous steps to visit mystical chapels. We saw *thangkas,* scrolls of scriptures, and images of deities and Tibetan leaders. In Kelsang Temple, chanting monks sat cross-legged on cushions before a throne for the Panchen Lama. Nearby, the Maitreya Chapel served as home to a tall, gold-leafed statue of Maitreya, Buddha of the Future. The Palace held the embalmed body of the tenth Panchen Lama, coated in gold.

Pilgrims put money by the sacred images or gave money to a monk. Many pilgrims were performing full-length prostrations before the images; some of them had fur- or carpet-covered boards strapped to their hands and knees for protection against the hard floor. In front of many images were butter sculptures—intricate, colorful art made from butter. The only light in the chapels came from flickering butter lamps. Pilgrims used plastic spoons to add more butter to the lamps, and when a butter lamp had filled, a monk scraped out chunks of butter and put them in a bag. "Take to other temples, to nomads," said Tara. "Butter shows interdependence of us all." As in most monasteries we visited, the air was putrid from the smoky butter lamps.

Like the other pilgrims, Karma carried a spoon and a bag of butter to put butter in the lamps. He prostrated himself and handed money to the monks. "So they get a good meal tonight," he said.

Back on the bus, Karen asked why a man had taken money from one of the chapels. Karma looked shocked, but then he chuckled, "Perhaps he needed cash . . . or maybe he was a Chinese spy."

Mutual Need

The bus rumbled toward Gyantse. In the distance, a farming village appeared. A man was plowing with two animals that wore bells around their necks and red feathers tied to their long horns. Ropes held the ancient wooden plow together. "Tibet has three traditional lifestyles: nomad, clergy, and farmer," said Karma. "We've seen nomads and monks. Now we'll meet farmers. They work with a yak or *dzo*, if they have one, or by hand." He pointed toward one of the animals: "That's a *dzo*, a cross between a bull and a female yak."

The villagers surrounded us, begging for handouts. "Let's do what we can for them," said Karma. "They need anything we can give them." He handed out pens, candy, and money, and the rest of us followed suit with gifts we'd brought from home. The children's eyes sparkled when Marge took Polaroid photographs and gave them away. Ken let the children look through his video camera, and Lisa showed them how to blow soap bubbles. All of us laughed together merrily.

"They want us to visit their mill for grinding *tsampa*," said Karma. He explained that most crops are hard to grow at that altitude. Tibetans live on a diet of *tsampa;* meat; cheese; and seasonal, noncultivated foods such as stinging nettles, wild leafy greens, and mushrooms. These foods do not provide enough nutrition for growing children. "Tibetans in Tibet tend to be smaller than Tibetans born in exile," he said. "My sons in the States are over six feet tall because of vitamins!"

The children led us to a shed by a narrow stream with very little water; I wondered how such a small trickle could accomplish anything. We took turns bending over to go through a small doorway and down steep steps. Below, the water worked to slowly turn one stone against another stone to grind the barley. The air was full of barley dust, and I quickly went outside again.

"Want to see where farmers live?" Tara asked. A lovely young woman wearing a turquoise and brown *chupa* led us to her house. Her black hair was pulled into a braid down her back. "Married daughter of household," Tara said. "Groom from another family. No children yet."

Karma explained to us that Tibetans are practical. Both women and men can own land and conduct business. A woman is permitted to have one or more husbands, just as a man can have one or more wives. For instance, a woman might marry two brothers in order to keep land in the brothers' family, or for security in remote areas.

Grandparents take care of the children, which means that the children learn from their elders—a crucial tie that keeps Tibetan society cohesive. At the same time, the daughter-in-law has the lowest status in the family and works the hardest. This can create a situation where she doesn't get enough to eat, which may affect her health and the health of her children.

The woman in the turquoise and brown *chupa* invited us into her courtyard. "For animals and storage," said Tara. "Second level for living." We climbed a ladder made of tree trunks and branches to a balcony, from which hung animal hides and yak cheese. The woman led us into an unheated room with a metal stove in the center. Translucent windows on one wall provided the only light. Around the room sat low, painted chests covered with Tibetan carpets. "Kitchen and eating and sleeping room," Tara said. "Sit or sleep on carpets. No electricity, plumbing, phone, heat. Use kerosene lamps."

"Family chapel," said Tara, as we entered a room with Buddhist images and sacred scriptures in glass cases. Before the images stood butter lamps and metal bowls filled with water. "Only monk sleep here. No one in family can read or write. Wait for monk to read scripture for special occasion—wedding, funeral. This family rich. Not everyone in village has statues and scriptures."

The woman showed us her sleeping and storage rooms. A beaming young man climbed the ladder and stood by her. "This groom," Tara said. She motioned toward excited adults and children crowding into the courtyard below. "Other members of family." I thought of Mark Epstein, an American psychotherapist and author, who observed that easterners meditate to transcend too much connectedness, whereas westerners meditate to overcome feelings of alienation and to establish connectedness.

A man offered *chang*, but only Karma accepted. Karma drank a shot in one gulp and held the glass out for more. The Tibetans chuckled. By the sixth drink, Karma looked shaky, but the man continued to pour. Finally, Karma put up his hand to signal that he'd had enough.

Several of us pressed currency into the woman's hands as we left her house. She stopped smiling and shook her head. We refused to take back the money and walked outside saying, *"Thu-je-chhe,"* Tibetan for "thank you." Finally, she agreed to keep the money, saying *"Thu-je-chhe"* in reply.

After emotional hugs, our new friends waved as we drove away. Feelings of mystical, universal love stirred deep inside me. A wave of indescribable exhilaration swept over me, and with it, an epiphany—a realization of how much we all need each other. No more would I be satisfied with trivial activities: I would focus on personal and societal healing. Tibet was transforming me.

Almost There

As the sun set, the bus reached Gyantse. "Not many Chinese," said Tara. "Gyantse still Tibetan." Ruins of the fourteenth-century Gyantse Dzong cast shadows. In 1904, British troops led by Sir Francis Younghusband stormed the fortress and killed a thousand Tibetans. During the Cultural Revolution of the 60s, the Chinese destroyed the fort again, but it was being rebuilt.

After another difficult night, Mike's temperature was 101°F. He had developed a respiratory infection on top of the altitude sickness. I gave him an antibiotic we had brought from home, and he and I swapped medications with other members of our group. I was feeling much better, for which I gave credit to the Tibetan herb.

On the way out of Gyantse, we stopped to visit Pelkor Chode Monastery, "the Pagoda of a Thousand Buddhas," founded in 1418. At one time, the compound contained fifteen monasteries that brought together three orders of Tibetan Buddhism, a rare instance of multidenominational tolerance. The other monasteries were destroyed during the Cultural Revolution. "Only a hundred monks," said Tara. "Formerly, over two thousand." In the compound stood one of Tibet's most revered and unusual architectural masterpieces, the multi-tiered, four-story, gold-capped Kumbum. Its four sets of protective eyes gazed serenely in each direction. The Kumbum was built in 1440 in the shape of a 108-sided mandala, with the Buddha or other deity as a central figure in each of its 112 chapels. The government was in the process of restoring three chapels destroyed during the Cultural Revolution, a new effort to encourage tourism.

The road started climbing and then disappeared altogether. We ended up by a Chinese industrial development. "They're desecrating our land," said Karma. "They're mining something valuable, and we don't know what. They say it's a water project, but we know it's mining." A Chinese soldier at the main gate of the compound motioned for us to leave. Ngawang maneuvered the bus until he found the road again.

As the road climbed through a series of switchbacks, Jack, who was sitting in the jump seat opposite Ngawang, staggered to the back, saying, "I can't handle being up front anymore." June took his place as we went by Jyenchen Khansar Mountain Glacier and crossed Karo La Pass. Karma told about history's highest battle, fought there in 1904 when a ragged band of Tibetans tried to stop the Younghusband expedition from going to Lhasa.

The road descended on the other side of the pass, and Yamdrok Tso Lake came into view, one of four holy lakes in Tibet. Where the ice had melted, blue-green water sparkled in the sunlight. "Tibetans walk on pilgrimage around it," said Karma, "which takes about a week. But the Chinese government is defiling it! Authorities have constructed a hydroelectric station here, despite protests that the lake is sacred and that solar energy is better. More than 1,500 troops guard the site and keep civilians away. See the long, thin stain in the water? It's from the chemicals they're using. Isn't that symbolic of what they're doing to Tibet?"

At the next pass, Khamba La Pass, June stumbled to the back of the bus saying, "Someone with a stronger stomach can sit up there." Ken made his way to the front. The descent was just as treacherous. "Ye gads!" Ken exclaimed as we rounded a blind corner: The road was climbing again. "One more pass," Tara yelled. "Then go down to Lhasa." When Ken gave up his seat, Lisa took his place. We crossed the pass, and the bus started another dangerous descent. Even Karma and Tara stopped chatting.

Abruptly, the road changed to a four-lane, paved highway. The engine purred and the tires rotated quietly. Finally, a level road surface! Ngawang clipped along at 40 miles an hour, by far the fastest speed of the whole trip. We crossed the first bridge we had seen since Friendship Bridge at the border with Nepal. "Yarlung Tsangpo River," said Tara. "Called Brahmaputra River outside Tibet." She told us that the river flowed 1,800 miles west to east across Tibet, then south into Bangladesh. Lhasa was situated on another river, the Kyi Chu.

Mike's color was still dusky, but we breathed easier in the lower altitude. "You feel better now," Tara said. "Lhasa 12,000 feet high, 3,650 meters. Same latitude as Delhi, Cairo, New Orleans. . . . Lhasa means 'abode of gods,' heart and soul of Tibet. Before Chinese, 20,000 to 30,000 people. Now 170,000 to 200,000. More Chinese than Tibetans, over 100,000 soldiers to guard us. Lhasa not our city. Chinese knock down old buildings, put up high-rise buildings. Another Cultural Revolution."

Up until then, Tara had faded into the background because of her humility. Now, dramatically, she glowed. "Lhasa, my hometown," she said. "I sing for you 'Lhasa Girl.' Welcome to Lhasa. About love for Lhasa. How we feel when we return to Lhasa. You feel that way, too?" In a strong, sweet voice, she sang Tibetan verses that moved everyone to tears. Along the highway, pilgrims were doing full-length prostrations. Like those pilgrims, we were nearing our goal. We had suffered, but now we were almost there.

Chapter 8

Impermanence

Emptiness

As the bus neared Lhasa, Karma announced, "We will learn about impermanence here. Lhasa is changing, like everything else." He explained that all phenomena, including each of us, is subject to change. Nothing is permanent, nothing unchanging. The Buddhists refer to this aspect of the universe as "emptiness," since everything is as evanescent as smoke, as fleeting as the reflections birds cast when they fly over a body of water. We suffer when we become attached to what is impermanent and "empty." To renounce our suffering, then, requires nonattachment. If we recognize the dreamlike quality of life, we'll be able to stop trying to make impermanent things permanent. We will no longer put energy into defending our ego, because we'll know at last that our ego doesn't really exist. Only then will we experience the true cessation of suffering, a peaceful state called *nirvana,* or buddhahood.

Tara spoke up. "Milarepa say, 'Seeing emptiness, have compassion.'"

"The realization that we're all suffering can lead to compassion," Karma explained. "As we release attachment, life's difficulties aren't disasters anymore. They remind us of impermanence and help us to develop compassion."

141

"Should we be compassionate toward the Chinese in Tibet?" Ken asked with a smirk.

"Certainly!" said Karma. "Tibetans aren't all good, and the Chinese aren't all bad. Some Tibetans are honest, and others aren't. The same is true for the Chinese. How Tibetans and Chinese differ is that most Tibetans want to follow Tibetan Buddhism, and the Chinese leaders try to stop them from practicing their religion."

The highway turned into Lhasa's main street. "Look how the authorities have razed old, beautiful, carved, decorated Tibetan buildings!" exclaimed Karma. "In their place are cement-block strip malls. See the blue reflective windows and garish signs? Fortunately, the construction and materials are shoddy and will crumble after a few years. Instead of the quiet I remember as a boy, boom boxes are blaring Chinese music." I felt disappointed that Lhasa looked like other Chinese cities with a wide boulevard, separate lanes for bicycles and pedestrians, and uniform blocks of cement apartments, shops, and karaoke bars. Drab Chinese office blocks were going up everywhere. A few cars, trucks, rickshaws, and army tanks were the only traffic.

Karma explained that, recently, Lhasa has changed more than in the last thousand years. "Each time I return to the city, it seems increasingly like a military garrison." Now, Chinese outnumber Tibetans in Lhasa by more than two to one. Only three hundred of the thirteen thousand shopkeepers are Tibetan. Few good jobs are available to Tibetans, many of whom are unwilling or unprepared to collaborate with the Chinese—they regard acculturation into Chinese ways as a step backward. Forced to do menial work, beg for a living, or resign themselves to unemployment, uneducated young Tibetans spend their time playing billiards and drinking cheap liquor, which the government makes readily available.

The bus skidded on a patch of ice. "We're fortunate to visit Lhasa in cold weather," said Karma, "because we won't see many foreigners. Most Western tour groups don't come until summer. Nomads are here, though. In cold weather, they come to shop and worship at Lhasa's shrines."

At our hotel, Karma's cousins welcomed us warmly before whisking him off to not one, but two family dinners in his honor. Family members who were collaborating with the government and therefore "prospering" gave him one celebration; the other dinner was given by family members who refused to accept Chinese rule and, as a result, were having a hard time. The two factions didn't get along, another tragedy brought on by the political situation.

The rest of our group trooped off to the hotel's heated restaurant to eat yak cheese and yak meat over rice, which we washed down with yak-butter tea. In the warmth, we laughed uproariously to relieve our tensions. Karen and I noticed a *China Daily* article, "Dalai Lama Trampled on Human Rights," which stated that, as ruler of Old Tibet, the Dalai Lama allowed the ruling class to trample willfully on serfs' rights. Because the traditional laws were the cruelest in the world, the article continued, the history of Old Tibet was written in the blood and tears of serfs. Now, though, Tibetans have equal rights in politics, production, daily life, and the economy. "A spy might be watching," Karen whispered to me. "Don't react!" We quietly put the paper back where we'd found it and continued eating.

After dinner I walked to the hotel gift shop, where I bought more of the Tibetan herb and some postage stamps. The Chinese proprietor counted out forty-eight stamps, two for each of my postcards. Two jovial Chinese women helped me to lick the stamps and put them on the postcards. We laughed together, and for a few moments I forgot about Tibetan-Chinese politics.

Our room had twin beds, hot and cold water, a Western toilet, and a television—all of which worked! A space heater made the room warm and cozy. For the first time since we'd entered Tibet, we removed our jackets and washed up. Tara had warned, "Don't take shower in high altitude: get dizzy, faint, hit head." I sat on the edge of the bathtub to lather myself before standing up briefly in the spray. Then I rested again to catch my breath and slow my heart before putting on pajamas and crawling into bed. At about midnight I woke up because Mike was gasping for air. The heater had stopped, and the room was frigid. I tried to comfort him as I called housekeeping for an oxygen pillow. "Let's fly home," I urged, more than a little frantic. He said he wanted to stay no matter how sick he felt.

Nonattachment

Snow had fallen by the time we woke up the next morning, and the air was crisp and cold. I put on my usual two pairs of long johns, warm-up suit, turtleneck, winter jacket, and gloves. "Today we visit the Potala Palace," Karma announced at breakfast, "the central symbol for Tibetans' hopes of self-government." Mike, Lorna, and Alice still had altitude sickness, but they boarded the bus with us, oxygen pillows in hand.

We drove past a garish, golden monument of two huge yaks. "The Chinese government erected them to celebrate their liberation of Tibet," Karma said, laughing. "Tibetans call them 'the Golden Bulls,' because the Chinese have behaved like bulls in Tibet."

Ahead we caught sight of the awesome Potala Palace, built on the summit of Red Hill. We gazed in silence at the thirteen-story, quarter-mile-long "Abode of the Gods." The enormous white-and-ocher building, topped with golden cupolas, dominated the Lhasa skyline. Meandering clouds hid the base of Red Hill, giving the illusion that the Potala was levitating in the turquoise sky under a blaze of shimmering gold. Mike leaned over and kissed me. Both of us were misty-eyed: We had risked so much to see it.

Part of the Potala was white, the rest was red. "When His Holiness lived here," said Karma, "the White Palace contained his private quarters. The Red Palace housed government offices, chapels, and tombs for all the Dalai Lamas. Tourists say that few sights surpass the Potala, but for Tibetans, it's an empty shell. His Holiness is not here. The soul of the Potala is gone."

He went on to say that the ancient village of Shoel used to stand at the foot of the Potala. The Chinese razed its historic buildings and forcibly relocated residents to slums a mile away. They brought in cleaning people to replace most of the monks who had lived in the Potala and taken care of it. Now Lhasa has its own Tiananmen Square, surrounded by barbershops, karaoke bars, discos, and shops. There the government puts on military parades to show off its tanks, artillery, and soldiers.

At the base of the Potala, Tibetan children surrounded us, begging for handouts. As usual, the children looked like they were starving and cold. Karma gave them money, and the rest of us followed his example. Tara led us up a steep incline, pausing periodically so we could catch our breath and slow our oxygen-starved hearts. Smiling pilgrims, some of whom were quite elderly, had no difficulty with the altitude. They walked around us, chanting and spinning their prayer wheels.

"Chinese spare Potala during Cultural Revolution," said Tara. "Many chapels and images intact from seventeenth century. Not heated. Rooms cold." She explained that *potala* means "Avalokiteshvara's Pure Land," the Dalai Lama being a reincarnation of Avalokiteshvara. Before 1959, the Potala Palace was full of life, for it served as the winter home and burial place of Dalai Lamas, the seat of the Tibetan government, and a training ground for monks. People worked in the offices, prayed in the chapels, and walked on the roof. At night, hundreds of butter lamps lit the windows. Now, she said, the Potala is a cold, lifeless museum, devoid of its past dignity, and only partially open to visitors.

We entered a courtyard of the White Palace, climbed steep steps, and walked through dimly lit, mysterious hallways to visit the Dalai Lama's bedroom, library, and meditation room.

Murals on the wall depicted the Buddha's life. In the chapels of the Red Palace, pilgrims put butter in the lamps and prostrated themselves in front of images of the Buddha, various Dalai Lamas, Avalokiteshvara, bodhisattvas, and other spiritual and political figures. In the Potala's most sacred room, the Lokeshwara Lhakhang, pilgrims prostrated themselves, touching their foreheads to objects embedded in the floor. On the Potala's flat roof, laughing women with red cloths around their heads were singing and dancing. Each woman held a long stick with a flat surface attached to one end, which she pounded against the roof. "This how Tibetans fix leaky roof," said Tara. "Put wet clay on roof. Sing and dance to harden."

On the square below the Potala, a man offered rides on a yak with a red Tibetan carpet on its back and red tassels dangling from its horns. The yak's head hung down as if all its dignity was gone; we took it as a symbol of the Potala and of Tibet in general. When the man beckoned me, I walked over to the yak and petted it. The yak nuzzled me, so I paid the fee and climbed on its back as the gathering crowd clapped enthusiastically. I wondered if I was exploiting the yak, or giving money so it could eat.

Back on the bus, I felt sadness wash over me as I looked up at the Potala. *Time to meditate on nonattachment,* I thought. The Four Noble Truths promise that, through meditation and ethical living, we can stop clinging to the people and things around us. "We're getting too attached to Tibet," I said to Mike. "How can the Dalai Lama advocate nonattachment, but show special concern for Tibet?"

"That's a universal ethical problem," Mike said, still weary but not too exhausted to present his views on this conundrum. "Love of one's own versus love of the good. Finding balance. In this case, it's love of Tibet versus the love of dharma. As a Tibetan, the Dalai Lama favors Tibet, but as a spokesperson for Buddhism, he has to advocate nonattachment. Let's develop equanimity, so we don't get so emotionally involved with what's going on in Tibet."

Equanimity

The next day, our group headed for Norbulingka Palace, the Dalai Lama's summer home in Lhasa. *Since all phenomena are impermanent,* I cautioned myself, *try to behave with equanimity. Stop taking things so personally and try to act from a less selfish, more peaceful place. If you detach from your reactive mind, you'll maintain your composure. You'll be open to whatever happens, without any attachment to the results.*

That was before the debate between Ken and Jack.

The two men felt safe enough on the bus to talk about the Tibetan situation. "I don't want to be discouraging," Ken began, "but I can't see how China will change its policy in regard to Tibet. China needs Tibet as an armed camp for its military security."

"I don't think so," Jack protested. "By occupying Tibet, China has to monitor two thousand miles of frontier with Burma, Bhutan, India, and Nepal. That's a huge expense. China's presence in Tibet irritates its largest neighbor, India, so China is less, not more, secure militarily. By demilitarizing Tibet, Beijing could use the money it saves to modernize China and improve its economy."

"China needs Tibet's lands and resources for economic prosperity," countered Ken.

"That's not necessarily true," replied Jack heatedly. "China spends millions to extract lumber, minerals, and other resources from Tibet. Chinese workers in Tibet get hardship pay and perks. China maintains a massive military to protect them and to suppress Tibetans. In developing countries, it's cheaper and easier to let local people run their government. They do a better job of handling their problems and delivering goods at competitive prices. If Tibetans are allowed to develop their highland, Chinese money can be used to create jobs for all the unemployed Chinese."

"But what about Chinese pride?" Ken persisted. "Chinese leaders can't bear to lose face by acknowledging that their past policies regarding Tibet were misguided and destructive."

My resolve to behave with equanimity went out the window as I jumped into the discussion. "Beijing would gain worldwide respect by giving Tibet autonomy," I burst out. "It would wipe out China's image of being an aggressive violator of human rights. Chinese leaders could say that the conquest of Tibet was the work of a previous era. They would be hailed as visionaries. The whole world would applaud China for adopting an enlightened course of action."

The discussion ended abruptly when Ngawang parked near a gate guarded by two stone snow lions. The seventh Dalai Lama designed Norbulingka as a summer retreat in 1755, Tara explained. But the thirteenth and fourteenth Dalai Lamas constructed most of the buildings. Each spring, a grand procession took the Dalai Lama from the Potala to the Norbulingka, and then returned to the Potala six months later. In 1959, the fourteenth Dalai Lama was at the Norbulingka when the Chinese invaded and he was forced to flee to India.

We walked through various palaces and paused to admire a picturesque pavilion by an artificial lake. *Like the Potala,* I thought, *this complex is a lifeless museum,* and again a wave of sadness washed over me. I tried to brush it away with a reminder about the need for equanimity.

Past Drunzig Palace and the library stood the fourteenth Dalai Lama's New Summer Palace, completed in 1956. In one room, 301 murals traced Tibetan history. "Before any people here," said Tara, "monkey come down from heaven to meditate. She-devil interrupt. Say, 'I want to mate with you.' Monkey say, 'No, I don't mate with she-devil.' She-devil pester monkey, but he keep meditating. Then she-devil say, 'If you don't mate with me, I mate with he-devil. We populate world with devils.' Monkey say, 'I better mate with you, so world not populated with devils.'

He mate with she-devil. They have six children. Their children become first Tibetans."

"This story reminds me of Adam and Eve," I whispered to Mike. "Such teachings blame women for evil in the world. They depict women as less spiritual than men and not capable of being spiritual or religious leaders."

Mike had a different view. "It's a profound story," he whispered. "It shows that humans are a combination of good and evil."

Leaving Norbulingka Palace, the bus bumped down a dirt road to Sera Monastery near Lhasa. The monastery looked like a village hugging a picturesque mountain ridge. Tara pointed to vultures circling a flat area high on the mountain. "Sky burial," she said. She explained that Tibetans, unlike Chinese, don't believe in ancestor worship. Since the introduction of Buddhism, sky burial has been the most common method for Tibetans to dispose of their dead. Designated individuals take the body to the sky burial site, where they chop it into pieces while performing religious rituals. They leave the remains for wild animals and birds. Because Tibetans believe in reincarnation, they view the body as temporary housing and sky burial as a humane way to feed wildlife.

Inside the monastery, Tara said, "Sakya Yeshe, disciple of Tsongkhapa, founded Sera in 1419. Second largest monastery in Tibet. Before Chinese, 5,500 monks. Now 600. Sera has colleges: Sera Me for philosophy, Sera Ngagpa for tantric studies, Sera Je for Tibetan healthcare and everything else. Study Tantra at Drepung, but monks at Sera get into Tibetan politics." She led us through various chapels to the roof, where men were repairing a massive, faded *thangka* by hand. One man powered an ancient treadle sewing machine with his feet. "Monks display *thangka* up there for religious holiday," Tara said, pointing to what looked like a movie screen on the mountain.

She led us to the debating garden, where a hundred monks, eighteen to thirty years old, were paired off. One monk in each pair was speaking rapidly to the other. "This how monks learn dharma," Tara said. "One stand, ask question. One sit, must answer. Make point, slap one hand in other. Answer wrong, hit head. Two or three hours every day unless meeting." Excitement filled the air, and I felt ecstatic. I yearned to understand what they were saying, to debate with them, and to ask them questions. When I recognized my emotional flip-flop, I reminded myself to behave with equanimity in all things.

◆ ◆ ◆

Back in Lhasa, Marge, Lisa, Karen, Mike, and I got off the bus to eat lunch at a restaurant that Karma said was well-known for Tibetan food. Wooden benches and chairs surrounded tables with faded oilcloths. Sunlight provided the only light and heat. When a young Tibetan woman came to take our order, we pointed to the word *momo* written on a small blackboard. About ten minutes later, she brought steaming dumplings filled with yak meat, the best we'd ever eaten.

Since we were alone in the room, we felt safe enough to talk quietly. "The Chinese presence is overwhelming," Karen said. "Chinese soldiers and shopkeepers are everywhere. I want to buy from Tibetan shopkeepers, but they're hard to find."

"Hopelessness seems to permeate the Tibetans we do see," said Marge. "Maybe they've lost pride in a home that's no longer their own. Perhaps they believe the official view that they're backward and uncivilized. We're seeing drawn-out ethnic cleansing, cultural genocide."

"What can we do?" Mike asked. "Protest? Monks and nuns do that and end up tortured, imprisoned, or even killed. With spies everywhere, we can't be too friendly with Tibetans. Who knows what the authorities will do to them after we leave? We could try to smuggle out letters, tapes, photographs, lists of prisoners, but the authorities might strip-search us at the airport."

"I feel helpless," Lisa said sorrowfully. "We're sick, and political activities could jeopardize our health. And I'm afraid of causing even more trouble for Tibetans."

"Being here must be hard on the Chinese, too, even if they make lots of money," I remarked. "The Chinese look as sad as the Tibetans do. The Tibetans don't want them here, and it must be difficult to live at this high altitude, to be so far from their families."

"Karma said that the Chinese never fully adjust to the high altitude," Mike commented.

"God is saying who should live here," Lisa said solemnly. None of us laughed.

When two muscular-looking Caucasian women walked into the room, we stopped talking, and Marge, Lisa, and Karen left to go shopping. Mike and I introduced ourselves to the women, who said they were from England. They had driven to Lhasa in a Land Rover. Their favorite hotel was in Nyalam, since it had mattresses—in most Tibetan hotels they slept on a dirty floor. "Nyalam!" Mike burst out laughing. "That was the worst night of my life. It's obvious you're younger than I am. If I don't have a sleeping bag, I need hotels to have mattresses!"

On the walk back to our hotel, Mike and I passed Chinese men and women selling mandarin oranges. *"Tashi delek,"* we said, but they didn't understand the Tibetan greeting. The Tibetans we saw seemed to have a baffled air about them, as if they were no longer familiar with their own country. When we smiled and said *"Tashi delek,"* their faces lit up and they replied, *"Tashi delek."*

Farther down the street, we saw a Chinese man stop an elderly Tibetan man who wore a wide, ancient-looking leather belt with a silver buckle. The Chinese man pointed to the belt and forced money into the Tibetan man's hands. The Tibetan man took off the belt and handed it to the Chinese man. Both men walked away in opposite directions. Mike and I felt bad for the Tibetan man, who apparently had been forced to sell his belt, but we didn't know what to do to help. Instead, we reminded each other of the need for equanimity and continued walking.

Spiritual Core

"Today we visit Jokhang Temple, Tibetan Buddhism's holiest shrine," announced Karma one morning. "It houses the Jowo Sakyamuni, Tibet's most revered image. Red Guards desecrated the Jokhang. They removed priceless images and made it a pigsty, but, miraculously, the Jowo survived the Cultural Revolution. Pilgrims from all over Tibet come to pray in the Jokhang."

Karma explained that pilgrims take three routes around the city. Lingkhor, the outermost and most important, circles the city's major religious sites. Barkhor, the middle and most popular route, is a half-mile circuit around buildings and streets surrounding the Jokhang. Nangkhor, the inner route, is inside the Jokhang. For centuries, the Barkhor ring has been the spiritual heart and commercial center of Lhasa. It is a popular meeting place for Tibetans. Since 1959, it has been the site of numerous independence protests and uprisings, most notably in 1987, 1988, and 1989.

Barkhor Plaza was crowded with pilgrims, monks, hawkers, and spies. Pilgrims carried babies on their backs and led children by the hand. On tables, blankets, and carpets, hawkers displayed religious items, boots, jewelry, hats, swords, rugs, prayer flags, *chupas, katas,* food, butter churns, boom boxes, false teeth, and anything else a pilgrim might need.

In an outer courtyard of the Jokhang, Tara pointed to the stump of an ancient willow tree inscribed with the terms of the Tibetan-Chinese Treaty of 822. "Guarantees mutual respect of Tibet and China border," she said without visible emotion. "Long ago," she continued, "demoness live in lake here. Tibetans drain water. Sacred goat carry stones to fill empty lake. Make solid foundation for Jokhang. King Songtsen Gampo start building Jokhang in 647. Four stories high, to house Buddha statue of Nepalese wife, Princess Bhrikuti. Then he build Ramoche Temple for Jowo Sakyamuni, statue of Chinese wife, Princess Wencheng. King died. Princess Wencheng put Jowo Sakyamuni in Jokhang."

Tara led us past the Four Guardian Kings, through the main assembly hall, and to various chapels: Chapel of Tsongkhapa and His Disciples, First Chapel of the Buddha of Infinite Light, Chapel of the Eight Medicine Buddhas, Chapel of Avalokiteshvara, First Chapel of Maitreya, Second Chapel of the Buddha of Infinite Light, Second Chapel of Maitreya, Chapel of Avalokiteshvara Riding a Lion, Third Chapel of Maitreya, and Chapel of the Hidden Jowo. The most important, Chapel of Jowo Sakyamuni, held the magnificent image of twelve-year-old Sakyamuni Buddha wearing a crown of gold, coral, and turquoise.

In contrast with Western cathedrals, which were built to awe believers, the Jokhang felt warm and intimate. Instead of soaring spaces, it consisted of rooms with low ceilings. Tara, Karma, and other devout pilgrims clustered together, fervently clutched bags of butter for the lamps, spun prayer wheels, counted prayer beads, chanted, offered money, and prostrated themselves before the gleaming, gilt images. The only light and heat came from the butter lamps. Some pilgrims were disabled and had to be carried; others wore dressings or had other visible health problems. Despite my feelings of compassion, a disturbing thought crossed my mind: They might have infectious diseases, such as tuberculosis, and we could become infected, too. In pitch-black corridors, members of our group held on to each other to avoid getting lost in the crowd. Because the air was nearly unbreathable, we didn't linger, as I'd hoped, but hurried through the chapels to go back outside.

We followed Tara to a room on the second level, where about twenty monks sat on the floor in two rows facing each other. They chanted and played musical instruments. One monk pressed a foot pedal that caused a padded, curved stick to hit a large, colorful drum. The deep, energizing boom made my heart beat faster. I felt mesmerized by the chanting; the drum beat; the readings from sacred scriptures; the rhythmic, brassy "shsssshh" of cymbals. The sounds were electric, comforting, addictive, and alien all at the same time. A monk whispered to me, "We meet again in free Tibet." I smiled and nodded my head, choked with emotion.

On the Jokhang roof, Mike and I gazed at the forlorn Potala Palace across town. We held hands, our hearts full. Thoughts about the need for equanimity disappeared. Unlike the Potala, the Jokhang was brimming with life and spiritual energy. I felt like crying, singing, chanting. Only in Jerusalem had I experienced such powerful emotions, and I wondered if the spiritual energy in Mecca, Islam's holiest site, was similar. In another epiphany, I knew that a spiritual force really did permeate me and everyone else. Despite—or because of—our suffering, this pilgrimage was causing me to wake up, as the Buddha had taught. In Socratic terms, I wanted to walk out of the cave and into the sun. I breathed deeply to oxygenate my lungs and rid them of the monastery's stale air. My body tingled from the pilgrims' devotion and the electric atmosphere of the upper room. I felt purified, transformed.

Disappearing Heritage

That afternoon, Mike and the other ill members of our group stayed at the hotel. The rest of us boarded the bus for a visit to an elementary school. As Ngawang drove through Lhasa, Karma said, "This morning, we experienced Tibet's rich heritage, but it's disappearing fast. Tibetans want their children to keep it alive. Many Tibetans send their children away with friends or relatives who are fleeing from Tibet, so the children can get a Tibetan education in Nepal or India. At the school we'll visit today, both the Chinese and Tibetan children learn Chinese. The school is unusual, though, for the Tibetans also study Tibetan, even though the Chinese don't."

Karma explained that in other schools across Tibet, classes are taught only in Chinese. Teachers indoctrinate Tibetan children with stories of Mao Zedong, Communism, and China's achievements. If the children don't answer ideological questions properly, they risk failing—and being beaten with clubs, whips, belts, electric wires, chairs, and bamboo sticks. Tibetan children can't honor Tibetan holidays, except the Tibetan New Year, but they must celebrate Chinese holidays. Usually, they are forbidden to wear Tibetan clothes to school except when officials or foreigners visit. Teachers promise them money if they spy on their families and report loved ones who talk about Tibetan culture, history, or religion.

Ngawang stopped by a two-story building, and a man with gray hair and a Mao jacket came out to welcome us. Karma introduced him as the school's director. We walked into the unheated building, up a flight of stairs, and down a hallway to the reception room. Faded curtains hung at the windows. The director motioned for us to sit on worn couches. I wondered how anyone could teach or learn in such cold. Teachers wearing heavy jackets over Western clothes passed around bowls of fresh bananas and mandarin oranges, then handed each of us a cup of hot tea. I eagerly ate an orange and banana—my first fresh fruit in Tibet—and warmed my hands with the tea cup.

In English, a woman explained that the eight-year-old school had 1,207 students, ranging from five to fourteen years old, and sixty-four teachers. School was in session from 9:00 A.M. to 6:30 P.M. Because it was after 6:30 P.M., the students' parents were outside waiting for them, but the teachers were keeping the children in school because of our visit. She spoke with deep emotion about the lack of funds, which meant that students had to do without resources that were available to most children in the world. When she finished, Karma chimed in, "If you wish to donate, we'll have a box by the door as you leave." I felt irritated by yet another sales pitch, but at the same time I wanted to help the school.

The teacher led us into a bleak room where children learned ballet. Next door was a math class of over fifty nine-year-olds and one teacher. Above the blackboard hung a large picture of Chairman Mao surrounded by red Chinese writing. Smiling children in faded jackets and no shoes sat crowded together, four students to a table. In a room nearby, third-year students were learning Tibetan. Down the hall, six-year-olds sat in tightly packed rows on Tibetan carpets, with boards behind their backs for support.

As we left, the director put a *kata* around each of our necks. Feeling deeply moved, I placed $20 in the donation box, all the money I was carrying. Bernie dropped in $100, and my remaining resentment toward him dissolved.

Back on the bus, I asked Karma, "What would you do for Tibetan children if you could?"

"First, I'd have the Chinese leave. Then I'd offer education to everyone, so they could do more with their lives and learn about their disappearing heritage. I'd encourage them to work like they did before the Chinese invaded. Begging is all right for elders and sick people, but not for anyone else."

Pema

"Tara has invited us to her home," Karma announced the following morning. "She has lived in Lhasa with her aunt, Pema, ever since her parents were killed in the 1989 Lhasa uprising. Tara got married, and fifteen months ago she had a son, Kunga. Now her husband and son live there, too."

Tara's home consisted of a walled complex with small, unheated buildings that opened to a dirt courtyard. The buildings had no plumbing, electricity, or telephone service. No plants or toys were in sight. Pema, a small woman with deep, sad eyes, shook our hands and then introduced little Kunga, who was dressed in a cap, faded jacket, and corduroy pants. She led us into the living room building, which was decorated with carved, painted wood. Colorful trunks topped by Tibetan carpets served as seats, and two trunks in the center were used as tables. On a red post hung a photograph of Tara's husband, who was at work. Pema passed around cups of hot tea and bowls of walnuts, bananas, and mandarin oranges. She also offered *chang*, but only Karma accepted.

The building next to the living room served as a bedroom for Tara, her husband, and Kunga. Across the courtyard was a tiny kitchen, with a table, a shelf for seasonings and dishes, and a stove for cooking over an open fire. The prayer room had an altar, burning incense, and lighted butter lamps before sacred images. Wooden cabinets held Buddhist scriptures. Trunks provided seating.

While Lisa and Marge took Polaroid photographs of Kunga, Pema invited me into her bedroom, which was only large enough for a small bed and an altar. She motioned for me to sit on the bed beside her. After glancing around to make sure no one was listening, she told me in broken English that she and her husband had worked for a rich family before the Communists invaded in 1959. The Communists considered this family, as well as Pema and her husband, to be class enemies. She was only nineteen years old when the government put her husband in prison, and she was allowed to visit him only once a year for the next three decades before he was released. Prison conditions were so poor that he developed many health problems, from which he died five years ago.

Every morning, she was forced to leave her baby son so she could do hard labor, quarrying stones from a mountain. Because no one was available to take care of the baby, she had to leave him alone, with only *tsampa* by his side for food. The baby cried, and she cried, but there was nothing else to do. When her son died from tuberculosis, she knew it was really because she had left him alone every day. Periodically, the Communists made her get up in front of everyone and confess her political errors. Since she was too young to have done anything wrong, she had to make things up, and they beat her for what she said. People who weren't from wealthy families didn't have to do that. Besides, if members of the aristocracy were so bad, why did Tibetans love them? After the revolution, her friends tried to help her because she didn't have enough to eat. Her story was sad, she said, but she wasn't the only one with such a story.

"How did you get through such a terrible time?" I asked, dabbing my eyes.

She said the Communists wouldn't let Tibetans practice Buddhism, but Tibetans did it secretly anyway. Tibetans couldn't read scriptures or talk to lamas, but they could remember what they had memorized as children. That's what got her through, she said, and that's what gets her through today. Things are better now, but they're still bad. The Chinese spy on them, regulate everything, and threaten them with prison. Tibetans don't dare talk or move around freely.

"Not good future," she said, her head hanging down. "Chinese take business, own everything, keep Tibetans out. Harass monks, nuns. Soldiers everywhere. Tibetans in prison. Tibet disappear. Become Chinese." I felt too choked up to speak. "You must help us!" Pema pleaded, holding my hand over her heart. She looked directly into my eyes. "In America, tell what happen in Tibet. Then everyone learn. Or we lose Tibet. Tibet no more. Tibetans no more."

Tara called out that it was time to leave. I hugged Pema and promised I would do my best to help Tibetans. "I feel like I've known you for a long time," I whispered. She replied that we must have been together in a previous life. Her serenity comforted me deep inside.

I saw Pema one more time during our stay in Lhasa. Late one night, she took a considerable risk to surprise us in our hotel room. After putting a *kata* around each of our necks, she bowed to us, and we bowed to her. With glistening eyes, she handed me a beautiful Tibetan door hanging with vertical blue, yellow, and red stripes and three white squares sewn across the top. Four blue, cloud-like figures decorated the corners. In the middle was a wheel of dharma, with eight spokes in green, brown, yellow, and red, surrounded by shades of blue. At the center were what looked like yin and yang in green and red, outlined in yellow and blue. The wheel appeared to be a turtle with legs, head, and tail. She told us that the image symbolized the wheel of dharma turning successfully. Then she hugged us and disappeared into the dark, cold hallway.

"She's giving us a message to develop good karma by helping Tibetans," I sniffled.

"For sure," Mike replied, wiping his eyes. "There goes our resolve to behave with equanimity. She doesn't want us to forget Tibet when we go home."

When we returned home to Minnesota, I hung Pema's gift on my office door. Its spiritual energy infuses the room, a reminder of Pema's plea and my promise to help Tibetans.

Chapter 9

Personal Healing

Mind-Body Interconnectedness

While we were in Lhasa, Karma took Marge, Karen, and me to visit the traditional Tibetan hospital and medical school established by the thirteenth Dalai Lama. Karma said that this institution had taken over the work of the Lhasa Chakpori Medical Institute, founded in the late seventeenth century by the fifth Dalai Lama. The Chakpori Institute stood on a hill in front of the Potala until the Chinese military destroyed it in 1959 during the Lhasa uprising. Under Chinese rule, Karma said, traditional care was being secularized and the medical school program had been reduced from fifteen to only five years. Many Tibetan medicinal herbs, once harvested in the high Himalayas, were now attributed to Chinese origin and grown on farms.

Karma led us to a large building decorated with Tibetan script and banners and surrounded by a metal fence with an open gate. He hurried us into the hospital, past beggars with crutches and soiled dressings, down an unlit hallway, and up a stairway to the second floor. Although I wore my winter jacket, I shivered and wondered how sick people could get well in the unheated building, much as I had wondered how children could

learn in an unheated school. In a sunny room, Karma motioned
for us to sit on built-in benches covered with Tibetan carpets.
The room was empty except for an ornate gilt case containing
statues of three men dressed in traditional robes.

A smiling man strode in wearing a blue Western suit. "I am
Dr. Tsetan," he said in English. "Welcome to Lhasa." He pointed
to one statue. "That is Yuthog Yontan Gonpo, founder of traditional Tibetan medicine. He lived 125 years, from 708 to 833.
Our traditional care works well." He chuckled and then continued, "The statue over there is the fifth Dalai Lama's doctor.
He founded the medical school. Next to him is Khenrab Norbu,
physician and first president of the hospital. He died in 1962.
This hospital has outpatient clinics and two hundred inpatient
beds. No maternity, for women help with babies at home. We
have over three hundred medical students, and 30 to 40 percent
of them are female. Tibet has other traditional hospitals, too."

Dr. Tsetan explained that traditional Tibetan medicine goes
back to the Buddha, "who taught that everyone seeks to be happy
and healthy." Happiness and health aren't accidental; rather, they
result from a balanced mind, spirit, and body, coupled with
peaceful relationships with family, friends, community, and environment. Happy, healthy people respect and value others, and
they feel respected and valued themselves. When they experience
disease, they are able to bring themselves into harmony again.
They use meditation techniques to purify the mind and become
enlightened, thus producing an improved state of health.

According to Tibetan medicine, five elements make up all
matter, including the body:

· Air governs movement in the body, including blood
  circulation and growth of skin.
· Fire drives growth, development, and the absorption
  of food.
· Water provides moisture and smoothness.

· Space allows the other elements to interact and coexist.
· Earth provides stability and structure.

Moreover, the body is composed of three humors, called *nyepas*, each of which has a counterpart in traditional Chinese medicine:

· *Rlung (qi),* also called wind and air.
· *Mkhris-pa (yang),* also called fire, tripa, or bile.
· *Bad-kan (yin),* also called water and earth, or phlegm.

Space pervades all three of these humors, and each has its own divisions and subdivisions. In a healthy individual the humors are balanced, but illness results when negative emotions cause disequilibrium. There are three kinds of negative emotions, or poisons of the mind:

· Attachment, greed, and desire.
· Anger, hostility, and aggression.
· Delusion, confusion, and close-mindedness.

Attachment will lead to *rlung* diseases, anger produces *mkhris-pa* afflictions, and delusion results in *bad-kan* illnesses. The three poisons cause us to make poor choices that result in disharmony and disease, Dr. Tsetan explained. The most common unwise choices include eating an unhealthy diet, leading an unhealthy lifestyle, and living in an unhealthy environment. Any of these unwise choices can result in illness. To heal from disease, we must root out the three poisons so we can make choices that promote health and happiness. Treating symptoms without addressing their underlying causes does not result in healing.

Diagnosis and Treatment

Dr. Tsetan led us into another sunny room. On one wall, two rows of ancient *thangkas* hung from ceiling to floor. A colorful painting of the Medicine Buddha dominated another wall. (The

Medicine Buddha is blue to represent the healing potential of
our buddha nature.) *Katas* were draped over a cord that stretched
from wall to wall in front of the painting. Flowers, fruit, and
small dishes filled with water adorned a large altar.

"From ancient times," said Dr. Tsetan, "physicians have used
thangkas to train medical students. These *thangkas* illustrate
human anatomy and physiology. See, this one shows how the
fetus develops. That one depicts the Tibetan calendar and
astrology. Over there are *thangkas* about how to make a diagnosis. Tibetans accurately diagrammed physiological phenomena long before the microscope was developed in the West."

According to Dr. Tsetan, traditional practitioners use three
diagnostic techniques:

1) Questioning the person about diet, lifestyle,
   environment, and behavior.
2) Visually checking the color and texture of the skin,
   eyeballs, blood, tongue, nails, sputum, feces, and urine.
3) Touching the body to identify pain, temperature, external
   growths, and other abnormalities.

Through pulse reading—the most important touch method—
a practitioner can identify abnormalities in the internal organs.
The practitioner places her or his right fingers on the person's
left radial artery and left fingers on the right radial artery. With
either hand, the practitioner then applies light pressure with the
index finger, moderate pressure with the middle finger, and
strong pressure with the ring finger. The right index finger feels
the pulse of the heart and small intestine, the right middle
finger feels the pulse of the spleen and the stomach, and the
right ring finger feels the pulse of the left kidney and the repro-
ductive organs. The practitioner's left index finger feels the pulse
of the lungs and large intestine, the left middle finger feels the
pulse of the liver and gall bladder, and the left ring finger feels
the pulse of the right kidney and bladder.

Dr. Tsetan led us into an adjoining room containing *thangkas* that explained how disequilibrium develops. He said that the art and science of healing involve aligning the three humors into a dynamic state of equilibrium so that the person will be healthy and free from psycho-physiological disorders.

Next, Dr. Tsetan pointed to glass cases holding herbal medicines and *thangkas* that illustrated which medicines are recommended for which conditions. Everything in the universe is considered to be potential medicine, he explained, so a traditional practitioner learns how to make medicines from herbs and other naturally occurring substances.

A traditional practitioner begins with gentle treatment, looking first at how the person's life is out of balance. Because all illness starts in the mind, the practitioner recommends prayer, meditation, and mantras, as well as behavioral and lifestyle modifications. The practitioner reminds the individual that the way to heal is to lead an ethical, spiritual life. An individual with *rlung* illness is encouraged to overcome attachment by meditating on impermanence. A person with *mkhris-pa* disorder is advised to meditate on compassion in order to heal anger. Someone with *bad-kan* disease is best off meditating on wisdom to cure delusion. A positive change in attitude can decrease and even eliminate the three poisons, thereby bringing the body into harmony.

Other recommendations given by practitioners include:

- Refrain from murder, theft, sexual misconduct, lying, gossip, harsh speech, divisive speech, covetousness, malice, and distorted views.
- Practice compassion.
- Remember the preciousness of human life.
- Keep your promises.
- Repay kindnesses and debts.
- Respect confidences.

- Be thrifty, but give liberally.
- Admit when you're wrong.
- Subdue your pride.
- Behave cautiously to avoid regret.
- Associate with peaceful people.
- Avoid stress and danger.
- Do what you enjoy, but don't overindulge in sensual pleasures such as eating and sex.
- Sleep in a comfortable position, and get enough rest.
- Bathe regularly, and keep your environment clean, quiet, and pleasant.
- Harmonize your body with environmental changes.
- Let nature take its course by not suppressing natural urges such as sneezing, defecating, and urinating.

"If illness persists," said Dr. Tsetan, "we try mild herbal medicines specific to *rlung, mkhris-pa,* or *bad-kan.* We advise the person to perform visualizations, and we also use acupuncture, massage, heat, cold, and exercise. For serious illness, we try stronger herbal medicine. We may perform venesection, which is a kind of bloodletting, or moxibustion, the application of heat by burning herbs over the area being treated. We only perform surgery if nothing else works."

Above all, he said, a traditional practitioner tries to create a healing environment by:

- Working with the individual and family, so each person feels valued and respected.
- Surrounding the individual with artwork, music, plants, and windows to the outside, allowing beauty and nature to promote healing.
- Encouraging clergy, family, and friends to sing, chant, meditate, dance, and engage in other spiritual activities that support their loved one.

Many people become ill if they lack kindness or are lonely. When individuals feel cared for and understood, they trust the healer and are more likely to recover. Before someone can become a healer, however, the person must first heal herself or himself. Only then can the healer exhibit true compassion and really listen to others.

As Dr. Tsetan talked, I thought of Rabbi Zalman Schachter-Shalomi's statement, that the best gift one person can give to another is to listen to the wounded child who weeps deep within the heart. My research participants concurred with this sentiment. To help them examine their ethical conflicts, I engaged in ethical listening. Ethical listening includes establishing a caring rapport, encouraging the person to talk openly, focusing on the person's ethical conflict, and being nonjudgmental. The participants told me that ethical listening helped them to resolve their conflicts in a way that allowed them to live with meaning and integrity. They expressed a profound longing for health professionals to really listen to them, just as Dr. Tsetan and Rabbi Schachter-Shalomi had described.

Dr. Tsetan paused to see if we had any questions. Karen asked what he thought of assisted suicide. "Tibetans don't request assisted suicide, and doctors don't offer it," he said, with apparent surprise at her question. "We believe in the preciousness of human life. If you end your life, you refuse what the Buddha gives you."

He allowed us to digest this concept before he continued. "There are two issues. One, should a doctor help someone die who can survive? Two, should a doctor help someone die who is dying? A doctor may give pills that help a person die if the person has a terminal illness and much pain. The result is virtuous if the doctor is motivated by compassion."

A Good Death

I asked Dr. Tsetan to describe a good death. "Dying peacefully, rather than fearfully," he said. "Death is a natural part of life. We can face death or ignore it. We will die peacefully or fearfully, depending on how we live and what happens as we die. To die peacefully, we need to live peacefully by leading a simple, ethical, and spiritual life. If we prepare well for death in this way, the three poisons—attachment, hostility, and delusion—won't influence us. We'll be able to let go of these poisons and cultivate peace in our thinking."

Dr. Tsetan explained that traditional practitioners take proactive steps to help a person die peacefully. "Most important is to show compassion so the person can talk freely, without fear. We encourage the person to resolve any conflicts and put their affairs in order. We say mantras, and we read from the Tibetan Book of the Dead and other sacred texts. We tell the person not to be afraid of dying, but to pray, focus on *thangkas,* think about love and peace. We encourage the person to let go. We tell about the physical changes that take place while dying." The picture he painted was one of natural processes: Water absorbs earth and vision becomes blurred; fire absorbs water and body cavities dry up; air absorbs fire and the body loses heat; space absorbs air and respiration ends.

"We remind the dying person that life doesn't end at death," he said. "A person goes through four stages, called *bardos:* life, dying and death, after-death, and rebirth. You can train in order to go through them smoothly. As the person moves from one *bardo* to the next, there is a corresponding change in consciousness. Through spiritual practice, the person can come to understand these stages and experience them without fear."

People who have a virtuous mind at death, he said, are more likely to experience profound spiritual insight and a favorable rebirth. They easily move from one *bardo* to another and bridge the dualities of human nature: self versus other and life versus death. It is the false perception of these dualities that causes suffering. Experienced spiritual practitioners meditate as they die and remain in a meditative pose for five to fifteen days after their last breath. Because they have prepared well, death is a triumph—the crowning and most glorious moment in their life.

I was fascinated, for Dr. Tsetan was addressing the central issues of dying, so often neglected by Western health systems: Is there a right way and time to die? Can we structure death by the way we live? If so, should health professionals teach individuals how to die well? Who would want to learn? What characterizes a good death?

Again I thought of Rabbi Schachter-Shalomi. He, too, advocates taking steps today to complete life and die well, rather than waiting until our deathbed. To reap the harvest of life, he wrote, we need to encounter our mortality and resurrect our unlived life. If we make amends and forgive ourselves and each other, we'll come to terms with our past, turn our perceived failures into successes, and heal our relationships. By doing this ethical and spiritual work on an ongoing basis, we'll develop into sages as we age. Then, at the time of our death, we'll be able to say that "we made a necessary and important contribution to the whole, which is a triumphant way to conclude this life."

The participants in my AIDS research came to mind. They had described the characteristics of a good death: acceptance, loved ones by one's side, dignity without suffering, personal control, peace with God or a Higher Power, belief in a pleasant afterlife, peace with other people, and a view of death as part of life. Looking back with regret, they felt bad about their perceived failures, missed opportunities, and ruptured relationships. They wanted to heal their lives, but they were concerned about the pain they might feel if they became reacquainted with the past. Having lived through the pain once, they were hesitant to reopen old wounds. They longed for health professionals to help them and their families reach into the past and repair events and relationships that they perceived as failures. If they did this ethical, spiritual work, they said, they could complete life and die a good death.

Five of the participants in my study stayed in contact with me until they died. Because they didn't want to leave "unfinished business" behind, they were repairing their lives. They were making amends for past wrongs, showering family and friends with love, completing tasks they had undertaken, and putting their financial and legal affairs in order. Once they developed a peaceful acceptance of death, they were able to plan their last days and even their memorial service.

Yes, I thought, *these values need development and application throughout life.* However, many people die without attending to these values, often because they, their families, and health professionals deny that they are going to die. What is lost by this denial? "An opportunity to become more fully human," the rabbi wrote. In the deepest sense, each of us wants to complete life and die triumphantly. To experience a good death, we'd be wise to listen to our inner voice now so that we can reframe and reshape the past. Then we'll be able to face death with peace and even joy.

Weak Digestive Pulse

Karma's voice broke into my reverie. "Thank you, Dr. Tsetan. Now Dr. Jhampa will give us a consultation. He doesn't speak English. Dr. Tsetan will translate." We followed Dr. Tsetan to the consultation room, where Dr. Jhampa met us. He wore a white lab coat and a white turban that nearly covered his eyes. Although he didn't smile, he emanated kindness.

Dr. Jhampa sat on a bench and motioned for me to sit by him. He gazed directly into my eyes for several moments before asking why I'd come to see him. I told him about my nausea and lightheadedness. Since taking the Tibetan herb, I said, my symptoms had decreased, but they weren't gone. He asked about my social history. Then, after asking to feel my pulse, he gently took my right wrist in both his hands, closed his eyes, and bowed his head. He concentrated for a long time, seeming totally attuned to everything about me. His touch felt good to me. He followed the same procedure with my left wrist. When he asked to look at my tongue, I stuck it out, and he put his face close to mine as he peered at the top, sides, and bottom. I thought of how Western health professionals' powers of observation can atrophy because of our reliance on technology. Too often, we don't look directly into an individual's eyes, and we fail to ask in-depth questions.

Then Dr. Jhampa proceeded to take the most comprehensive health history I've ever given. He asked a wide range of questions. "Do you like to eat sweet things? Do you have heart palpitations or feel short of breath when you stand up? Do you have trouble sleeping?" He turned to my mental state. "Are you under stress? Do you get headaches? Have you been concerned about depression? Do you use alcohol or drugs?" When I kept saying no, he asked, "Do you have pain?" I shook my head, but he wanted to feel my abdomen. I unzipped my jacket, and he pressed below my breastbone. "That hurts!" I burst out in surprise. After palpating my abdomen, he spoke in Tibetan to Dr. Tsetan.

"All your internal organs are normal, except some indigestion," Dr. Tsetan said smiling. "Your diagnosis is a weak digestive pulse. That's why you have pain below your breastbone. Keep taking the Tibetan herb while at a high altitude. Be careful what you eat. Don't eat too much food, not much fat. Not too cold or too hot. Don't eat sour or spicy food. Not too many sweets. Avoid foreign food. When you get home, eat what you're used to, and you'll be fine. It will go away."

"How can I avoid foreign food in Tibet?" I chuckled to myself. Excited and relieved, I said, "Thank you. I feel better already." Their advice was sound. When I later flew to sea-level Hong

Kong and ate familiar food again, my symptoms disappeared and I stopped taking the Tibetan herb.

Karen told the doctors that for several months she'd felt less energetic than usual. Her physician at home wanted to conduct tests to determine what was wrong, but she was suspicious of Western healthcare because of its focus on medications and surgery. After Dr. Jhampa examined her, Dr. Tsetan said, "You are in good health, but you need to take better care of yourself. Be careful what you eat. Don't work too hard. Do what you enjoy. Sleep well. Lifestyle changes: Make them and your energy will return." Karen beamed, nodding her head in agreement.

As Marge was taking Karen's place, Dr. Tsetan walked over to me and asked, "You take photo and send to me?" I smiled and said, "I'd be happy to. Would you like Dr. Jhampa to be in the photo, too?" He nodded, and I took photos of both physicians, promising to send the photos after I returned home. Then they turned their full attention to Marge.

Marge described her history of migraine headaches. The physicians spent a long time asking about her and her mother's bouts with depression. Karen whispered to me, "Incredible! For years, Marge has been going to doctors in the States. None of them ever asked about her mother. I've always thought that her migraines have a lot to do with her mother's problems. The Tibetan physicians are very good at asking questions, aren't they? They get right to the heart of the problem."

"We recommend an herb for migraines," Dr. Tsetan said to Marge. "You buy it here. Costs less than $10 for six months. Crush it, pour on boiling water, drink as tea. Also, change your lifestyle. Eat healthy food, sleep well, exercise, don't worry, pray, meditate. You'll feel better soon. The herb won't hurt you, and it might take away your migraines. Do you want to try the medicine?"

Marge hesitated, but when Karma and Karen nodded, she said, "I've tried everything else. Nothing has worked. What do I have to lose?" Dr. Jhampa left the room and returned with three plastic bags filled with small black pellets. Dr. Tsetan wrote on a prescription pad the name of the herb, instructions for taking it, and the name and address of someone Marge could contact in the United States if she had questions or wanted to obtain more. Marge, Karen, and I thanked the physicians. We each gave them $25 and then giggled like excited teenagers as we followed Karma out of the hospital.

Tibetan Bioethics

The next day, Dr. Tsetan and I ate lunch together to discuss bioethics. I asked what he thought about organ transplantation. He approved in cases where the donors aren't killed for organs, the recipients will die without donated organs, and the system is fair about rationing organs. It isn't right to transplant organs from prisoners, he said, into people who pay large sums of money for them, as is rumored to occur in China. This disregards the sanctity of life and gives preference to the rich. Dr. Tsetan hadn't seen transplants, for his hospital focused on preventative care and gentle treatment.

I asked if he agreed with the use of animals for research. "Human life is precious," he said, "because of human intelligence, but humans don't have the right to exploit other forms of life. If the only way to conduct health experiments is by using animals, then it's all right to reduce human suffering. We should minimize animal experimentation, though, and find alternatives when possible. Humans are the cruelest species. We must make sure that animals have rights, too."

I wanted to know his perspective on cloning. "Cloning can accomplish much good," said Dr. Tsetan, "if it isn't used in harmful ways. An example of good is cloning new organs and tissue for sick people. Cloning new human beings would give them the opportunity for precious human life. In Tibet, we're a long way from cloning. We're just trying to survive here."

Then I asked if he thought abortion is ethical. "What are its benefits and disadvantages?" he asked. "In Tibetan medical texts, the Buddha says if you destroy a human, you're a sinner, with two exceptions: When a baby will be born out of wedlock, a woman can have an abortion; or abortion can be done when a family has too many kids, the mother is sick and weak, and she can't support her kids. Then the Buddha permits abortion. Abortion is still a sin, but a minor sin.

"A Chinese woman employed at the hospital came to see me," he said. "She was six months' pregnant. I told her I could feel the baby's heartbeat. She screamed, 'No!' Because she already had a child, she was afraid she'd lose her job. The Chinese have a policy of one child per couple. I said, 'Let the baby be born. I'll try to find someone to adopt the baby, even a Tibetan.' She said, 'If they find out, they will fine me and fire me.' She pushed hard. Finally, I called friends. We gave her an abortion, and she didn't lose her job."

I questioned how he was able to resolve such heart-breaking conflicts. "I get up at 3:00 A.M. and pray until 6:00 A.M. each day," he said. "A doctor's most important character-istic is compassion. I can't be compassionate without spiritual practice." Looking around to make sure no one was listening, he whispered, "The Chinese should not force Tibetan women to have abortions. The one-child policy is wrong for Tibetans. There are few of us left."

Not wanting to get him or myself into trouble with the authorities, I quickly changed the subject and asked about AIDS. "I haven't seen AIDS," he said, "but that doesn't mean it's not here. I think it's already in Tibet. We haven't done research on how many people have AIDS, or who has it. Most drug abusers in Tibet use opium. We have some prostitution, primarily by poor Chinese women, but we don't know how much. Doctors who see people with AIDS should treat them like anyone else and not discriminate."

I asked whether everyone has the right to healthcare in Tibet. He said that anyone can come to his hospital. Farmers are given medicine and most other treatments at no charge; other people pay up to 80 percent of the cost of treatment. Most traditional care can be done in the home, which costs little or no money. He added that rich countries like the United States should provide free quality healthcare to all their citizens.

When I asked if resources should be distributed more equally throughout the world, he said, "That's a tough question. It has many parts—politics, technology, education, research, cooperation, natural resources. In Tibet, we have natural resources, but problems with politics. I wish for a high standard of living in Tibet, but not for taking anything away from another country. A high standard of living doesn't necessarily mean happiness. We need rich countries to help Tibet with technology, financing, and research—and Tibetans can help rich countries with happiness."

I nodded vigorously and then asked how elders should be treated. "In Tibet, we honor elders," he replied. "Tibet doesn't have nursing homes. Families take care of their own members."

Leaning toward me, he whispered, "I'd like to ask a question. How do the different races get along in America? We don't manage well here. Is it better to be Tibetan and poor, or Chinese and rich? Tibet or China . . . resist, or give in to China? Tibetans don't know what is the right thing to do."

Our conversation was about to take a dangerous turn—spies might be listening. Steering the discussion to a safer subject, I told him that race relations pose tough ethical problems in America. Western bioethics addresses race as it relates to genetics, adoption, and access to healthcare, but until recently, most bioethicists have been Caucasian males. Bioethics needs non-Caucasians—women and men—to lead, teach, and publish in the field. Then, ideally, healthcare will reflect the best values of the individuals who provide and use it, regardless of their ethnicity. If all of us work together, I said, we can distribute health resources more equitably.

He compared my description of American bioethics with the situation in Tibet, where government officials decide policies about healthcare. Hospitals are handicapped by the lack of sanitary conditions, food, heat, electricity, hot and cold running water, and other basic resources. Bioethics education would help the authorities to make better decisions, if they would open their minds to it. I cautioned him that bioethics can also be dangerous, because it encourages independent thinking. Bioethics provides a language for putting conflict into words, and it promotes doing the right thing, which may be different from what the government demands.

Tibet needs bioethics, he said, not propaganda. Tibetan bioethics programs could be developed if Western bioethicists were to work with health professionals in Tibet and award scholarships so Tibetans can study bioethics in the West.

It was at this point that we noticed two men in black suits edging toward us. Dr. Tsetan stood up and said loudly, "Keep taking the Tibetan herb, and you'll feel better soon. *Tashi delek.* I hope we meet again. Be sure and come back to Tibet." He shook my hand and walked out of the restaurant.

Western Healthcare

That evening, Karma introduced Mike and me to Dr. Tsering, a Tibetan physician who practiced Western medicine. After advising me to keep using the Tibetan herb while in Tibet, Dr. Tsering asked Mike about his fever and cyanosis (the bluish color of his fingernails and skin). Mike produced his antibiotic. "That's good," Dr. Tsering said. "I'd give you a different one, but we have a shortage here. If you keep using yours, your cold will get better, and the altitude won't affect you as much. Your respiratory infection has been making your altitude sickness worse. Your symptoms are common among visitors to Tibet. When you go to a lower altitude, your symptoms will disappear." His advice was good: Mike's temperature dropped to normal two days later, and his cyanosis gradually disappeared after we left Tibet and returned to a lower altitude.

Because I wanted to learn about the nature of Western health-care in Tibet, I offered to treat Dr. Tsering to lunch. I asked him to invite a Tibetan nurse to accompany us. Two days later, over *momos,* he told me, "To practice Western medicine, a person studies for five years at a medical college in Beijing or Lhasa. My work appointment is at First People's Hospital of the Tibet Autonomous Region. It's the largest hospital in Tibet, with 500 beds and 800 staff, of which 220 are physicians and 280 are nurses. We have several units: surgery, pediatrics, emergency, cardiology, intensive care, and obstetrics, which includes a newborn nursery. We specialize in Western care, but we also have a department for traditional Chinese medicine."

I asked how Western and traditional care differ. He said that a Western practitioner identifies a sick person's symptoms and history, and then reaches a diagnosis through a process of elimination. Treatment is based on statistical data regarding groups of people, with little attention given to any underlying disharmony or how different individuals experience a particular disease. Because of research and technology, Western practitioners can make quick, detailed diagnoses. Often, they can effectively treat acute illnesses with medication, surgery, and other technological advances. They have been less successful with chronic diseases, however, and powerful Western treatments may harm the person being treated.

In contrast, he said, a traditional Tibetan practitioner believes that illness is rooted in a person's unique background and situation. During an examination, the practitioner considers not only the chief complaint and symptoms, but also the individual's personal, health, dietary, and spiritual history. The practitioner tries to understand and treat the root cause of the entire complex of symptoms and disharmony. What a Western practitioner might perceive as one disease, such as cancer, the traditional practitioner understands as a range of conditions.

Dr. Tsering explained that Western care is effective for acute illnesses that respond to medication and surgery, such as bacterial pneumonia, tuberculosis, and appendicitis. Tibetan care is good for chronic illnesses like arthritis, cancer, asthma, and viral infections. Tibetans use both Western and traditional care, depending on their needs. Dr. Tsering's own practice integrates Western care with Tibetan herbs, diet, exercise, meditation, and visualization. Moreover, he encourages his patients to live an ethical, spiritual life that promotes positive thinking and restores balance.

"Tibetans' knowledge of herbs and minerals and their recommendations for healthy behavior can assist the West," he said. "In Old Tibet, people survived by living in harmony with nature. What they learned can help the world's ecological problems. Everyone benefits if westerners and Tibetans collaborate."

"That's ideal," I said with a grin. "Western technology for health emergencies and acute illness, and more traditional approaches for balanced living and chronic illness. We're starting to do that in the West. Insurance companies are happy, because traditional care costs far less than Western technology!"

A man entered the restaurant and sat down at our table. Without a word of introduction, he engaged Dr. Tsering in an hour-long conversation in Tibetan. After the man left, Dr. Tsering apologized and said the man wanted advice about his mother, who probably was suffering from stomach cancer. Because she was afraid to see a doctor, her son was treating her at home. She most likely would die soon, so he suggested herbs to help her feel more comfortable. "I'm impressed with your compassion," I told him. "Ordinarily, health professionals in the U.S. don't give so much time to a stranger outside the office."

Dr. Tsering laughed, and then grew serious. "Our biggest health problem is alcoholism. That's probably why the most common cancers are gastrointestinal. Our infant mortality rate greatly exceeds China's. The nearest health facility for most rural Tibetans is far away. If no one in their village has a car, sick people must walk or ride a yak or horse. We are undergoing unheard-of changes in our environment, diet, crops, values, and religion. All these changes cause stress, and this impacts our health."

He gave me a copy of a study conducted by Americans who found that an entire generation of Tibetan children is severely malnourished. The children suffer from rickets, intestinal parasites, and respiratory diseases. Many toddlers fall far short of international standards for growth and development. School-age children are extremely small for their age. They are at risk for irreversible, decreased intellectual capacity and increased likelihood of death before age seven. To reduce child morbidity and mortality, the researchers are working with Chinese and Tibetan leaders to initiate education programs. They hope to empower families to find their own solutions to health and nutrition problems. For example, the researchers are teaching hand-washing techniques to women and elders, the primary persons responsible for healthcare and childcare in rural areas.

As Dr. Tsering spoke, a woman wearing pants and a well-worn Western suit jacket came over to us. "This is Senior Nurse Nyima from my hospital. She dressed up to meet you. I'll translate, as she doesn't speak English." Nyima took both my hands and then sat next to me, her shoulder touching mine. She was deeply moved that an American nurse wanted to meet her.

Until recently, nurses didn't work in traditional Tibetan hospitals, she said. Instead, medical students assisted physicians. Today, traditional Tibetan practitioners are starting to follow the example of Western and Chinese physicians, and they now incorporate nurses into their work. Nurses assist physicians, give medications, and perform acupuncture and moxibustion. After completing junior high school, nursing students enter the three-year nursing school. Since 1997, graduates have had to pass a licensing exam. A nurse works fifteen to twenty years to become a senior nurse. The majority of Tibetan nurses are women, as very few men study for this career.

Nyima told about an American nurse who taught sanitation techniques in Lhasa's six hospitals. The American nurse helped Tibetan nurses design carts for holding a basin, towel, container of water, and other supplies. Now, nurses move the carts from unit to unit, which means fewer trips to wash their hands and get supplies.

When I asked how Western health professionals could help Tibetan nurses, Nyima listed needed resources: educators, researchers, journals, textbooks, basic supplies (such as dressings and intravenous equipment), dietary supplements, and prescription and nonprescription drugs. But most important was emotional support from the outside world. If Western healthcare professionals send friendly cards and letters, Tibetan nurses won't feel so alone. I told her that my travel group was leaving Lhasa the next morning, or I would offer to give lectures. She thanked me and invited me to return to Tibet. Then she announced that she had to go back to work. With tears in her eyes, she put a *kata* around my neck and hugged me close before walking out of the restaurant.

The following morning, Dr. Tsering came to the hotel to bid our travel group farewell. Mike and I handed him a large bag containing all of our over-the-counter and prescription medications, with the exception of Mike's antibiotic. We knew we might need them, but the Tibetans needed them more.

"Thank you very much," Dr. Tsering said, visibly moved. "You must be feeling much better to give away your medications. Now, please come back and see us in Lhasa."

Chapter 10

Buddha Nature

Nature of the Mind

"All aboard for Tsetang!" said Tara.

Karma announced, "Our bags are on the luggage truck, and it's time to say goodbye to Lhasa." As our group boarded the bus, several of Karma's cousins came to say goodbye. "I never know if I'll get back into Tibet and see them again," Karma said in a husky voice as he closed the bus door. Ngawang cranked up the engine and turned the bus onto Lhasa's main street.

All of us were on the bus, even Lorna. In Lhasa, she had been too ill to participate in most group activities, and Karma had told us she might fly home early. Dr. Tsering's house calls must have worked, though, since she felt well enough to continue. As we drove out of town, no one talked; everyone seemed to be grappling with complicated feelings about Lhasa. It was Tibet's holy city, but it also served as the focal point for intense strife between Tibet and China, East and West, the spiritual and the temporal, peace and violence, ancient ways and technology. In Lhasa, these extremes were inextricably connected—and ever present.

As we left the city limits the pavement ended and the road turned to gravel. The bus bumped along, and Karma took the microphone. "Today we'll drive to the Yarlung Tsangpo River.

We'll take a ferry to Samye, Tibet's first Buddhist monastery. Afterward, we'll drive to Tsetang, where we'll stay two nights."

"Photo op!" Marge yelled from the lookout seat. Out from under a cliff near the road jutted a large Buddha, with a smaller Buddha on either side. The three figures were painted red, blue, yellow, and green, in stark contrast to the surrounding moon-scape's infinite variations of brown. No one had sculpted these Buddhas, Karma said reverently. They came out of the rock by themselves, but someone painted the figures so we can see them clearly and be reminded of our buddha nature.

The bus left the three Buddhas behind, and I thought of what Sogyal Rinpoche wrote about buddha nature. Tibetans use the word *sem* to describe the ordinary mind. *Sem* is what thinks, plots, desires, and manipulates. To confirm its existence, *sem* asserts, validates, confirms, fragments, conceptualizes, and solidifies our experience. Because *sem* creates and indulges in negative emotions and thoughts, it is chaotic, confused, and undisciplined. External influences constantly affect *sem*. Like a candle flame in a doorway, *sem* is vulnerable to the winds of circumstance.

In contrast, buddha nature is the innermost essence of the mind, untouched by change or death. Sogyal Rinpoche wrote that buddha nature is clear, perfect, free, and beyond mere words. Simple and natural, it can't be complicated, corrupted, or stained. It is the seed of enlightenment, the birthright of everyone. Instead of being limited to one person, buddha nature is the true nature of everything, the knowledge of knowledge itself—"a primordial, pure, constantly creating, pristine awareness that is both intelligent and awake."

Sogyal Rinpoche cautioned that the busyness of the ordinary mind obscures buddha nature. We may catch glimpses of it, though, as when the clouds shift to reveal the shining sun. Buddha nature is our inner teacher. When our vision clouds over, our buddha nature works tirelessly and ceaselessly to awaken us and guide us back to our true selves. With infinite compassion, it encourages us to evolve spiritually.

Buddha nature is like the space in an empty vase. The space both inside and outside the vase is the same, but the fragile walls separate one space from the other. The ordinary mind is the vase that encloses buddha nature. The vase shatters as we become enlightened, and the space inside merges with the space outside. Then we realize that they were never separate, but always the same.

As Sogyal Rinpoche wrote, once we come to trust our buddha nature, we more easily accept our own and others' negativity and deal with it kindly. We can learn to recognize our buddha nature through meditation. The traditional meditative pose is to imitate the Buddha by sitting cross-legged, like an unshakable mountain. A mountain is completely natural and at ease, no matter how strong the winds that batter it or how thick the dark clouds that swirl around its peak. If we let our mind rise and soar when we meditate, we will feel the self-esteem, dignity, and humility of the buddha that we are becoming. We will realize our ageless, radiant, fathomless, eternal buddha nature.

I thought of Maimonides and his explanation for why so many of us ascribe human characteristics to the sacred: We don't know how to relate in any other way. Various names for buddha nature flooded through my mind. Jews, Christians, and Moslems pray to "God." Sufi mystics talk about "Hidden Essence." Native Americans refer to the "Great Spirit." Aristotle wrote about the "unmoved mover" and "first principles." Although the various wisdom traditions use different names, faces, and interpretations, all of them recognize that each of us has the sacred opportunity and responsibility to realize what Tibetans call buddha nature—the fundamental truth about the nature of the mind.

As I meditated, I noted the air moving through my nostrils. In yoga philosophy, breathing is a way to access *prana,* the life-force that permeates everything. It occurred to me that *prana* is, in fact, buddha nature, or God. If God is *prana,* God is all around us, inside us, giving us life and replenishing us. God connects us with each other. We're never alone—when we feel alienated from God, it's only because we've put up obstacles, not because God isn't there. That's a reason why breathing is so important: It can remove blockages and fill every cell in the body with God, promoting the healing of body, mind, and spirit.

Clouded Over

The bus arrived at the Yarlung Tsangpo River. All of us got off the bus except Lorna, who still felt ill. Karma directed us to climb onto the local ferry—an old flat-bottomed barge, big enough to carry about two dozen people and powered by a motor that looked too small. Because the ferry had no seats, we leaned against the sides or sat on supporting beams. Tara said that the ferry would leave when there were enough passengers to fill it. We waited for passengers to come.

Two men arrived pushing a wooden cart that carried an iron plow and a large barrel of gasoline. "I hope they don't intend to put the gasoline on board!" said Ken in alarm. "The boat could catch fire and sink!"

That was exactly what they planned to do. A crowd of women and men soon gathered. Amid laughter, several men worked for over an hour to get the barrel and plow on board. Finally someone produced a wooden plank, and the men rolled the barrel up the plank onto the barge. Then they carried the plow up the plank. The barge bobbed lower in the water, but it didn't sink. After several tries, the driver started the motor, and we took off. Although this part of the river was less than two miles wide, the ride took an hour and a half, for the driver had to navigate between sandbars.

I studied the two Tibetan men by their barrel and plow. The
older man reeked of alcohol; he wore a Chinese army uniform and
a Tibetan fur hat, the mixed symbols of his life and his country. He
smiled, revealing large gaps between his yellow teeth. The younger
man wore an old Western jacket and dirty-white woolen gloves. He
crouched with his head bent down, as if he were afraid to look up.
When I asked Tara about the men, she said, "Older man is farmer,
sixty-one years old, lives near Samye Monastery. Just bought fuel
and plow. Now going home. Has ten children. Youngest son over
there is nineteen. Things better for him now. Chinese lightening up
and economy improving. He doesn't mind Chinese being here." I
was surprised to hear this view, the first positive statement I'd
heard from a Tibetan about the Chinese in Tibet.

Jack asked Karma why we didn't see more wildlife. "There used
to be a lot of wildlife, such as ducks," answered Karma, smiling
ruefully. "But the Chinese killed them for 'Peking duck.'"

When the ferry safely reached the Zurkar shore, our group
applauded in relief. Men helped us climb out of the barge, up
the steep bank, and onto the back of an old flatbed truck. "We'll
ride with local people to Samye Monastery," Karma said. "To
keep from falling down, you'd better stand where you can hold
on to something—the ride will be bumpy." Mike and I grabbed a
bar attached to the truck. Colorfully-dressed Tibetans climbed
on board and grabbed the bar, too.

As the truck chugged across the sand dunes, I felt like I was in
an electric blender. Even though I braced myself against the
tractor, my teeth rattled. The ride was so noisy it was impossible
to hear anyone.

We passed five small, white stupas with spires on top. Tara had
told us that King Trisong Detsen built them to commemorate
Padmasambhava's arrival in Tibet. When the king asked for
proof of the visiting monk's powers, Padmasambhava stretched
out his hand, and fire shot out of each finger. The five spires
represented his fingers.

Samye's ancient, gleaming facade appeared before us like an oasis. The Buddha's eyes—the same eyes we'd seen in Nepal—stared serenely at us. When the truck stopped, children with runny noses and threadbare clothing surrounded us. Now quite used to the routine, we gave them candy and money.

Those of us who felt well enough followed Tara into the monastery. She told us that King Trisong Detsen had founded Samye between 765 and 780. The Indian master, Santarakshita, trained and ordained Tibet's first seven monks there. Eventually, disputes arose between Indian and Chinese Buddhists. In 799, the Great Debate of Samye resulted in Tibetan Buddhism following the Indian school. Since then, Samye had been damaged and restored many times. "All but first floor destroyed during Cultural Revolution," Tara said sadly. "Now being renovated. Golden roof rebuilt recently. Before, 400 monks live here. Now 130 monks."

In the assembly hall, monks sat in rows. Incense filled the air and butter lamps flickered in front of sacred images and *thangkas*. We heard the now familiar sounds of chanting, as well as the deep tones of the long trumpet, the booming of the drum, the clashing of cymbals, and the tinkling of bells. On the second floor, a statue depicted a male deity having sex with a female consort, illustrating that the "whole" consists of both female and male. I asked why the male was a deity with a name, but the female wasn't. "Tantra," Tara said, offering no other explanation. "Only for advanced spiritual practitioners." In the last chapel, a monk was chanting, reading scriptures, and using a foot pedal to beat a drum. He smiled at us, the first expression of warmth I had experienced at Samye.

A flight of precarious steps took us up to Samye's flat roof, a suitable place to eat our box lunches. The view was spectacular. In one direction, sand dunes stretched to the river. On the other side, a mountain guarded the ancient village. I felt warm enough to take off my jacket, a rare luxury in this climate. The heat of the sun contrasted sharply with the cold air inside the chapels.

But soon the sun clouded over and I put my jacket back on. I felt sad that this famous monastery, like the Potala Palace, seemed to be a museum rather than a thriving monastic community. Just as the clouds hid the sun, the political situation was obscuring buddha nature at Samye.

A flatbed truck arrived and our group climbed on board. So many Tibetans packed in with us that there was no danger of falling down during the jarring ride. A young man with a red tassel braided into his long, shiny black hair flirted with two young women wearing *chupas*. We reached the river, where two ferries waited. The younger Tibetans climbed on the first barge, which promptly headed across the river. Our group and the older Tibetans boarded the second one.

On the other side of the river, we joined Lorna at the bus and continued our trip to Tsetang. At the edge of town, the gravel changed to pavement. We drove down a street between Chinese-style cement buildings with small shops. "Third largest city in Tibet," said Tara. "Now 70 percent Chinese. Tibetans disappear. Tonight we stay in three-star hotel. Not like three stars in States." Even so, Mike and I enjoyed our accommodations, which included a bathroom with cold running water.

A Glimpse

The following morning, our bus chugged through the village of Trandruk toward Yumbulagang, the oldest building in Tibet. Tara explained that King Nyentri Tsenpo, who came from heaven, built Yumbulagang in 126 B.C.E. Eventually it was enlarged into a fortress, and in the seventh century it became a monastery. Now it was being restored.

Ahead, a square white-and-gold structure sprouted from a mountaintop. "Remember story I tell about origin of Tibetans?" asked Tara. "This is sacred mountain where monkey meditate. Monkey mate with she-devil. Have six children. First Tibetans.

Mountain made of crystal. Pilgrims chop out crystal, take home. Help them, heal them, give them long life."

Ngawang drove part way up the mountain and then stopped the bus. Everyone but Lorna got out. A narrow dirt track wound up the steep slope. "We'll walk up that path," said Karma.

"You must be kidding!" Mike said laughing. "In this altitude?"

"We'll go slowly," Karma said reassuringly. "You'll be glad you did it."

Tara led the way, stopping frequently so we could catch our breath, calm our pounding hearts, and enjoy the spectacular view of the valley below. "They've spotted us!" Karen said, pointing to four children who raced toward us. They begged us for food and money, but we had left everything on the bus. Nevertheless, they walked with us, holding our hands until we reached precarious steps. Then they turned around to go back down again.

As there was no guardrail, Tara showed us how to climb the steps safely. We soon came to an old, wooden plank over a deep ravine. "Bridge," she said. "Go across to chapel." Karen and I, who enjoyed heights, quickly crossed to the other side. The others balked, but they were able to proceed with Karma's help.

Inside the chapel, a friendly monk sat by a colorful altar. I wondered if he lived there, or if he climbed the mountain each day. *Thangkas* and butter lamps surrounded the central golden Buddha. Along the walls stood images of Songtsen Gampo, Trisong Detsen, and the twenty-eighth Tibetan king, Lha-tho-tho-ri, who lived to be 120 years old. During Lha-tho-tho-ri's reign, Tara said, Buddhist scriptures fell from heaven and landed on Yumbulagang.

Perhaps it was the altitude, or the excellent light and ventilation. But in that meditative, joyful atmosphere, I caught a glimpse of buddha nature. Karen and I explored the second-floor chapel and climbed rickety stepladders to the top of the three-story building. We gazed down on the valley and shared several minutes of ecstasy. I felt in harmony with myself, Karen, and everything else.

Then came the dangerous adventure of climbing back down the mountain. A stiff breeze had arisen, strong enough to blow a person over the side; however, all of us reached the path safely. The children met us with hands full of crystals. Back at the bus there was a flurry of activity to get money for the children.

Two boys walked up wearing thick robes and carrying wooden sticks. Strapped to their backs were packs nearly as large as they were. Several adults and children soon joined them. Karma told us that the boys were twelve years old, and the whole family was on a pilgrimage from eastern Tibet to Yumbulagang. They used the sticks to keep away dogs. Their backpacks were full of supplies for eating and camping along the way.

As we drove back to Trandruk, Karma said, "We'll visit the monastery here. In 1959, His Holiness took this road when he fled from the Chinese. He stopped in Trandruk, where they gave him provisions. It took him two weeks to ride on horseback from Lhasa to India. All the time, the Chinese were looking for him. Imagine what a long, arduous, dangerous, frightening trip that was!"

Ngawang parked the bus on the narrow dirt street, between whitewashed buildings with black paint around the windows and doorways. Two cows nuzzled another cow that was lying in the street, lazily chewing her cud. A man rode by on a bicycle. Several people jaywalked. An elderly woman hobbled along with a cane. High above, on either side of the monastery entrance, a rope of faded prayer flags stretched across the street. The ropes were attached to poles on the monastery roof. Feathers painted blue, white, green, red, and yellow adorned the poles.

Tara led us through the monastery entrance into a court-yard. "Songtsen Gampo built in seventh century," she said. "Same ground plan as Jokhang in Lhasa." Two elderly men sat on steps leading into a large building at the rear. One was blind and the other apparently couldn't walk. A woman who looked sick crouched nearby. They begged for money, and Karma gave them cash.

We visited the assembly hall and chapels, where smoky butter lamps provided the only light. During the Cultural Revolution, Tara said, Red Guards damaged the monastery, but now it was being rebuilt.

Next, we crowded into a small dark room that held the monastery's most important treasure. Behind a dusty glass hung the magnificent *thangka* of Avalokiteshvara, made from thirty thousand pearls. "Resting God of Mercy," Tara said. "Very famous. From seventh century." She said that a lama once brought a Buddha statue from India to Tibet. When the king and queen came to see it, the statue spoke to the queen and told her she was beautiful. In her delight, the queen offered gold to the statue. The statue was so surprised that it became speechless, and the queen interpreted this as rejection. To please the deity, the queen took pearls, gold, diamonds, turquoise, and jade from her crown and made them into this *thangka*. Monks hid the *thangka* in the ground during the Cultural Revolution. Recently someone found it, and now it hung before us in the monastery.

The *thangka* seemed to reach out to me. Captivated by its power, I again caught a glimpse of buddha nature; I wanted to spend more time in this sacred place. When Tara motioned for us to leave, however, I followed her outside into the fresh air, which I breathed in deeply.

A flight of steep steps led to an outdoor walkway encircling an inner courtyard. Young monks smiled shyly as they caught sight of us. I stooped through a low doorway into the monastery kitchen, where the only light came through the doorway and from an open fire over which two monks were cooking. After sneezing in the hot, smoky air, I went back outside again.

"Folks," said Karma, "do you remember the blind man at the front entrance? He's eighty-three years old. Ordinarily, I wouldn't ask you to help a beggar, since I don't believe in begging. I think people should work for a living. In his case, though, it would be beneficial to help, for he needs it badly." The blind man held out a tattered hat and opened his mouth as if to say something. Several teeth were missing. His clothes were dirty and filled with holes. My heart went out to him, and I gave him money. For me, buddha nature was evident in Karma's compassion and the blind man's strength.

Healing Presence

That afternoon, Karma announced, "We're going to a nunnery. This is something most tourists in Tibet never get to do." He told us that nuns have a lower status than monks, and that Chinese authorities treat them even more brutally, imprisoning, beating, and raping them, sometimes with electric cattle prods. Yet nuns, more so than monks, stand at the forefront of the Tibetan independence movement.

"Chinese authorities must be stepping up pressure on nuns and monks," Jack said. "Today's *Tibetan Daily* is calling for major policy changes, or Tibet won't be in compliance with China's socialist system. The paper says that religion exerts too powerful an influence in Tibet."

Trudi asked about the Chinese political "reeducation sessions" for the clergy. Karma explained that these sessions are based on five principles:

- Opposition to separatism.
- Unity of Tibet and China.
- Recognition of the Chinese-appointed Panchen Lama.
- Denial that Tibet was or should be independent.
- Agreement that the Dalai Lama is destroying unity.

Clergy are ordered to accept these principles and admit that the Dalai Lama indulges in "splittist activities." Nuns and monks express their opposition by coughing, sleeping, and shaking their robes during the sessions. Sometimes they are taken into a room and interrogated. Those who give unsatisfactory answers are ordered to leave their nunnery or monastery, and often they are arrested and jailed.

Ngawang parked the bus at the end of a narrow dirt road that turned into a path up a mountain. As we got off the bus, Tara pointed to a cluster of Tibetan buildings high above. "Nunnery up there," she said. She slowly started up the path, nimbly picking her way around rocks and crevices. Halfway up the mountain, we reached mani stones. Tara suggested that we repeat the Tibetan mantra, *"Om Mani Padme Hum,"* to make the climb easier.

When we reached the nunnery, Tara knocked on the door but no one answered. She opened it and looked in. All was quiet. We entered the dirt courtyard, a peaceful place surrounded by traditional buildings. When no one appeared, she ran down the mountain to find out where the nuns were. We sat on a low wall to catch our breath from the climb.

Eventually, Tara returned and spoke to Karma in Tibetan. He must have thought we were alone, because he let down his guard. For the first time, I heard anger and sarcasm in his voice: "The nuns are at a mandatory meeting called by the Chinese government. The purpose is to straighten them out about their proper role in liberated Tibet, to reeducate them about His Holiness' abuses of human rights. It's propaganda. Basically, the Chinese are informing the nuns about the consequences of their actions if they engage in protests against the government."

Mike motioned for Karma to look behind him at three men in dark suits who had entered the nunnery. I clutched my throat in fear. When Karma saw the spies, he returned to his jovial self and said, "Isn't this a lovely, peaceful place? We'll rest a few minutes. Then we'll go back down to the bus."

Two nuns entered the courtyard, the older one dressed in maroon robes and a maroon jacket, her shaved head glowing in the sun. The younger one wore brown robes with a maroon sweater and matching knit hat. Ignoring the spies, they smiled at us warmly, and our tension dissipated. Ken whispered to me, "I

wonder how they can be so serene in these circumstances? I
don't know what I think of religion, but their serenity is enough
to turn me into a religious man!"

Karma translated as the younger nun answered our questions.
"She said the nunnery was built in the eighth century. There
used to be more nuns, but only twenty-five live here now. The
other nuns are at the mandatory meeting, but these two were
excused because of their age. She says she entered the nunnery
when she was thirteen; now she is fifty-eight. She left the nunnery for several years because of political turmoil, but she came
back six years ago. Most nuns here are about forty. The youngest
is twenty and the oldest is seventy-three. Today, girls may join
the nunnery when they are seventeen. Chinese officials don't
allow younger girls to join; by reducing the number of girls
going into nunneries, they hope to limit protests against the
government. The nuns are supported by pilgrims and their families. There are far more monks than nuns, but now nuns can
become lamas, too.

"They are inviting us to visit their chapel," Karma said, aware
that the spies were watching. "They are poor. If you give them
money, they can eat tonight."

The chapel had a low ceiling and an intimate feel. We saw no
magnificent images presiding over an ornate altar. Only three
butter lamps flickered before small images and *thangkas*. Yet, for
all the sparseness of the furnishings here, I felt mothered and
comforted in a way I hadn't experienced in the monasteries.

The younger nun asked if anyone wanted to see her bedroom.
Karen and I followed her up narrow wooden steps to a small
room with a tiny window covered by white paper. When I stood
up, I hit my head on a wooden beam. Her sleeping mat was
rolled out on the wood plank floor. A tiny altar stood in the
corner. She reached into a crevice and produced a faded photo of
the fourteenth Dalai Lama. Karen and I took turns holding it
reverently. *"Thu-je-chhe,"* we said as she hid it again.

Back in the courtyard, I noticed a tiny, elderly nun wearing a maroon robe, sweater, and hat, with prayer beads around her left wrist. I smiled at her, and she walked over to me. She radiated such compassion that I felt chastened, cared for, and exhilarated all at the same time. My attachments, resentments, fears, delusions, and sadness melted away to reveal my buddha nature. No longer did I need to defend my ego, for I didn't have an ego. Feelings of goodwill rolled over me. I could afford to forgive myself, my family, and everyone else; I was connected with all sentient beings everywhere. It all seemed so simple, this interconnectedness of life. We were all blessed— even oppressive, autocratic government officials. I felt grateful and joyful.

Instead of being weakened by suffering, this little nun stood tall and strong like a mountain. Realizing that my life had been too self-indulgent and unfocused, I wanted to shout out that, from now on, I would use each day well and grow into a mountain, like her. But words would ruin "my intuitive grasp of first principles," as Aristotle might have said. As I stood silently in the nun's healing presence, I relaxed deeply and my thoughts slowed. My mind became still. I felt serene.

Karma spoke to the nun. "She's seventy-two years old," he said to me. "She became a nun at the age of twelve. When the Chinese took over, her life was in danger, so she left the nunnery and went to live with her family. She returned here as soon as it was safe again, and she has lived here ever since."

"Please tell her I can feel her faith, her serenity, and her strength," I said in a husky voice, wanting to fall at her feet. "Let her know how deeply moved I feel by her. And thank her."

I reached out to shake her hand. She pressed it between both her hands. I bowed to her, and she bowed to me. Tears streamed down my cheeks. I was sure that if I could just stay in her presence for a while, I'd figure out why I was crying, and my remaining sadness would wash away.

Mike walked over to me and said gently, "Everyone's gone. We had better go, too, so we don't keep them waiting."

Saying *"Thu-je-chhe,"* I bowed to her again and then hurried to catch up with the others. By now, I was crying uncontrollably. Everyone else was crying, too, even the men. These three nuns had moved us more profoundly than all the monks in all the monasteries put together.

Karma asked me if anything was wrong. "I didn't think I believed in saints," I said, "but I feel as if I was just in the presence of a saint, a truly godly person." Smiling, he put his arm around my shoulders and assured me that this experience would make me into a better person.

On the bus, everyone was subdued as Ngawang drove back to Tsetang. I tried to figure out what had affected me so deeply. Certainly, my intense emotions resulted from an accumulation of experiences on the trip. The next morning, we'd fly to Chengdu, China, and I hadn't yet come to terms with my ambivalent feelings about China and Tibet. I was exhausted and developing a cold. But most of all, I had cried because I'd experienced the nun's buddha nature—and my own. Her serene, compassionate presence had opened my heart, and I could feel my deep sadness and pain. I felt purified and healed, if only for a few moments.

I wanted to hold on to these insights after returning home. Radiating a healing presence might awaken the heart of someone who is ill and lead to recovery. *But,* I wondered, *What does it mean to awaken the heart? We say, "I took her into my heart" and "My heart goes out to him." Perhaps these statements mean letting others in, or going out to meet others.* As the bus bumped along, I felt enveloped by buddha nature, *prana,* the Divine, God. I reached over and hugged Mike.

We got off the bus at the Tsetang Free Market. Still teary-eyed, we walked by tables laden with grains, religious items, rugs, cheap jewelry, clothing, and furniture. Hawkers called out for us to buy something, but we were too preoccupied with the nuns to be interested. A woman pushed something in my face. "How much?" she demanded. "She's trying to sell you snuff!" Mike said with a chuckle. Several women surrounded us, and soon all of us were laughing together.

Why Doesn't God Do Something?

Our group gathered in the hotel's heated restaurant for our final dinner in Tibet. Marge and Lisa took Polaroid photos of the staff members, who wore traditional Tibetan and Chinese clothing. The five young women pranced around in delight as they served a delicious Tibetan and Chinese feast. No other patrons were in the restaurant. After the women cleared the table and left the room, we felt free enough to talk openly about our reactions to Tibet.

Marge blurted out, "I don't see how God can sit by and let China take Tibet away from the Tibetans. It's unfair. Isn't there a divine law about right triumphing in the end?"

"There isn't a god!" Jack declared. "Otherwise, he or she would help the Tibetan people. Ever since I went to Catholic school, I've been an atheist. The clergy use guilt to hold on to members and get money from them. I stopped going to church because I didn't like feeling guilty all the time."

"God can't do anything because we have free will," said Mike. "If God interfered, we wouldn't have free will. It's up to us to work together and create a better world."

"Jack, if God is a person, I'm an atheist, too," I said. "But if God means 'life-force,' I can't be an atheist, and I don't think most other people are, either." I spoke about my research participants. Their perspectives on God varied widely, yet all of them wanted to live with meaning and integrity. To me, this suggests developing whatever view of a "life-force" that will help us become better, happier people.

"I don't know how people get along without some kind of spirituality," said Karen. "I've sure needed spiritual strength to get through the hard times in my life."

"When my husband died," said Lisa, wiping her eyes, "I blamed God, but then I got depressed. Now I'm finding new ways to relate to God. I may join a convent and become a nun."

"An ancient Buddhist prophecy said Tibetans would be forced out of Tibet in order to bring Tibetan Buddhism to the world," said Karma, looking at Lisa sympathetically. "That's the good part of what's happening. Wherever Tibetans go, we bring with us our religion, culture, and values."

Mike said that two thousand years ago, Jews experienced something similar when the Romans destroyed their temple in Jerusalem. Jews fled all across the world, bringing with them values about justice and the rule of law. These values have become a cornerstone of Western civilization. In 1990, the Dalai Lama invited Jewish leaders to Dharamsala to learn about the survival strategies Jews had developed during their diaspora. Rodger Kamenetz wrote about this meeting in *The Jew and the Lotus*. The Jewish leaders described how Judaism evolved from a religion based on priests and the temple, which was located in Jerusalem, to a religion with rabbis (teachers) and synagogues (houses of study) all over the world. A new way of "being Jewish" had come out of the destruction, one that was portable and adaptable. Now the heart of Judaism is in the home, and Judaism can be practiced anywhere. The Jewish delegation to Dharamsala told the Dalai Lama that Judaism is still here because of this evolution, and the way for Tibetans to survive their diaspora is to develop values that can be followed inside or outside of Tibet.

"His Holiness knows that Tibetans need to do the same thing," said Karma. "Lamas are reinterpreting Tibetan

Buddhism to fit into the Western lifestyle. If Tibetan Buddhism doesn't evolve, Tibetans in the West won't find it relevant and will turn away. Then we'll lose our strength."

"Christianity is going through the same thing," said Karen. "That's why there's so much conflict over abortion, birth control, women's rights, homosexuality, celibacy of clergy, and other issues. How can it be recast in order to be spiritually relevant in the twenty-first century, so people will continue following it?"

Toward the end of the evening, Karma stood up and thanked Tara, Ngawang, and Thupten. Honorable Treasurer Bernie gave them the group's tips, and Lisa and Marge handed out chocolates from the Tsetang Free Market. Afterward, the servers came back into the room and asked to sing Tibetan songs for us. Their haunting music elicited images of nomads herding yaks on snowy mountains. Tibetans had sung these songs for centuries, but with the way things were going, the songs might one day be lost forever.

Freedom

The next morning, the same women served us *momos,* scrambled eggs, and fruit before bidding us a warm goodbye. It was still dark as our bus bumped along to Gonggar Airport near Lhasa. A rosy glow appeared behind a mountain range and slowly became bigger. Then the sun appeared in a spectacular display of fiery reds, oranges, and yellows—a final gift from the land of Tibet.

As the bus approached the terminal, Karma took the crackling microphone for the last time. "This morning we're going to fly to Chengdu, China. Are you ready to leave Tibet?"

"We're all sick," sniffed June. During most of the trip she had felt good, but now she, too, had a swollen nose and red eyes. "We'd like to stay, but it's time to go home. You know it's time to go home when you look worse than your passport photo!"

On the ride from Kathmandu to Lhasa, Mike and I had felt so ill that we counted the days until we could fly home. Now I was ambivalent about leaving Tibet. I felt deeply connected to the people, culture, and religion. Tibet was transforming me, and I wasn't ready for this process to end. Yet, Tibet's problems weighed heavily on me. Moreover, Mike's skin was still dusky because of the lack of oxygen, and I was getting a cold from exhaustion. It was time to go home.

Inside the terminal, Tara collected our passports and tickets and went to get our boarding passes. Suddenly, government officials began yelling and gesturing angrily at us. "They say our luggage is over the weight limit," said Karma. "They're trying to make money off us. We have to pay extra money. This has happened all along, having to bribe the Chinese officials so they'd let us continue. They'll weigh the luggage, and then I'll pay them. Afterward, I'll divide the amount by the number of people in our group, and you can reimburse me. Is that all right?"

We had no choice, of course, so we nodded. In a few minutes, Karma returned and collected $20 from each of us. Although $20 was small compared with the cost of the trip, it was just enough to trigger our anger. Ever since the bus seat situation had been straightened out, our group had functioned like a loving family. Now we were tired and sick. We weren't in a mood to accommodate each other. "Those who did all the shopping should pay, not the rest of us," Ken grumbled loudly. "If our bags are overweight, it's because of them!"

Notwithstanding these complaints, it was time to say goodbye to our Tibetan guide. Tara bid our group a painful farewell, and we boarded an old Chinese plane. The plane took off from the airport and climbed above snow-covered mountain peaks. Although food stains covered my broken tray table and passengers' bags were piled everywhere, even in the aisle, Mike and I sighed with relief. We didn't have to deal with the authorities in Tibet anymore. We were free—at least, freer than in Tibet. Liberty felt intoxicating.

Freedom increased progressively as our group traveled from Tibet to Chengdu to Hong Kong, and then back to the United States. However, we continued to experience ethical problems wherever we went.

Chapter 11

More Ethical Problems

Should We Speak Up?

"Meet Lily, our Chinese guide," Karma said with a smile as he introduced a young woman at the Chengdu airport. I wondered how Karma could treat Lily so graciously, since she represented the people whom he viewed as Tibetans' oppressors. The rest of us didn't follow his kindly example—with memories of Tibet fresh in our minds, we were aloof toward her.

"Welcome to Sichuan Province in China," Lily said, trying to connect with us. She noted how exhausted we were, with soiled clothes, dark circles under our bleary eyes, and red, swollen noses from colds. "You are tired. Chengdu is at sea level. We enjoy a subtropical climate, so this will feel good after traveling in Tibet." I warmed to her and gave her a smile.

Outside the terminal, the air felt warm, humid, and heavy after the cold, dry, thin air of Tibet. Fragrant flowers bloomed everywhere. Green trees and bushes waved in the mild breeze. I breathed deeply to cleanse my lungs of the putrid air from Tibet's monasteries. As the sweet, oxygenated air filled my body, I felt a surge of energy. We climbed into a modern bus. The engine purred as we rolled down paved streets lined with prosperous-looking businesses.

"Sichuan is the most populous Chinese province." Lily's voice came strong and clear over the microphone, which was a relief after the crackling microphone on the rickety bus in Tibet. "We have many minorities, including Tibetans, Yi, Miao, Hui, and Qiang." She pointed out landmarks, but most of us were falling asleep, not listening. To get our attention, she told a joke. "In China, we throw away the chicken's buttocks. On a map, China looks like a chicken, and Tibet is the buttocks, so we throw Tibet away." She laughed heartily. When no one else joined in, she grew silent. Evidently, she realized she had offended us, but she wasn't sure why.

In his seat by the driver, Karma glowered. Everyone else peered out the bus windows.

"That so-called joke was flat-out racist!" Mike whispered to me. "I wonder if this is the prevalent view in China. If so, no wonder the Chinese people don't object to their government's treatment of Tibet."

"Perhaps we misunderstood her meaning because of cultural differences," I whispered back. "She may only know what her government says about Tibet. Should we say something?"

"I'm too sick to deal with this now," Mike replied wearily. "Let's find a better time later."

I sat back in my seat to ponder this ethical problem: Was it right to judge a culture far older and in many ways wiser than American culture? Then I thought of Pema and the little nun. Perhaps raising the consciousness of one Chinese woman would help Tibetans in some way.

Lily took a different tactic to connect with our group. "Have you heard of *Wild Swans* by June Chang?" Mike and I had, indeed, read this disturbing book, which describes three generations of women in one Chinese family: a grandmother with bound feet who was a concubine to a warlord, her daughter, and her grand-daughter. The granddaughter, who was, in fact, the author, became a "barefoot doctor" during the Cultural Revolution before fleeing China. "June Chang is from Chengdu, and we're proud of her. She wrote about her life here, the suffering we endured during the Cultural Revolution. The Chinese government outlawed the book, but people all over China have read it. We think it's quite accurate. Now she lives in England because she isn't safe from the government here." Lily's new strategy worked, and the tension decreased. She had reminded us that the Chinese people also suffered during the Cultural Revolution, and for this she blamed the government.

After a delicious Sichuan feast, Mike and I took Lily aside. We told her that our group saw firsthand the plight of the Tibetan people, which is why everyone reacted to her joke. "Now I understand," she said, giving us hugs. "Thank you very much." Back on the bus, I questioned whether we'd said enough. "I think she got the point," Mike said. "At least we tried."

"I know you're tired and want to rest," Lily said once everyone was on board, "but your hotel rooms aren't ready. We're going to visit Riverside Park Bamboo Garden. It was built one thousand years ago in memory of Xue Tao. He was a famous poet during the Tang dynasty. Walking in the park will help you feel good." I groaned, because I wanted nothing more than to take a hot shower and crawl into a clean, warm bed. Lily was right, though, for as Mike and I walked along the lush bamboo- and flower-lined pathways, we breathed deeply to fill our lungs with oxygen. Mike's skin color changed dramatically from dusky to pink, and our fatigue began to lift in this joyful, beautiful place. Surprisingly, China was healing us from the rigors of Tibet.

We watched people doing *tai chi*. Grooms with brides in white, Western-style wedding gowns waited to be photographed in front of picturesque pavilions. Women marched by playing drums. At an embroidery factory, artists sewed exquisite images of animals, flowers, and picturesque scenes. Friendly sales clerks gathered around us, more interested in practicing their English than in selling. "Where from?" a woman asked me, "Chicago?"

I replied, "Minneapolis," and drew a map of the United States to show where we lived. Soon all of us were laughing together.

Despite our experiences in Tibet, China was seducing us, just as it had on our previous visit.

Finally, our group checked into the hotel. Mike and I took showers and weighed ourselves. I'd lost ten pounds and he'd dropped fifteen. On CNN, scenes of flooded cities and farmlands in the United States flashed across the screen. After dry Tibet, so much water seemed unreal. I fell asleep thinking about yin and yang, that most things aren't good or bad in and of themselves. Too much water leads to suffering from floods, while a shortage results in suffering from drought. The Buddha, Aristotle, Confucius, and Maimonides were right about the need for a middle path: not too much and not too little. We awoke refreshed, and I said to Mike, "It's time to go back to a middle path when it comes to how we treat both the Tibetans and the Chinese."

Are We Disloyal to Tibetans If We're Friendly to the Chinese?

As I settled into my seat for the flight from Chengdu to Hong Kong, a Chinese woman dressed in a Western suit sat next to me. "I'm Wendy," she said. Wendy told me she wasn't married, and this concerned her family. Chinese women were expected to marry and have children, but she worked too hard at her job to meet a suitable man, much less get married and raise a family. A year ago, she was so burned out from work that her boss gave her a year off, all expenses paid, to recuperate at her sister's home in San Francisco. She hoped to travel to America again soon. "It's worse for women in China," she said. "We don't have the freedom you do in the States."

When I told her that Mike and I were on our way home from Tibet, she said, "I've always wanted to travel to Tibet! Lhasa is a holy city, and I'd like to see it." She said she managed sales in Sichuan for her company. If her company expanded into Tibet because of the excellent business opportunities there, she'd be the head of the Tibetan branch. I told her there were many political problems in Tibet. She said she knew that, but she didn't get involved in politics.

So many thoughts swirled in my head, I didn't know how to respond. *I like Wendy, but her apparent insensitivity upsets me. By doing business in Tibet, she might exploit Tibetans. Still, why shouldn't she work in Tibet if she hires Tibetans and pays them good wages? But don't most Tibetans want China out of Tibet? Yes, I must say something to Wendy. . . . But what do I really know about the situation? After all that we've been through, I still have no clear answers about the conflict in Tibet. I can relate to Socrates when he said the only thing he knew for sure was that he knew nothing.*

More immediately, I thought of any spies who might over-hear us and make trouble for Wendy—or for me. Mike and I still felt weak and exhausted. Engaging in a potentially dangerous conversation about human rights in Tibet with a Chinese woman on a Chinese airplane didn't seem like a good idea.

By the time we landed in Hong Kong, I still didn't know how to resolve my ethical conflict. Wendy must have sensed my tur-moil, for she confided that her parents and most other Chinese people she knew grew up in poverty. They suffered greatly during the Cultural Revolution and political changes since. Things were improving, however, and her job was providing the means to a better life than her parents had. If she managed the Tibetan branch, she'd work longer hours, but she'd make more money, which she would give to her parents to improve their lives.

"Be sure and hire Tibetans," I said, "and pay them good wages."

Karma walked by, and I introduced Wendy. He seemed sur-prised that I was being friendly with a Chinese woman. Had I forgotten Tibet already? I felt somehow disloyal. Then I remem-bered that Wendy wanted to go to Tibet, and that perhaps Karma could take her. At my request, he gave her his business card. She looked dubious but accepted it. Then she hugged me, picked up her luggage, and walked out the door of the terminal.

How Should We Help Tibetans?

Marilyn, our guide in Hong Kong, led us to a luxurious bus. "I'm Chinese, but I grew up in Hong Kong," she said, as we drove to our Kowloon hotel. "In 1997, Hong Kong went back to China. We Chinese in Hong Kong have mixed feelings. No one asked what we wanted to do. The British and Chinese governments decided for us, and we didn't have a choice. The British didn't want us. They wouldn't even give us passports, for they don't want Chinese people to move to England. China wants us—after all, we're Chinese. But we're afraid of Beijing. I don't think the Chinese authorities would dare to curtail our rights in Hong Kong. The whole world is watching. If Beijing interferes and Hong Kong stops thriving, China will lose a moneymaker."

First Lily, then Wendy, and now Marilyn. Even with Tibet fresh in my mind, my heart went out to all three women. Like everyone else, they wanted to be happy and avoid suffering. "It's not right to penalize Marilyn for China's actions in Tibet," I said to Mike. "But if the Chinese people aren't responsible, who is? We promised Pema to help Tibetans. How can we keep that promise?" We decided to invite Karma to dinner and ask him.

"Three ways," Karma answered, as we stuffed ourselves with naan, curried chicken, dal, and yogurt. "First, encourage other Americans to go to Tibet and see what's happening. Second, send postcards to political leaders to let them know you care about Tibet. Third, support organizations that assist Tibetans. As friends like you become aware of Tibet's desperate situation, the movement to help will grow. We are dependent on grassroots support."

Karma looked exhausted. "We were fortunate to have Tara while we were in Tibet," he said sadly. "From now on, only guides trained in China will be allowed to work with tourists. The Chinese government doesn't care if they speak English or if they have any knowledge about Tibet, as long as their political views are 'correct.' I'm concerned that Tara will lose her job."

To cheer him up, I handed him a gift of money in appreciation for the trip. "You said the purpose of life is to become a better person, and to help others become better people. You've encouraged me to rise up and be my best self. That's the greatest gift of all from Tibet!"

"Thank you," Karma replied, breaking into a grin. "Let's stay in touch after we get back to the States. I'd like for us to remain friends."

The next morning, Mike and I sampled our hotel's American and Chinese breakfast buffet. Then we took the Star Ferry from Kowloon to Hong Kong Island. We walked past double-decker buses to the tram, which we rode to the top of Victoria Peak. For the next three hours we hiked on mountainous trails cutting through dense jungle on the far side of the island. Tree frogs croaked and colorful birds chirped. Giant butterflies fluttered by. Colorful flowers lined the trails. Boats meandered lazily in the sparkling South China Sea far below. We inhaled the warm, humid, oxygenated air. Suffering and politics seemed far away.

"I think Plato and Aristotle were right about *akrasia,*" I said. "When we behave in harmful ways, we're acting out of ignorance. We don't know that our actions will lead to unhappiness. This applies to Chinese and Tibetan leaders, too. Evidently, they each think that they're doing the right thing for Tibet, and that the other one is wrong. The question is, do they know what will promote happiness? The extent to which they base their views on ignorance is the extent to which their actions produce suffering, rather than happiness."

"There aren't monsters on either side of the Tibetan situation," said Mike. "It seems to be human nature to make monsters out of enemies. Our society views the Nazis as monsters. If we do that, though, we don't acknowledge the good and bad in each of us."

"In my research, some participants were what society would define as outstanding people," I said. "Others were the opposite—

they had a long history of violence, drug abuse, and trouble with the law. But even the finest people had a mean streak, and the worst demonstrated some goodness. No matter how praiseworthy—or not—each person wanted to be happy and avoid suffering, but they varied greatly as to whether they were taking appropriate steps toward happiness."

"This is more complicated than putting people into categories of good or bad," said Mike. "When we started learning about the Tibetan situation, we saw the Tibetans as victims and the Chinese as aggressors. Now we realize that Tibetans and Chinese are more complex than simply good or bad. Also, we've seen variations within Tibetan and Chinese communities."

"This conclusion makes it more difficult to decide whom to help and whom not to help," I said. "Since all of us have some good and some bad, should we just sit back and not take a stand about anything? Are we justified in helping Tibetans? If so, what actions will lead to happiness and not more suffering?"

"To help Tibetans," said Mike, "I don't think we have to say that Tibetans are all good and Chinese are all bad. Tibetans are suffering. Part of being happy is to reach out to suffering individuals. We can do our small part to preserve the best values of the culture that has produced Tibetan Buddhism, Tibetan medicine, and the Dalai Lama. If Tibetan culture dies, the world will lose an important asset. Also, let's do what we can to promote a peaceful solution to the Tibetan situation. An amicable approach will illustrate the wisdom of nonviolence."

"Okay, so we're going to help Tibetans," I said. "Individuals, or the Tibetan community? Tibetans in Tibet, or in exile? What's a middle-road approach?"

"Give money to Tibetan organizations," said Mike, "but also help individual Tibetans. When we see something to do, let's do it. We'll avoid being critical of the Chinese."

"That's a sensible middle road," I agreed. "We can be friends with Chinese people, too. From now on, how's this motto? 'Do what needs to be done, what no one else is doing, and what we can and are willing to do.' This way, we can try to make a contribution without becoming embroiled in the politics of helping. Applied to Tibetans: They need help, not enough people are helping, we can help, and so let's help. When Tibetans no longer need our assistance, we can help someone else. There's always plenty of work to do."

With this resolution, we felt free to enjoy Hong Kong. That evening, our group took a harbor cruise to celebrate the last night of the trip. We ate from a lavish Chinese buffet while a woman performed juggling acts and a man sang in Chinese. Mike and I held hands and gazed across the beautiful moonlit harbor. Back on Kowloon, we walked past upscale stores selling designer clothes, shoes, and luggage. Outdoor restaurants displayed roasted chickens and kittens, as well as live snakes, lizards, and eels. At the Night Market, customers purchased goods from all over the world.

The next day, we said emotional goodbyes to our fellow travelers before boarding our various flights to the United States. Mike and I arrived in Minnesota with our luggage still soiled from the dirt roads in Tibet. I put the Tibetan rugs we had purchased on the floor of our house and tacked Pema's door hanging on my office door. Every day it reminds me to help Tibetans.

Ethical Problems of Tibetans in the United States

Mike and I reached out to help Tibetan immigrants in the U.S., and they responded warmly with friendship. We learned that many of them have never seen Tibet, having been born in exile, and that visiting Tibet would be dangerous for them. Often, U.S. immigration laws have separated them from their family members back in Tibet, India, and Nepal. Although they are grateful to be in the United States, they suffer from homesickness, and they feel guilty about doing well while their families are enduring hardships in Asia. Moreover, they experience conflict about how to be both Tibetan and American at the same time.

One day we stood with a friend, Pempa, on the front steps of the inner-city apartment building where he and other Tibetans live. Smells of Tibetan cooking wafted through open windows. Prayer flags tied to a flagpole blew in the evening breeze. "Here are new values, more individual freedom, less male dominance," he said. "That changes the relationship between husband and wife. We Tibetans didn't expect to find problems here, for we had a rosy picture of life in America. Now we wonder how to preserve our values."

A number of Tibetan friends have echoed this sentiment. Dolma, who is studying to be a registered nurse, met me for tea one day before beginning her afternoon shift as a nursing assistant at a nursing home. "I'm questioning my Buddhist faith, now that we're living in America," she said, distraught. "My mother-in-law has cancer, and I don't know how to deal with her. She demands that my husband stay home with her, so he can't work, and we don't have enough money. I work half-time, but I might have to quit school and get a full-time job. My mother-in-law was a strong Buddhist all her life. Now she's angry about Tibet, and she's taking out her anger on us. I'm afraid my husband will get sick. High lamas came to see her. They said she's mentally ill. She refuses to go to a doctor— Tibetan or Western—and sits in a chair all day. This must be happening because of her karma and ours. I say mantras, but it doesn't help. My neighbor is trying to get me to become a Christian. I wonder whether I should go to church with her."

Several weeks later, I sat with another friend, Kalsang, on a large Tibetan rug in the prayer room of her house. Her baby daughter lay sleeping nearby. In front of us, a Buddha statue and a picture of the fourteenth Dalai Lama stood on an altar decorated with *thangkas*. Kalsang lit incense on top of the altar. A brass bell tinkled. A singing bowl chimed. The sights, smells, and sounds instantly transported me back to Tibet's monasteries. The baby woke up but didn't cry, and Kalsang nursed her.

In this meditative atmosphere, Kalsang and I discussed her conflicts in America. She and her husband work alternating shifts so they can take turns caring for their baby. They have invited her elderly mother to come to the United States to baby-sit and teach their daughter about Tibetan culture. Her mother refuses, for she doesn't speak English and she'd be lonely staying home all day with a child. Kalsang said she's concerned that Tibetan-American children are adopting Western, consumer-oriented values. Tibetan parents value an American education, but they want their children to grow up Tibetan and to help their relatives in Tibet. The children need to learn about Tibetan culture to have a sense of community and continuity, or what makes them Tibetan will disappear.

Dr. Gompo, a Tibetan physician trained in Western medicine, described Tibetans' conflict about how to integrate Tibetan values and Western healthcare. "We use traditional Tibetan medicine for chronic illnesses, such as arthritis, and Western medicine for acute conditions, like a heart attack. When Western health professionals prescribe treatment, we try to be true to our Tibetan values, but it's not easy. In the United States, women have babies in hospitals, but Tibetan women prefer to have babies at home so new mothers can rest for forty-nine days afterward. We don't know what to do when a Western physician says we need surgery; we're scared of surgery because it isn't part of our background. Many Americans ask for aggressive treatment even if they are dying, but we want to die peacefully and naturally, and we don't like heroic efforts to keep us alive. Here, after someone dies, the body is quickly taken away. We believe in reincarnation, and we want a Tibetan lama to visit the dead person before the body is moved. It's a problem, how to have a foot on each side: in the U.S. and in Tibet, and in the two healthcare systems."

A Solution?

As Tibetans opened up to us, Mike and I came to see how deeply troubled they were about the Tibetan situation. Like many Jews, Tibetans often used humor to express their anxiety, but finding an equitable solution was foremost in everyone's mind.

A peaceful end to the conflict seemed far away until we attended a panel discussion at a local college. Karma told us about the panel because he was flying in to be a participant. Besides Karma, the panel consisted of Dr. Bob Russo, a pro-Chinese anthropologist, and Dr. Beth Huber, a Buddhist scholar.

Bob began by saying that the fourteenth Dalai Lama has been conducting an international campaign to marshal Western support for Tibet. Is this strategy working? Yes and no. Yes, for the Dalai Lama is as well known as any rock star, and he has developed sympathy for Tibet around the world. No, because he has publicly humiliated China, making it difficult for China to offer concessions. Rather than court the West, Bob said, the Dalai Lama should make the best deal he can with China.

"His Holiness hasn't made any mistakes," Karma protested, "but the Chinese have. They aren't doing the right thing in Tibet."

"Chinese leaders aren't dumb or ignorant," Bob replied. "If the Dalai Lama treats the Chinese as demons, he simplifies things so much that he can't deal with them at all."

"His Holiness doesn't take an anti-Chinese stance," Karma said. "He's pro-justice."

"Most Chinese leaders don't agree," said Bob. "In my view, the Dalai Lama has made a second mistake, one that affects his credibility. He portrays Old Tibet as a romantic Shangri-la. Tibetans were happily, peacefully devoted to Buddhism, or so the myth goes, when the forces of evil invaded their ecologically enlightened land, which was ruled by a god-king. This Pollyanna perspective denies Tibet's feudal past. The Dalai Lama needs to argue for Tibetan autonomy without Shangri-la."

"If His Holiness took that position," said Karma, "who besides Tibetans would pay any attention to Tibet? One of the reasons the world cares about Tibet is because of Shangri-la."

"Third," Bob persisted, "the Dalai Lama hasn't developed Tibetan nationalism enough. Old Tibet wasn't a nation in a modern sense, with a global economy, secular laws, and citizenship. It didn't have diplomatic relations with other countries, or industrialism. Even today, Tibetans in the United States say they are from a region in Tibet, not from Tibet itself."

Karma countered by saying that Tibetans have more of a sense of nationalism than people from many other developing countries do. Tibetans all around the world are asking if Tibetans in the United States are the same or different from Tibetans in Tibet, India, and Nepal. Also, they question whether Tibetans who don't speak Tibetan are still Tibetan. Jews and many other ethnic groups ask similar questions about themselves.

Bob kept going. "The Dalai Lama has made a fourth mistake, in my view. He claims that Tibetan Buddhism is Tibet's gift to the world. But instead of teaching historic Tibetan Buddhism, he's reformulating it into a universal wisdom tradition, a science of the mind. This isn't consistent with true Tibetan Buddhism. In fact, Tibetan Buddhism has a lot of superstition in it."

Beth broke into the debate. "It depends on how you view Tibetan Buddhism, or any wisdom tradition. Some people call wisdom traditions superstitious; others say they are spiritual. Reformulating Tibetan Buddhism into a universal wisdom tradition isn't a mistake. It's a brilliant strategy to attract non-Buddhists! Wisdom traditions change over time. The dharma mutated in its travels from India to China, Southeast Asia, Japan, Tibet, and the West. Tibetan Buddhism is inclusive enough to incorporate both traditional Tibetan beliefs and Western practices."

"Worshippers of Tibet's regional deities wouldn't agree," said Bob. "Which leads to a fifth mistake. The Dalai Lama says that support for Tibetan autonomy is not just politics, but dharma. That makes no sense."

"He's offering Tibetan Buddhism in exchange for Tibetan autonomy!" Karma declared.

"Autonomy is essential for Tibetans to fulfill their historic role of priest," said Beth. "After Tibet's submission to the Mongols in the twelfth century, Tibetans viewed the relationship between China and Tibet as one of patron-priest, with China the patron and Tibet the priest. When the Qing dynasty fell, the priest aspect ceased, but the patron relationship continued. Now China is attempting to play the role of the priest, too, by selecting Tibet's religious leaders, as in the case of the Chinese-appointed Panchen Lama. In response,the Dalai Lama has turned to patrons throughout the rest of the world. Tibetans once again perform the role of priest, and their patrons give them financial contributions and political support."

Bob said the historic patron-priest relationship would go well with what many people suggest is a reasonable way to resolve the Tibetan situation. China could offer Tibet the status of a "special administrative region," SAR, with a high degree of autonomy. SAR is the same designation that China has given to Hong Kong. Beijing would be responsible for Tibet's foreign affairs and defense. In other areas, including religion and culture, Tibetans would be free to make their own decisions. However, if Tibet was granted autonomy, other minority groups in China might demand it, too.

"Radicals on both sides would complain," said Karma, "but His Holiness would welcome such an event as a genuine attempt to resolve the Tibetan situation."

"Bob, you claim that the Dalai Lama has made political mistakes," said Beth. "Let's look at the Tibetan situation in another way. From an ethical and spiritual perspective, universal Tibetan Buddhism is an enormous contribution to the West. Old Tibet was no dark, primitive place of feudalism and slavery. Instead, Old Tibet was an ethically and spiritually sophisticated civilization. Tibetans' greatest treasures aren't historical relics; their most important gift to the world is the profound knowledge the lamas developed—and continue to refine—about the nature of the mind and the way to promote individual and collective understanding. This inner science complements the West's understanding of the physical world, and it remains just as vibrant and relevant today as it did in Old Tibet."

Bob sounded irritated. "Let's not forget that China has been pumping millions of dollars into Tibet and modernizing it. No one, including the Dalai Lama, wants to go back to the primitive lifestyle of Old Tibet."

"I don't advocate life without modern conveniences," said Beth. "However, it seems to me that individuals with a materialistic view analyze the Tibetan situation one way, and those who value dharma see it in quite another. According to dharma, compassion and wisdom—not airplanes and bombs—characterize true civilization. Old Tibet's culture didn't develop industrially or militarily, but it wasn't backward. I agree with Professor Robert Thurman, who is a friend of the Dalai Lama. Thurman wrote that in many ways, Old Tibet had a more sophisticated culture than our own, for it advanced ethically and spiritually. The lamas knew that happiness results from inner work—from inner revolution, actually—not from material wealth, and that we must be ethical and spiritual in both our personal and political life."

"His Holiness' experience with China has taught him the importance of uniting personal ethics and public responsibility," said Karma. "He's a role model for how to view ourselves as global citizens, not just private individuals." Karma suggested a curriculum to produce global citizens: Read Eastern literature alongside the Western canon; study the histories and philosophies of countries around the world, not just in Europe and the Middle East; and include yoga and *tai chi* in sports. The goal would be to produce ethical individuals who demonstrate spiritual intelligence, not just rational intelligence, and take seriously their responsibility as contributors to the world.

"China needs the Dalai Lama to guide its development," said Beth. "Otherwise, the Chinese people may discard their ethical, spiritual values in the rush to accumulate material goods. If China grants Tibet SAR status, China and Tibet can go back to a patron-priest relationship."

"As a young man," said Karma, "His Holiness was shocked when Mao told him that religion is poison, the opiate of the masses. The organized worship of Mao had already become China's state religion. His Holiness' teachings can be the antidote to the opiate of Maoism."

"Interesting turn in our debate," said Bob, attempting to sum it all up. "Working together would benefit Tibet and China. Of course, this won't eliminate every problem, but we'd all breathe more easily if the Tibetan situation were resolved in this peaceful way."

◆   ◆   ◆

Following the panel discussion, the audience buzzed with excitement about the possibility of a peaceful end to the Tibetan situation. Karma seemed particularly cheery. With intense emotion, he told Mike and me what a relief it would be for him, his family, other Tibetans, the Chinese, and the world if the conflict between Tibet and China could end well.

"All this talk about the Dalai Lama," I said, "but Mike and I have never seen him in person. Is there any way we can go to hear him when he's in the U.S. next?"

"Matter of fact, His Holiness is coming to the United States to give teachings about compassion," said Karma. "Would you like to go? I'll get tickets for us." Two months later, Karma, Mike, and I were on our way to hear the most extraordinary Tibetan of all.

Chapter 12

Compassion

Universal Compassion

Karma, Mike, and I walked up the steps to the auditorium where the Dalai Lama would present three days of teachings. Tibetans wearing *chupas* smiled at us. Although most people entering with us were Caucasian, every ethnic group was represented, including persons from as far away as Taiwan and Chile. A placard listed languages into which the teachings would be translated as the Dalai Lama talked. Police checked tickets and directed the crowd through metal detectors. Such heavy security illustrated a paradox: The Dalai Lama taught nonviolence, but he had received death threats.

Volunteers handed out the text to accompany the teachings, *The Stages of Meditation, Middle Volume,* a handbook on meditation written by the Indian master Kamalasila. The text explained that by the second half of the eighth century, Buddhism had become entrenched in Tibet. However, the Tibetan Buddhist community was divided into two factions, the "Simultaneists" and the "Gradualists." Because these factions disagreed, a debate was held at Samye, the first Buddhist monastery in Tibet, to determine the right Buddhist path. Karma, Mike, and I had visited Samye when we were in Tibet.

The Chinese *Ch'an (Zen)* master Ho-shang Mo-ho-yen headed the Simultaneists. The Simultaneists believed that meditative practice should consist solely of thought cessation—the stoppage of any kind of mental activity whatsoever—which induces a simultaneous or instantaneous realization of awakening. For them, meditative insight alone is sufficient to achieve awakening. They considered the practice of compassion to be superfluous, or even obstructive to meditative insight. On the other side of the debate was Kamalasila, who led the Gradualists. They viewed human thought as an instrument for developing compassion, asserting that compassion was an essential component of spiritual growth. Advocating a step-by-step approach to spiritual development, they claimed that each stage of growth served as a foundation for the next. The Gradualists prevailed, and the Simultaneists were told to stop teaching their interpretation of dharma.

As we sat in the packed auditorium, the audience suddenly grew silent and everyone stood up. People put the palms of their hands together and bowed toward the stage. The Dalai Lama entered, wearing his characteristic maroon and saffron robes. He was accompanied by his translator, a Tibetan man in a business suit. They bowed and then sat in chairs, as if they were going to have a fireside chat with the audience. On either side, nuns and monks with shaved heads and black or maroon and saffron robes arranged themselves on the floor. An altar loomed over the back of the stage, above which hung a huge *thangka* of thousand-armed Avalokiteshvara, the deity of compassion and patron deity of Tibet.

"I'm not singing, and I'm not dancing," the Dalai Lama began, punctuating his words with smiles and laughter, "so I don't know why such big numbers came out today. I have nothing to offer you except some of myself—my thoughts, beliefs, and experience. Because we are the same human beings mentally, emotionally, and physically, you may find some ideas to cope with your daily problems." His face looked jolly, even when he wasn't smiling. He spoke primarily in Tibetan, but periodically he burst out in English.

Everyone wants to be happy, he said. The purpose of life is to be happy. When we're happy, we enjoy pleasant feelings without being attached to them. But we can be mistaken about how to be happy. If our goal is to accumulate material possessions and engage in sensual pleasures, we may feel good temporarily, but these activities interfere with our development of ethical and spiritual qualities, which leads to suffering. We need to figure out which conditions result in our happiness and which ones don't, and then increase the former and decrease the latter.

What brings the greatest joy and satisfaction in life, he said, are actions we take out of concern for others. The more we desire to benefit others, the more happiness we experience. Thus, the way to be happy is to develop good karma by practicing compassion without religious dogmatism or complicated philosophy. Compassion gives meaning to life and makes our actions ethical, which leads to happiness for both ourselves and others.

At first, disciplining ourselves to act with compassion may be a struggle, for there are no shortcuts. Eventually, feeling compassion for everyone, including those who have harmed us, becomes a habit. This equanimity isn't an end in itself, but a springboard to even greater compassion. He said we can even develop unconditional, undifferentiating, universal compassion. For three days, the Dalai Lama talked about how to practice compassion, let go of negativity, transform ourselves through meditation, and use compassion to transform society.

Practicing Compassion

In the Tibetan language, said the Dalai Lama, the word for compassion connotes a rational, conscious activity that needs cultivation. Compassion includes love, affection, kindness, caring, patience, humility, gentleness, forgiveness, peace, generosity, and tolerance, but it doesn't imply condescension or pity, that I'm fortunate and you're not. Instead, compassion is a feeling of connection with others. Compassion arises from our innate reason and empathy, our ability to enter into, and to some extent share in, others' suffering. We recognize ourselves in others, especially those who are disadvantaged, for we realize we're all sisters and brothers with no substantial differences. Each of us has an equal right to develop happiness. Since compassion is not the desire for attachment to a person, we can show compassion without harming ourselves or each other.

Because our true nature is compassionate, our potential to develop compassion is stable and continuous. We think it's natural when one person takes care of another person. Murder, not good deeds, becomes news, since that is an unnatural occurrence. People do kindly things for each other all the time, something that is easy to take for granted. For example, during the Holocaust, some people behaved altruistically by saving Jews. "Remembering their compassion gives me joy and relief," he said.

"Compassion acknowledges that my interest is dependent on the interest of others," the Dalai Lama continued. "We can't be happy by focusing on our own self-interest. Thinking primarily of 'my life, my life, my life' destroys happiness, for small problems appear gigantic and lead to frustration, insecurity, and fear. When we reach beyond the confines of narrow self-interest, our hearts fill with kindness. The more we care about the happiness of other people, the greater is our own happiness."

As we transform our innate capacity for empathy and reason into compassion, he said, we develop inner restraint, and our behavior becomes more ethical. We avoid harming and, if possible, we do good. Our actions are ethical when our hearts are filled with compassion. If we lack compassion, our behavior can turn destructive. Compassion provides the necessary foundation and motivation for both inner restraint and virtue.

Gradually, we extend our compassion to the point where we feel responsibility for others, and we dedicate ourselves to helping them overcome their suffering and the causes of their suffering. We long for others to find lasting happiness, and we act to secure that happiness.

Having concern for others breaks down barriers that inhibit healthy interactions. Compassion helps remove our fears and insecurities, gives us the strength to cope with obstacles, and displaces our self-centered motives that cause us to deceive and misuse each other. Developing a warmhearted feeling for others puts our mind at ease, and we develop lasting friendships. We experience a sense of liberation from our habitual preoccupation with self, which, paradoxically, gives rise to strong feelings of confidence.

The principle source of success in life is compassion—a combination of individualism and emphasis on others. Compassion in our hearts brings loving kindness to everyone who comes in contact with us. We promote understanding and harmony with family, friends, community, workplace, and the world.

Compassion is necessary to the survival of our species, he said, for all of us need to love and feel loved. If we don't feel loved, we find it hard to love others, and this undermines our health. Anger is a primary source of high blood pressure, sleeplessness, degenerative diseases, and other health problems. Our bodies can heal if we are affectionate rather than fearful and angry. When we practice compassion, we are healthier and more peaceful, and our bodies function better.

The Dalai Lama explained that some people dismiss compassion as impractical and unrealistic. But compassion can be powerful. A good heart is a sign of inner strength and courage, not weakness. It sustains peace of mind through difficult circumstances, and life becomes more stable.

Someone in the audience asked if only Buddhists act with compassion. "No," replied the Dalai Lama with a grin. "Compassion is not a Buddhist monopoly." He said that each of the world's major wisdom traditions helps individuals to restrain their narrow, selfish impulses and to develop compassion. We see compassionate Jews, Christians, Moslems, and Hindus. Mother Teresa, a Christian who spent her life caring for the poor, demonstrated the very heart of compassion. Of course, to be good human beings, we don't need to become religious or adhere to a complicated ideology. All we need to do is develop our basic human qualities. The Dalai Lama himself takes a nonsectarian approach, making an effort to practice all wisdom traditions simultaneously. Buddhism is most suitable for him, but is not necessarily best for everyone else. The world has many different people, so we need a variety of wisdom traditions.

Another member of the audience asked if the Dalai Lama experiences anger. "Of course, I occasionally do," he said. "When I was young, I was excitable. At age fifteen or sixteen, I began to take serious interest in spiritual practice. Meditation on compassion helps me to cope with anger. If I get disturbing news, I'm like the ocean during a storm. The waves churn, but deep down the ocean is calm. If Tibet's political situation is resolved, I can take a long time off. Then no work, all rest. I like that best." He laughed heartily.

Healing Negativity

The Dalai Lama explained that negativity keeps us from practicing compassion. Positive acts arise from positive emotions and thoughts, whereas negative acts result from negative ones. Positive acts are ethical, helpful, right, and virtuous, while negative acts are unethical, unhelpful, wrong, and lacking in virtue. For example, when the desire to harm someone motivates a seemingly positive act, the act is negative. The way to be happy is to curb our negative reactions to life's troubles. By developing insight, we will engage in acts that lead to happiness, not suffering.

From a Buddhist perspective, said the Dalai Lama, all things originate in the mind. Thus, we have everything we need for happiness. Our perception is important, not the situation itself. Every painful thought, emotion, and event can be a source of anger and despair, but also of ethical and spiritual growth. Moreover, negativity may become positive, just as positivity can turn into negativity. We can choose how we view life's inevitable difficulties. If we take a positive approach, things will go better than if we make negative decisions. The outcome is up to us!

Negativity deceives us, for it seems to offer satisfaction. Coming in the guise of a protector, negativity gives us boldness and strength, but it destroys one of our most precious qualities: our capacity for discriminative awareness. Negativity robs us of the ability to judge between right and wrong and to discern the likely outcome of our actions. Decisions made under the influence of negativity are often a source of regret.

Negativity also encourages us to assume that appearances are the same as reality. For example, when we become angry, we tend to view others as if their negative characteristics are unchanging. We forget that they, like us, are merely suffering human beings who want to be happy. When our anger diminishes, we see them in a more positive light.

The more we give in to negativity, the less room we have for compassion, and the less able we are to solve our problems. If we do not restrain our negativity, it has a propensity to increase, like a river that floods when the snow melts. Negativity enslaves the mind and renders it helpless. When we indulge in our negative feelings and thoughts, we become accustomed to them. Far from free, we gradually become habituated to behaving negatively in the face of trying circumstances.

In all this, negativity has one good quality: We can heal it. We may mistakenly deny and suppress our negativity, as when we hide our anger to present a facade of self-control. However, this lack of honesty can lead to more negativity, which will eventually burst out physically and emotionally when we can't contain it any longer. The process of healing negativity doesn't mean denying or suppressing our feelings and thoughts, but facing up to what troubles us. An infected wound needs to be cleansed before it can heal.

We can heal our negative actions by expressing sincere regret and making amends. To keep from behaving negatively in the future, we can learn to let go of negative emotions and thoughts, allowing them to pass through our mind just as clouds drift by in the sky. Letting go will keep them from lodging in our consciousness. We may want to express our negative feelings and thoughts, but then we run the risk of overreacting and causing harm. After careful consideration, we'll know whether or not to express our negativity, and how we can do so in a compassionate manner.

In trying times, we can heal our negativity by shifting our focus from ourselves to others. Practicing compassion, taking into account the needs of others, causes our own problems to diminish. If we aren't able to change our negative reactions, we can avoid individuals and situations that give rise to this negativity, surrounding ourselves instead with those that lead to happiness. For example, if we become angry whenever we meet someone, it may be best to stay away from that person until we develop the necessary internal resources to resist a negative reaction. Meanwhile, we can spend time with people we enjoy.

To truly heal negativity, we must root out anger, hostility, resentment, confusion, pride, anxiety, lust, greed, and envy, and replace them with compassion. We can do this by noticing when our negative thoughts and feelings arise. We learn to critically examine them, analyze them, determine their causes, and figure out how to deal with them. Looking for the slightest negativity, we pay close attention to our body, our speech, and all our behavior. We think, think, think—like a scientist who collects and analyzes data and then draws appropriate conclusions. This is not easy. For example, hatred is a strong emotion when fully developed, but in its beginning stages we may notice only a subtle aversion. Gaining insight into ourselves is a lifelong task, but unless we undertake it, we won't see how to make positive changes. The more we develop compassion, the more we increase its force.

A member of the audience asked how to deal with people who hurt us. The Dalai Lama said that occasionally we may need to protect ourselves from such people. If we are being physically threatened, it's best to run away, rather than give in and get injured! Injustice may make us angry, and though this anger may be justified and even produce good, negativity increases if anger becomes personal and turns into malice. That is why we practice nonviolence and refrain from physical reactions, even if we are provoked. We do not return harm for harm. Since we are inherently good, goodness and justice will prevail. With this positive view, we'll be able to cope fairly well.

When people hurt us, said the Dalai Lama, treat them well. Otherwise, we get hurt twice—first by their actions, and then by our response. If two people disagree, and one of them takes the conflict lightly while the other is obsessed with getting revenge, what happens? The second person broods, and this can lead to eating problems, insomnia, ill health, and miserable days and nights.

People who hurt us do so because they are suffering. We need to avoid an angry response, for this causes more suffering. Instead, we might recognize that their behavior results from a vast and complex web of interrelated causes and conditions. Yes, it's easy to care for our friends and hate our enemies, but if our attitude changes, we may see our friends as enemies and our enemies as friends.

Attitudes do change. We would be wise to not base our compassion on people's attitude toward or treatment of us. Hostility will not disturb us if we practice compassion toward everyone.

When someone hurts us, patience can give us the strength to resist a negative reaction. Then, in the face of adversity, we'll experience composure and a sense of being unperturbed. Instead of reacting negatively, we can forgive people who hurt us. One of the hardest tasks in life is to forgive. Forgiving doesn't necessarily consist of forgetting, reconciling, condoning, denying, or excusing. Instead, forgiveness means to drop the burden of resentment and to forego revenge. We refuse to let negativity take over. Forgiveness helps us move forward and increases our optimism. It lessens our suffering and adds deeper meaning to life.

It is best to do everything in our power to resolve our problems. If we can't change other people's harmful actions, though, we can learn to accept them. Then we won't compound trouble with emotional suffering.

Often, the greatest spiritual growth occurs during times of difficulty. Suffering can open our eyes to reality and help us to empathize with each other. The Dalai Lama quoted a prayer: "May I be able to maintain my calmness even if the whole universe rises against me."

Meditation

By meditating regularly, the Dalai Lama said, we can overcome negativity and transform ourselves into compassionate, happy individuals. But an ethically disciplined life is a prerequisite for effective meditation. Unethical behavior causes turmoil that interferes with meditation.

Meditation doesn't necessarily mean sitting cross-legged on the floor. Simply observing our thoughts throughout the day is a form of meditation that yields excellent results. The Dalai Lama described two kinds of meditation: placement or tranquilization meditation, and analytic or insight meditation.

Placement meditation means to focus single-mindedly on an object or the breath. Through this kind of meditation we can

develop mindfulness, or a sense of being fully present in the
moment. Our body and mind become more flexible, and we
experience joy.

The Dalai Lama explained that our mind, or consciousness, is
like a crystal-clear lake. When a storm stirs the water, mud from
the bottom of the lake makes the water appear opaque. Through
placement meditation, we can calm the water, allowing the mud
to settle so the lake becomes clear again. In other words, placement meditation can help focus the mind so its true, good, and
beautiful nature shines through.

When used alone, placement meditation will not erase our
negativity or lead to enlightenment. To transform our mind, we
also need analytic meditation. Through this kind of meditation,
we can contemplate positive concepts, such as compassion and
happiness, and cultivate them in our heart and mind.

The Dalai Lama listed two stages for meditating on compassion. First, meditate on equanimity to develop a compassionate
attitude toward all sentient beings. Start with those we cherish.
Then meditate on neutral persons, those for whom we don't
have feelings. Finally, meditate on our enemies. As we transform
the mind, we become more compassionate. The Dalai Lama
quoted another prayer: "For as long as space endures and sentient beings remain, until then may I, too, abide to dispel the
misery of the world."

Once we have conditioned ourselves to equanimity, the second
stage is to meditate on the awakened mind. The Dalai Lama
described two types of awakening: temporary freedom from suffering, which can be experienced during meditation, and total liberation from suffering, a state of mind called enlightenment,
omniscience, nirvana, or buddhahood. This ultimate, awakened
mind is transcendent, radiant, unmoving, and unwavering.

The Dalai Lama went on to describe two obstacles to meditation. Mental sinking occurs when we feel sluggish or sleepy. We
can counteract this obstacle by thinking about something joyful,

splashing water in the face, or taking a walk. Mental excitement is the opposite state. The way to counteract this obstacle is by reflecting on something somber, such as how procrastination keeps us from meditating.

Someone in the audience asked, "Is it better to take care of my two-year-old or go to your lectures?" The Dalai Lama responded by talking about the relationship between practical attachments—such as children or a career—and spiritual practice. Ideally, society would encourage us to spend half our time on material concerns and half on spiritual practice that results in spiritual power. He quoted Milarepa: "May the benefactors who live in town and the meditators up in the caves obtain liberation together." Ultimately, each of us must decide how best to balance our responsibilities and spiritual practice.

"In meditation and all spiritual practice," the Dalai Lama cautioned, "I believe in the middle way, for I distrust extreme positions. Western thought seems greedy for certitude, which may neglect the gray zone. We need to develop more comfort with uncertainty, with mystery, and with the constant flux of things. As Kamalasila wrote, enlightenment doesn't occur instantly, but as a result of a long process. Buddhism isn't a quick fix, like taking a pill. There's no such thing as instant nirvana."

Another member of the audience asked if the Dalai Lama has reached enlightenment. The Dalai Lama threw his head back and laughed merrily. "On a good day, when all my mental faculties are working, I'm at a point where I can just see where the path lies. I'm giving my personal experience now, not to proclaim my goodness, but to inspire you to transform your mind and society." Several pigeons flew into the auditorium and perched on the rafters. Looking up, he joked, "We're about to receive a blessing!" Evidently, the pigeons lost interest, for after a few minutes they flew away. He chuckled, then continued with his teachings.

Universal Responsibility

In addition to transforming ourselves, said the Dalai Lama, we can transform society by developing an attitude of universal responsibility. Because all of us are interconnected, we are responsible to and for each other. Violence, human rights violations, cultural genocide, unsanitary conditions, environmental desecration, and lack of basic essentials such as food, clothing, housing, heat, and healthcare occur all over the world, including in the United States, and affect everyone. Only by working together to solve these problems can we live in harmony with each other and the environment.

"I am seeking autonomy for Tibet, not separation from China," he said in English. "More and more Chinese are sharing our concern about Tibet. I will give all my authority to the autonomous Tibetan government. That government should be an elected government. Then I am no longer the head of the Tibetan government, and I will truly be a simple Tibetan monk. My ambition for the rest of my life is to spend time in meditation and things like that." Reiterating the pledge he made in 1992, he said that if China grants Tibet political autonomy, he will relinquish his role as temporal leader of his homeland. He also stated his belief that political and economic liberalization in China will promote public awareness of human rights abuses in Tibet.

"Perhaps I'm being nosy," he continued, "but we need to think about nuclear proliferation and the arms trade. Instead, value nonviolence and a contented lifestyle. There is too much difference between rich and poor. Some people consume too much, and others don't have enough. Governments don't necessarily represent everyone, so we need a body representing all humanity to govern the world."

The Dalai Lama called for individual, scholarly, and political attention to the discipline of compassion. "We need to cultivate not only the rational mind, but also the human spirit.

Western educational systems are not paying enough regard to development of the heart, compared with the brain." This comment drew a strong round of applause. "Compassion should be taught to children, because this concept is difficult for adults to understand. If families and teachers are role models, children will grow up understanding compassion. This is the proper way to transform society."

A member of the audience asked about his greatest delight in this lifetime. "When I am able to help someone," the Dalai Lama quickly answered in English. Another person wanted to know if he thinks that world leaders will ever see political problems through the eyes of compassion. "Things are changing," said the Dalai Lama. "I see many acts of compassion. The signs are hopeful, but we need to make more of an effort. Some people live in societies that don't have much compassion. Then it's difficult for them to understand compassion. Our whole society is responsible for being compassionate."

On stage, the nuns and monks assisted the Dalai Lama in performing an ancient ceremony for sustaining his long life, then he offered the audience the opportunity to take the vows of a bodhisattva. His translator explained that the Dalai Lama is a special manifestation of Avalokiteshvara, the Bodhisattva of Compassion and patron deity of Tibet. Receiving empowerment from the Dalai Lama could help us all to develop compassion. Karma, Mike, and I joined the audience in taking the vows to become a bodhisattva.

Tibetans walked to the front of the auditorium as everyone else filed out. The Dalai Lama pulled his chair close to them and spoke in Tibetan. Later, Karma told Mike and me, "His Holiness talked to us as a loving parent. He said, 'Be Tibetan. Follow dharma. Maintain your integrity. Work hard so you're self-sufficient. Obey the laws of the country where you live. Education is important. Go as far as you can in your field. Get along. Support each other. Don't fight. Two Tibetan men got into a fight in New York, and now one of them is in jail. Don't worry about me, for I'll be fine. Things are changing. Eventually, we'll go back to Tibet, so don't give up hope.'"

As Karma bid us goodbye, he said in a husky voice, "Now, I'm more firmly committed than ever to living up to the values of His Holiness." We nodded, overcome with emotion.

Home in Judaism

Back home, Mike and I discussed how to fulfill our vows to behave as bodhisattvas. But what does this mean, we wondered, as far as everyday life? Is a bodhisattva the same as a mensch, the Hebrew word for a good person? Or is a bodhisattva a step higher—a *tsaddek,* the Hebrew word for righteous person? As I thought about this, a yearning for Judaism came over me. "Buddhism has become an important part of my life," I told Mike, "but I miss the Torah, Hebrew prayers and music, and Judaism's focus on justice."

The following Friday evening, we attended services at our synagogue, and the next morning we went to Torah Study. We made this Saturday class a part of our weekly schedule. During the teachings, I noticed many similarities between Buddhism and Judaism. Surprisingly, my insights into Buddhism gave new meaning to Judaism.

Both wisdom traditions teach the importance of direct experience. In Torah Study one Saturday, Rabbi Lerner described two kinds of faith. "One kind is when we see someone cross a precarious bridge and we have faith that we can cross it, too. The second kind of faith is when we cross the bridge ourselves. Then we really know, for we know from the inside out." This metaphor brought to mind Karma's description of mindfulness and what Tara said about the need to experience ourselves directly.

During another class, Rabbi Lerner discussed how biblical Hebrew words characterize the nature of the Divine. He translated *YHVH* as "the Lord" and *Elohim* as "God." Attributes of YHVH and Elohim include justice, strength, goodness, compassion, graciousness, kindness, faithfulness, forgiveness, and responsibility—all attributes that Buddhists try to cultivate during meditation. "When Moses saw the burning bush," said the rabbi, "he asked God's name. God replied, 'Ehyeh.' *Ehyeh* refers to the Divine's active, hidden, mysterious, eternal nature. Unlike *YHVH* and *Elohim*, *Ehyeh* is a verb—the first person singular of 'to be.' Because the tense is unclear, it could mean 'I am' or 'I shall be.' Jewish philosopher and theologian Martin Buber translated *Ehyeh* as 'the One unalterably persisting in being here, in every now and in every here.'" I noted that *Ehyeh* was similar to Dorjee Rinpoche's teachings about buddha nature—not an external creator-god, but the active, hidden, mysterious, eternal, intelligent, awake, and true nature of everything and everyone.

"The Divine is being (Yesh) and emptiness (Ayin) at the same time" Rabbi Lerner continued. "*Yesh* describes the Divine as a separate entity, whereas *Ayin* indicates that all separation is illusory." Likewise, Sogyal Rinpoche wrote that buddha nature is both being and emptiness, inside and outside, for buddha nature transcends opposites and is untouched by change or death. The rabbi went on: "These Hebrew words—*YHVH, Elohim, Ehyeh, Yesh,* and *Ayin*—affirm that the Divine is not anthropomorphic or finite. As Maimonides put it, 'God does not change, even though our perception of God may change.' In other words, because we are human beings, we can't fully comprehend the Divine."

Another Saturday, Rabbi Lerner spoke to the class in terms reminiscent of the Dalai Lama's teachings: "Meditation is meant to transform our ignorance and suffering into wisdom and happiness. We learn to focus less on our own ego and more on the Divine, on God. The essence of serving God is to be empty of self. Only then can we be an open channel for God. Happiness dawns when we come to realize that there is nothing but God. We can hear God in silence, when one breath stops and another breath starts. If we avoid thinking and our mind becomes still, we can have an experience of God. But if we think too much, we'll miss this opportunity." Both the Jewish and Buddhist perspectives teach that meditation can help us awaken to our emptiness—that we can catch a glimpse of the Divine by experiencing the Divine.

One Sabbath, Rabbi Lerner talked about karma, without using the actual word. "When you toss a stone into a lake, what happens? The ripples extend far beyond where the stone falls. If you open a feather pillow in the wind, can you retrieve all the feathers? No, they blow away. Similarly, a good deed has consequences, not only at the time it is done, but long afterward. The merit of a good deed stays with the person who does it, and with the person's children. Conversely, bad deeds come back to haunt us, as well as our children and even our children's children. It's up to each of us to make good choices.

During another Torah Study, Rabbi Lerner quoted an ancient rabbinical text about healing, which reminded me of the Dalai Lama's teachings on compassion. Even if we think someone is completely bad, the text stated, we must find something good in the person. Through this process we can raise the individual from unworthiness to worthiness. We can raise ourselves in the same way by attempting to avoid depression and to be in a state of happiness at all times. Rather than looking inward and seeing ourselves without worth, we must search for and focus on the iota of good inside, even if it seems full of blemishes and ulterior motives. By distinguishing the good from the bad, we'll be able to gather up the good, and then look for even more good! Rejoicing in this bit of good—no matter how small—will revive us, give us strength, and keep us from falling into depression. When we heal ourselves in this way, we become happy and we pray and sing. We can heal the world when we behave this way toward one another.

After Torah Study that day, I said to Mike, "I feel at home in Judaism. Yes, I draw from Christianity, yoga, the Twelve-Step Program, bioethics, and most recently Buddhism—and I want to learn more about other wisdom traditions. Like the Dalai Lama, I practice many wisdom traditions at the same time. But my roots are in Judaism. That's my ethical, spiritual foundation."

"Same for me," Mike said. "We can keep learning from Buddhism and other wisdom traditions, and we'll do what we can for Tibetans, but our home is in Judaism."

"Remember after Sara and Mom died?" I asked. "I felt completely drained physically, emotionally, and spiritually. My philosophy of life was no longer sufficient, and I felt confused and dissatisfied. It was as if I'd lost my voice, for all I could hear were other people's voices. I felt an inner void, a vacuum of the spirit. Something important was missing, but I didn't know what."

"So, what was lacking?" Mike asked. "Do you know now?"

"A path with heart," I said, "one that's based on the Doctrine of Karma. I still visualize my wisdom traditions as overlapping circles. Christianity gives me the desire for a personal relationship with the Infinite. Judaism offers detailed ethical and spiritual guidelines to follow. Yoga reminds me to harmonize my body, mind, and spirit. The Twelve-Step Program suggests how to develop healthy relationships. Bioethics focuses on rationality, which helps me make wise choices."

I paused to think a moment. "And Buddhism, the sixth circle, explicitly addresses the interdependence of ethics, spirituality, and healing—that happiness and suffering aren't accidental, for they result from our actions. The reason to behave ethically and spiritually is because it's the happiest way to live. Yes, bad things happen to seemingly good people, and good things happen to seemingly bad people. Over all, though, good choices lead to a happier, healthier life than poor choices do. If I live in this way, I'll bring healing to myself and the world.

"If we hadn't reached out to the Tibetans," Mike said, "we wouldn't have taken our Tibetan odyssey. We wanted to help them, but they turned around and benefited us at the same time. Individual Tibetans have become family for us. Our life is more meaningful because of them."

"Karma . . . Dorje Rinpoche . . . Tara . . . Pema . . . Dr. Tsetan and Dr. Tsering . . . Nurse Nyima . . . the nuns in Tibet . . . the Tibetans here in the United States . . . and, of course, the fourteenth Dalai Lama," I said. "Each of them has opened our eyes to a larger and more inclusive ethical, spiritual, and healing perspective."

"This philosophy of life isn't final," said Mike with a grin. "Judaism and Buddhism teach that we're constantly changing. We won't be fully alive unless our thinking continues to evolve."

Laughing, I put my arms around him and kissed him. "Thank you for sharing this Tibetan odyssey with me. In the words of the ancient Jewish prayer, 'Blessed art Thou, Adonai, Who, with great mercy, has restored my soul. Blessed is Adonai, the Source of healing.'"

Epilogue: Healing the World

Diversity of Values

Now, a year after going to the Dalai Lama's teachings, I am reflecting on the effect that this Tibetan odyssey has had on my life. Perhaps my most profound transformation has been from private individual to global citizen. Traveling in Tibet and other developing countries and becoming friends with Tibetans have opened my eyes to the importance of moving beyond the personal to the political. As the Dalai Lama and other sages teach, ethical, spiritual behavior requires an attitude of universal responsibility. They assert that, because all of us are increasingly interconnected in this shrinking world, we're responsible to and for each other, and we must work together to live in harmony with one other and with the environment.

Research suggests that much personal and interpersonal turmoil results from conflict over values. The participants in my research studies described a stressful clash of their deeply held values about what to believe, about who to be, and about what to do in a given situation. On a societal level, conflict over values has led to untold suffering. In my view, the Tibetan situation is an example of what can occur when one group, Chinese leaders, forcibly imposes its values on another group, Tibetans who want to follow different values.

Clearly, self-interest lies in tolerating each other's values. John Locke advocated tolerance because of our human fallibility and mutual needs. He wrote that intolerance, not diversity of values, leads to societal conflict. Because no one knows for sure about the right way to conduct our lives, we're best off acknowledging our fallibility. If we learn to live together peacefully, he stated, we will be able to meet our mutual needs.

Ideally, we'll learn not only to tolerate each other's values, but also to celebrate them. That means respecting each other's wisdom traditions. No two individuals are identical, and each of us needs something different from a wisdom tradition. Rather than being threatened by the various belief systems, we can choose to learn from them.

Diverse wisdom traditions have not only added richness to my philosophy of life, but also helped me to deal with life's inevitable difficulties. Moreover, I enjoy studying wisdom traditions. Mike and I have been reading the Bhagavad-Gita in preparation for our upcoming trip to India and Nepal. The purpose of the trip is to celebrate Losar, the Tibetan New Year, with Tibetan friends in Dharamsala and Kathmandu. However, we look forward to learning more about Hinduism, and we plan to visit mosques in Old Delhi so we can expand our knowledge of Islam.

I've come to relish the benefits of various wisdom traditions. If all wisdom traditions were standardized, the world would lose the uniqueness of each. Wisdom traditions can be compared with world cuisines, which vary in sight, smell, texture, nutrition, and taste. Tibetan *momos,* Jewish matzo balls, Chinese wontons, and Italian gnocchi are all dumplings, but each has different characteristics. I wouldn't want to eat only lutefisk (cod soaked in lye and salt water), lefse (thin, rolled pancakes), and other food from my Scandinavian-American background. Life would be boring if all food—and wisdom traditions—were the same.

A lovely Jewish story illustrates the problem with sameness. A wheat farmer traveled to the city where he visited one bakery after another to sample the pastries. In each bakery he asked what the pastries were made of, and the baker replied, "Wheat." When the farmer returned home, he said to his family, "The pastries were the same—they were all made of wheat." Because he couldn't see beyond the wheat, he wasn't able to appreciate each individual pastry. Similarly, life is bland if we don't recognize and enjoy the diversity of wisdom traditions.

Experts advise parents not to show favoritism toward any of their children, but to appreciate each child's personality, strengths, and weaknesses. I like to think of the various wisdom traditions as God's children, each with its own personality, strengths, and weaknesses. A strength of Judaism is its focus on justice and rule of law, yet this strength can become a weakness when compassion is lacking. For Buddhism, the emphasis on compassion is a strength, but without justice it can become a weakness. Rather than argue about which tradition is superior, we can develop collective wisdom by encouraging "cross-fertilization" among the traditions. Then, instead of dividing us, they will bring us together.

Unity of Values

Although wisdom traditions differ, they share the same ethical and spiritual goal: to help individuals live and die well. Many of the world's troubles arise when we forget the basic oneness of our wisdom traditions.

Wisdom traditions more or less link ethics, spirituality, and healing. They address the basic ethical problem: How should I conduct my life, knowing I will die? Though they may not use the term *karma,* they advocate living by ethical and spiritual values, for this is the best way to be happy and healthy and to create a better world. Each tradition offers solace in times of suffering and advocates social justice through individual and collective action. Any of these traditions can lead to personal peace, peace with others, and peace with the environment.

Tibetans have reminded me that not only do wisdom traditions share a basic oneness, but so do human beings. Even though each of us is a unique individual, we hold some values in common. What are those values? Happiness, for one. Everyone I've ever met, regardless of age, gender, ethnicity, sexual orientation, education, or socioeconomic level wants to be happy. Moreover, my research suggests that each of us wants to live our lives with meaning and integrity.

I've come to agree with the Dalai Lama and other sages: To get along with each other, we must create nonsectarian ways of working together without demanding that individuals abandon their own values. One way to do this is by conducting research and engaging in philosophical analysis about the ethical and spiritual values on which we can all agree. We will need to draw from diverse wisdom traditions and develop common values that address both individual and universal responsibility for personal happiness and world peace.

To stimulate dialogue about the values we hold in common, I will suggest seven ethical values and seven spiritual values as I come to the end of this book. I have observed these values in individuals, regardless of their circumstances, wherever I have traveled. Wisdom traditions teach these values as well. Yes, they represent ideals, and most of us only adhere to them to some degree. Nevertheless, I think that deep down we yearn to rise up to our best selves by living in accordance with these values.

As Aristotle noted, ethics is not an exact science. Moreover, ethics and spirituality aren't distinct categories. For this reason, the ethical values I propose can be viewed as spiritual values as well, and vice versa. My list of ethical and spiritual values won't fit everyone, nor will everyone agree with my definitions. In other words, my list is only a beginning. That being understood, I'll go ahead and suggest these values anyway, hoping they will stimulate discussion and lead to a more comprehensive understanding of our best values.

(In my descriptions, the ethical values indicate actions we can take to behave ethically. The spiritual values describe beliefs or states of being.)

Ethical Values

Beneficence—Remove, prevent, and avoid evil or harm. Do or promote good. Strive to be a good human being and behave virtuously. Transform suffering into happiness.

Honesty—Be truthful, trustworthy, and honorable. Rather than manipulate anyone, communicate in a sincere, genuine, fair, meaningful way. Avoid half-truths and misrepresentations.

Justice—Treat everyone fairly. Address the gap between rich and poor, and allocate scarce resources equitably. Behave with moderation and self-discipline.

Nonviolence—Avoid physical, mental, and sexual abuse. Instead of spending money on weapons, develop programs to eliminate poverty and disease. Do away with a culture of aggression by developing peaceful means for resolving conflict.

Peace—Develop internal and external harmony. When change is impossible, accept what is. Support others instead of fostering division. Choose leaders who help everyone to live with meaning and integrity. Use resources to improve people's lives rather than hurt them.

Respect for the Environment—View natural resources as a sacred trust. Use and replenish these resources wisely. Clean up the air, water, and food. Live in harmony with plants and all sentient beings, including animals.

Respect for Human Rights—Follow the United Nation's Universal Declaration of Human Rights, which states that all human beings have the right to life, security, expression, education, religion, movement, peaceful assembly, participation in government, fair employment, an adequate standard of living, and equal treatment before the law, with the presumption of innocence until proven guilty.

Spiritual Values

Compassion—A good heart filled with loving kindness. We love and are loved. Because we view others as being "of our own kind," we realize that everyone is suffering and has an equal right to happiness.

Divine—God, Ultimate Concern, Sacred, Buddha Nature, Life-Force, Underlying Order, Higher Power, Infinite, Great Spirit, Unmoved Mover. These names are inaccurate and limiting, for the Divine is not anthropomorphic.

Happiness—Well-being, self-actualization, human flourishing, and human excellence, which are not necessarily the same as temporary, sensual pleasure. After basic physical needs are fulfilled, happiness results from inner peace, not material wealth.

Integrity—Excellent character that is sound, incorruptible, and complete. We live in harmony with our best values, which are ethically and spiritually justifiable.

Meaning—A sense that we are connected to something larger than ourselves and that we are contributing to "the whole." In both suffering and happiness, we believe that life has purpose and value.

Meditation—A process that promotes awareness of the inner self and of the Divine. We learn to calm the whirl of thoughts that occupy the mind and to develop wisdom. As we transform ourselves, we become an expression of the Divine.

Spirituality—Cleaving to and experiencing something higher, deeper, and greater than ourselves. We develop love, compassion, kindness, contentment, responsibility, altruism, peace of mind, joy, patience, humility, tolerance, and forgiveness. Fully alive, we feel deeply replenished to the core of our being.

More work needs to be done to describe these values. If we—as a society, a civilization, a world—can come to some agreement about the best values we hold in common, then we'll be more likely to realize how similar we are, that all of us are "of the same kind." With this attitude, we will have an easier time treating each other kindly and working together to heal the world. Then, as the Hebrew prophet Isaiah put it, "They shall beat their swords into plowshares, and their spears into pruning hooks. Nation shall not lift up sword against nation, neither shall they learn war anymore."

Glossary

Avalokiteshvara: Bodhisattva of Compassion, the patron deity of Tibet. His Tibetan name is Chenrezi. The Dalai Lama is a manifestation of this deity.

bardos: Four stages that each person goes through: life, dying and death, after-death, and rebirth.

bodhisattva: A person who is gentle and not abusive, without deceit and fraud, and full of love toward all beings; a highly accomplished spiritual practitioner who has attained enlightenment for the sake of liberating all sentient beings from suffering.

buddha: One who is awake, who is enlightened; the historical Buddha.

buddha nature: The luminous, pure, Buddha-like quality inherent in all beings; our true nature.

chang: Tibetan beer, usually brewed from barley.

Chenrezi: Tibetan name for Avalokiteshvara, the Bodhisattva of Compassion, the patron deity of Tibet.

chupa: Traditional Tibetan dress worn in slightly different versions by both men and women.

Dalai Lama: "Ocean Teacher," honorific title for the temporal and spiritual leader of Tibet.

dharma: Buddhist teachings revealing the ultimate truth, reality, and universal law; literally "the Path."

dri: A female yak.

dukkha: Suffering; dissatisfaction.

dzo: Cross between a bull and a female yak.

dzong: Castle, fortress, or district.

Gelugpa: One of the four Tibetan Buddhist sects; the Yellow Hat sect.

incarnate lama: Reincarnation of a famous teacher, usually recognized in childhood and educated to fill the teacher's former position.

Jokhang Temple: Great central cathedral of Lhasa and holiest temple in Tibet, built in the eighth century.

kata: A ceremonial scarf presented upon meeting or departing as a token of friendship or respect. Also spelled *khata.*

lama: Highly respected religious teacher or elder; the Tibetan equivalent of a guru.

Losar: Tibetan New Year, which occurs at the new moon during the Western months of February or March. It is not the same as the Chinese or Korean New Year.

Mahayana Buddhism: The branch of Buddhism that spread to Tibet, Korea, China, and Japan.

Maitreya: Buddha of the Future.

mandala: A sacred diagram, used in visualization and meditation.

mani stones: Stones on which the mantra *Om Mani Padme Hum* is written.

mantra: Verbal formula repeated as part of meditation.

Milarepa: Great Tibetan poet and teacher in the eleventh century who attained enlightenment in one lifetime.

momo: Tibetan steamed dumpling filled with meat or vegetables.

Monlam: Great prayer festival in Lhasa held during the first fifteen days of the new year.

moxibustion: A traditional Tibetan treatment that consists of applying heat by burning herbs over the area of the body to be treated.

namaste: Hindu greeting meaning "The spirit in me greets the spirit in you."

nirvana: Cessation of desire; freedom from suffering and rebirth.

Norbulingka Palace: "The Jewel Park," summer palace for the Dalai Lamas in Lhasa.

Om Mani Padme Hum: Sanskrit mantra translated as "Jewel in the Lotus," meaning "the thought of enlightenment in the mind" or "the union of compassion and wisdom, through which we can transform our impure body, speech, and mind into the pure exalted body, speech, and mind of a buddha"; the mantra of Avalokiteshvara; Tibet's national mantra.

Padmasambhava: Indian Buddhist teacher who traveled to Tibet in the eighth century and helped establish Buddhism. Also called Guru Rinpoche.

Potala Palace: Winter residence of the Dalai Lamas in Lhasa and seat of the Tibetan government, built by the fifth Dalai Lama in the seventeenth century.

prana: According to yoga philosophy, the life-force that permeates everything and is most accessible in the air we breathe.

prayer wheel: Device for mechanically producing a mantra. May take the form of a large cylinder in a temple or a small handheld cylinder with a handle that is whirled.

regent: Monk who heads the Tibetan government during the minority or absence of the Dalai Lama.

rinpoche: Literally "precious one"; the respectful title used for incarnate lamas and other great teachers.

root lama: One's most important personal spiritual guide and mentor.

Sakyamuni: Buddha of the Present; historical Buddha who lived during the sixth century B.C.E. in what is now a village on the border between India and Nepal, and who attained enlightenment under a *bodhi* tree. His subsequent teachings developed into Buddhism.

samsara: This world, which is a world of delusion.

sem: Ordinary mind, in contrast with buddha nature.

stupa: A dome-like mound containing a Buddhist shrine.

Tantric Buddhism: Esoteric Tibetan Buddhism, which includes advanced meditation teachings that can lead to enlightenment in one lifetime. Same as Vajrayana Buddhism.

Tara: Feminine aspect of compassion who has twenty-one different manifestations, the most frequent being Green Tara and White Tara.

Tashi delek: Traditional Tibetan greeting that means "good luck, good health, and peace be unto you."

thangka: Tibetan painting on a scroll.

Theravada Buddhism: The branch of Buddhism that spread to Southeast Asia.

Thu-je-chhe: Tibetan for "thanks," "thank you very much."

The Three Jewels: Buddha as the teacher of refuge, dharma teachings as the actual refuge, and *sangha* as spiritual community or helpers toward that refuge.

tsampa: Roasted barley flour, a staple food of Tibet, often used in religious ceremonies.

venesection: A traditional Tibetan treatment that consists of bloodletting.

Bibliography

Al-Anon Family Group Headquarters, Inc. *Al-Anon's Twelve Steps and Twelve Traditions.* New York: Author, 1989.

Alcoholics Anonymous World Services, Inc. *Alcoholics Anonymous.* New York: Author, 1983.

Appel, A. *High Holiday Sutra.* Minneapolis: Coffee House Press, 1997.

Aristotle. *The Nicomachean Ethics.* Translated by D. Ross. New York: Oxford University Press, 1987.

———. *The Politics.* Edited by S. Everson. New York: Cambridge University Press, 1988.

Avedon, J. F. *In Exile from the Land of Snows.* New York: HarperPerennial, 1994.

Beauchamp, T., and J. Childress. *Principles of Biomedical Ethics.* New York: Oxford University Press, 1994.

Black, A. H. *Man and the Nature of Philosophical Thought of Wang Fu-Chih.* Seattle: University of Washington Press, 1989.

Boorstein, S. *It's Easier Than You Think: The Buddhist Way to Happiness.* New York: HarperCollins Publishers, 1997.

———. *That's Funny, You Don't Look Buddhist: On Being a Faithful Jew and a Passionate Buddhist.* New York: HarperCollins Publishers, 1997.

Buber, M. *I and Thou.* Translated by R. G. Smith. New York: Charles Scribner's Sons, 1958.

———. *The Origin and Meaning of Hasidim.* Edited and Translated by M. Friedman. New York: Harper Torchbooks, 1960.

———. *Kingship of God.* Translated by R. Scheimann. New York: Harper Torchbooks, 1973.

Chang, June. *Wild Swans.* New York: Doubleday, 1991.

Chödrön, P. *The Wisdom of No Escape: And the Path of Loving-Kindness.* Boston: Shambhala Publications, 1991.

———. *Start Where You Are: A Guide to Compassionate Living.* Boston: Shambhala Publications, 1994.

Clark, B., trans. *The Quintessence Tantras of Tibetan Medicine.* Ithaca, NY: Snow Lion Publications, 1995.

Coulter, A. H. "Overview of Tibetan Medicine." *Alternative and Complementary Therapies* 4 (1998): 338–42.

Craig, M. Kundun: *A Biography of the Family of the Dalai Lama.* Washington, DC: Counterpoint, 1997.

Dahl, N. O. *Practical Reason, Aristotle, and Weakness of the Will.* Minneapolis: University of Minnesota Press, 1984.

Dalai Lama, the Fourteenth (Tenzin Gyatso). *Compassion and the Individual.* Boston: Wisdom Publications, 1994.

———. *A Flash of Lightning in the Dark of Night: A Guide to the Bodhisattva's Way of Life.* Boston: Shambhala Publications, 1994.

———. *The Way to Freedom.* Edited by J. F. Avedon and D. S. Lopez, Jr. New York: HarperCollins Publishers, 1994.

———. *Awakening the Mind, Lightening the Heart: Core Teachings of Tibetan Buddhism.* New York: HarperCollins Publishers, 1995.

———. *The World of Tibetan Buddhism: An Overview of Its Philosophy and Practice.* Edited and translated by G. T. Jinpa. Boston: Wisdom Publications, 1995.

———. *Ethics for the New Millennium.* New York: Riverhead Books, 1999.

———. *The Dalai Lama's Book of Transformation.* London: Thorsons, 2000.

———. *The Power of Compassion.* Translated by G. T. Jinpa. New Delhi, India: HarperCollins Publishers India, 2000.

———. *A Simple Path.* London: Thorsons, 2000.

———. *Transforming the Mind.* London: Thorsons, 2000.

The Dalai Lama, et al. *MindScience: An East-West Dialogue.* Boston: Wisdom Publications, 1991.

The Dalai Lama, and J. C. Carriere. *Violence and Compassion.* New York: Doubleday, 1994.

The Dalai Lama, and H. C. Cutler. *The Art of Happiness: A Handbook for Living.* New York: Riverhead Books, 1998.

Dash, V. B. *Tibetan Medicine: Theory and Practice*. Delhi, India: Sri Satguru Publications, 1997.

David-Neel, A. *Initiations and Initiates in Tibet: An Extraordinary Woman Traveller Uncovers the Spiritual Practices of Tibet*. Edited by F. Rothwell. London: Rider and Company, 1973.

Davis, A., ed. *Meditation from the Heart of Judaism*. Woodstock, Vt.: Jewish Lights Publishing, 1997.

Dhonden, Y. *Healing from the Source: The Science and Lore of Tibetan Medicine*. Translated by B. A. Wallace. Ithaca, NY: Snow Lion Publications, 2000.

———. *Health through Balance: An Introduction to Tibetan Medicine*. Translated by J. Hopkins, L. Rabgay, and A. Wallace. Delhi, India: Motilal Banarsidass Publishers, 2000.

Dummer, T. *Tibetan Medicine and Other Holistic Health-Care Systems*. New Delhi, India: Paljor Publications, 1998.

Epstein, M. *Thoughts without a Thinker: Psychotherapy from a Buddhist Perspective*. New York: Basic Books, 1995.

Evans-Wentz, W. Y., ed. *The Tibetan Book of the Dead: The After-Death Experiences on the Bardo Plane, According to Lama Kazi Dawa-Samdup's English Rendering*. New York: Oxford University Press, 1960.

Fitzgerald, R., trans. *Homer: The Odyssey*. Garden City, NY: Doubleday and Company, 1963.

Flack, H. E., and E. D. Pellegrino, eds. *African-American Perspectives on Biomedical Ethics*. Washington, DC: Georgetown University Press, 1992.

Frankena, W. K. *Ethics*. 2nd ed. Englewood Cliffs, NJ: Prentice-Hall, 1973.

Frankl, V. E. *The Doctor and the Soul*. Translated by R. Winston and C. Winston. New York: Bantam Books, 1965.

Gilligan, C. *In a Different Voice*. Cambridge, Mass.: Harvard University Press, 1982.

Goldstein, M. C. *The Snow Lion and the Dragon: China, Tibet, and the Dalai Lama*. Los Angeles: University of California Press, 1997.

Goldstein, M. C., and C. M. Beall. *Nomads of Western Tibet*. Berkeley, Calif.: University of California Press, 1990.

Goldstein, M., W. Siebenschuh, and T. Tsering. *The Struggle for Modern Tibet: The Autobiography of Tashi Tsering.* Armonk, NY: M. E. Sharpe, 1997.

Gyeltsen, G. T. *Compassion: The Key to Great Awakening.* Boston: Wisdom Publications, 1997.

Hanh, T. N. *The Miracle of Mindfulness.* Translated by M. Ho. Boston: Beacon Press, 1987.

———. *The Blooming of a Lotus: Guided Meditation Exercises for Healing and Transformation.* Translated by A. Laity. Boston: Beacon Press, 1993.

———. *For a Future to Be Possible: Commentaries on the Five Wonderful Precepts.* Berkeley, Calif.: Parallax Press, 1993.

———. *Being Peace.* Berkeley, Calif.: Parallax Press, 1996.

Harrer, H. *Seven Years in Tibet.* New York: G. P. Putnam's Sons, 1996.

———. *Return to Tibet: Tibet after the Chinese Occupation.* New York: Tarcher/Putnam, 1998.

Hicks, R., and N. Chogyam. *Great Ocean: An Authorized Biography, the Dalai Lama.* New York: Penguin Books, 1990.

Hoffer, E. *The True Believer.* New York: Harper and Row Publishers, 1951.

Johnson, S. *The Book of Tibetan Elders: The Life Stories and Wisdom from the Great Spiritual Masters of Tibet.* New York: G. P. Putnam's Sons, 1996.

Josayma, T. T., and K. Dhondup. *Dolma and Dolkar: Mother and Daughter of Tibetan Medicine.* New Delhi, India: Yarlung Publications, 1990.

Kamalasila, A. *The Stages of Meditation: Middle Volume.* Translated by V. G. L. Sopa, V. E. W. J. Newman, and J. Newman. Madison, Wis.: Deer Park Books, 1998.

Kamenetz, R. *The Jew in the Lotus: A Poet's Rediscovery of Jewish Identity in Buddhist India.* New York: HarperCollins Publishers, 1995.

———. *Stalking Elijah: Adventures with Today's Mystical Masters.* New York: HarperCollins Publishers, 1997.

Kant, I. *Grounding for the Metaphysics of Morals.* Translated by J. W. Ellington. Indianapolis: Hackett Publishing Company, 1986.

Kerr, B. *Sky Burial: An Eyewitness Account of China's Brutal Crackdown in Tibet.* Chicago: The Noble Press, 1993.

Kling, K. *Tibet.* New York: Thames and Hudson, 1990.

Kornfield, J. *A Path with Heart: A Guide through the Perils and Promises of Spiritual Life.* New York: Bantam Books, 1993.

Labowitz, S. *Miraculous Living: A Guided Journey in Kabbalah through the Ten Gates of the Tree of Life.* New York: Fireside, 1998.

Lerner, M. *Spirit Matters.* Charlottesville, Va.: Hampton Roads Publishing Company, 2000.

Lew, A. *One God Clapping: The Spiritual Path of a Zen Rabbi.* Woodstock, Vt.: Jewish Lights Publishing, 2001.

Locke, J. *A Letter Concerning Toleration.* New York: Macmillan Publishing Company, 1950.

Lopez Jr., D. S. *Prisoners of Shangri-la: Tibetan Buddhism and the West.* Chicago: The University of Chicago Press, 1998.

Matt, D. C. *The Essential Kabbalah: The Heart of Jewish Mysticism.* New York: HarperCollins Publishers, 1996.

———. *God and the Big Bang: Discovering Harmony between Science and Spirituality.* Woodstock, Vt.: Jewish Lights Publishing, 1996.

Mehta, S., M. Mehta, and S. Mehta. *Yoga the Iyengar Way.* New York: Alfred A. Knopf, 1999.

Men-Tsee-Khang (Tibetan Medical and Astrological Institute of H. H. the Dalai Lama). *Fundamentals of Tibetan Medicine: According to the Rgyud-Bzhi.* New Delhi, India: Author, 1995.

Miles, J. *God: A Biography.* New York: Vintage Books, 1996.

Mill, J. S. *Utilitarianism.* Edited by O. Piest. New York: Macmillan Publishing Company, 1986.

Mirel, J. L., and K. B. Werth. *Stepping Stones to Jewish Spiritual Living: Walking the Path Morning, Noon, and Night.* Woodstock, Vt.: Jewish Lights Publishing, 1998.

Noddings, N. *Caring: A Feminine Approach to Ethics and Moral Education.* Los Angeles: University of California Press, 1984.

Nussbaum, M. C. *The Fragility of Goodness: Luck and Ethics in Greek Tragedy and Philosophy.* New York: Cambridge University Press, 1994.

Patt, D. *A Strange Liberation: Tibetan Lives in Chinese Hands.* Ithaca, NY: Snow Lion Publications, 1992.

Pellegrino, E. D. "Toward a Virtue-Based Normative Ethics for the Health Professions." *Kennedy Institute of Ethics Journal* 5 (1995): 253–77.

Plato. "Gorgias." In *Plato,* translated by W. R. M. Lamb. Cambridge, Mass.: Harvard University Press, 1961.

———. "Protagoras." In *Plato,* translated by W. R. M. Lamb. Cambridge, Mass.: Harvard University Press, 1967.

———. *The Republic.* Translated by A. Bloom. New York: Basic Books, 1968.

Prabhavananda, S., and C. Isherwood, trans. *The Song of God: Bhagavad-Gita.* New York: Penguin Books USA, 1972.

Quing, Ven S. Y., ed. *Lotus Fragrance.* Hong Kong: The Hong Kong Buddhist Association, 1992.

Revel, J. F., and M. Ricard. *The Monk and the Philosopher: A Father and Son Discuss the Meaning of Life.* New York: Schocken Books, 1999.

Rinpoche, H. H. D., trans. *Sadhana of the Medicine Buddha.* New York: Yeshe Melong, 1998.

Rinpoche, L. Z. *Transforming Problems into Happiness.* Boston: Wisdom Publications, 1993.

Rinpoche, P. *Liberation in the Palm of Your Hand: A Concise Discourse on the Path to Enlightenment.* Edited by T. Rinpoche, translated by M. Richards. Boston: Wisdom Publications, 1997.

Rinpoche, S. *The Tibetan Book of Living and Dying.* Edited by P. Gaffney and A. Harvey. New York: HarperCollins Publishers, 1994.

Rousseau, J. J. *Emile: Or on Education.* Translated by A. Bloom. New York: Basic Books, 1979.

Ruderman, A. C. *The Pleasures of Virtue: Political Thought in the Novels of Jane Austen.* Lanham, Md.: Rowman and Littlefield Publishers, 1995.

Saddhatissa, H. *Buddhist Ethics.* Boston: Wisdom Publications, 1997.

Schachter-Shalomi, Z., and R. S. Miller. *From Age-ing to Sage-ing: A Profound New Vision of Growing Older.* New York: Warner Books, 1995.

Seeskin, K. *Maimonides: A Guide for Today's Perplexed.* West Orange, NJ: Behrman House, 1991.

———. *Searching for a Distant God: The Legacy of Maimonides.* New York: Oxford University Press, 2000.

Shainberg, L. *Ambivalent Zen.* New York: Vintage Books, 1997.

Smith, H. *The Illustrated World's Religions: A Guide to Our Wisdom Traditions.* New York: HarperCollins Publishers, 1994.

Snellgrove, D., and H. Richardson. *A Cultural History of Tibet.* Boston: Shambhala Publications, 1995.

Sparshott, F. *Taking Life Seriously: A Study of the Argument of the Nicomachean Ethics.* Toronto: University of Toronto Press, 1996.

Spiegelberg, H. *The Phenomenological Movement.* Boston, Mass.: Martinus Nijhoff Publishers, 1984.

Taylor, C. *Tibet.* London: Lonely Planet Publications, 1995.

Tendzin, O. *Buddha in the Palm of Your Hand.* Edited by D. Holm. Boston: Shambhala Publications, 1987.

Thiroux, J. P. *Ethics: Theory and Practice.* 3rd ed. New York: Macmillan Publishing Company, 1986.

Thurman, R. *Inner Revolution: Life, Liberty and the Pursuit of Real Happiness.* New York: Riverhead Books, 1998.

Thurman, R., and T. Wise. *Circling the Sacred Mountain.* New York: Bantam Books, 2000.

Trungpa, C. *The Myth of Freedom and the Way of Meditation.* Edited by J. Baker and M. Casper. Boston: Shambhala Publications, 1988.

———. *Shambhala: The Sacred Path of the Warrior.* Edited by C. R. Gimian. Boston: Shambhala Publications, 1988.

Van Beek, S. *Tibet: Lhasa to Kathmandu.* Singapore: Insight Pocket Guides, 1994.

Welwood, J. *Awakening the Heart: East/West Approaches to Psychotherapy and the Health Relationship.* London: Shambhala Publications, 1983.

Wilson, J. Q. *The Moral Sense.* New York: The Free Press, 1993.

Yeshe, L. *Becoming Your Own Therapist: An Introduction to the Buddhist Way of Thought.* Boston: Lama Yeshe Wisdom Archive, 1999.

Yeshe, L., and L. Z. Rinpoche. *Wisdom Energy: Basic Buddhist Teachings.* Boston: Wisdom Publications, 2000.

Yuthok, D. Y. *House of the Turquoise Roof.* Ithaca, NY: Snow Lion Publications, 1995.

Zhisui, L. *The Private Life of Chairman Mao.* New York: Random House, 1994.

Zion, N., and D. Dishon. *A Different Night: The Family Participation Haggadah.* Jerusalem: The Shalom Hartman Institute, 1997.

Author's Related Publications

Cameron, M. E. *Hello, I'm God and I'm Here to Help You.* New York: Warner Books, 1980.

———. "The Moral and Ethical Component of Nurse Burnout." *Nursing Management* (Critical Care Management Edition) 17, no. 4 (1986): 42B–42E.

———. "Justice, Caring and Virtue." *Journal of Professional Nursing* 7 (1991): 206.

———. *Living with AIDS: Experiencing Ethical Problems.* Foreword by E. D. Pellegrino. Newbury Park, Calif.: Sage Publications, 1993.

———. "Ethical Problems Involving Death." *AIDS Patient Care* 8, no. 5 (1994): 269–78.

———. "Ethical Problems Involving Health Care." *AIDS Patient Care* 8, no. 4, (1994): 212–19.

———. *Tell Me the Right Answer: A Workbook for Learning about Nursing Ethics.* Seoul, South Korea: College of Nursing, Seoul National University, 1994.

———. "Yoga." In *Independent Nursing Interventions,* 2nd ed. (Japanese), by M. Snyder. Tokyo: Medicus Publishing, 1994. First published in *Independent Nursing Interventions,* 2nd ed., by M. Snyder. New York: Delmar Publishers, 1992.

———. "The Relationship between Toleration and Entitlement in Health Care Policy." *Journal of Nursing Law* 2, no. 3 (1995): 55–65.

———. "Virtue Ethics for Nurses and Health Care." *Journal of Nursing Law* 3, no. 4 (1996): 27–39.

———. "*Akrasia,* AIDS, and Virtue Ethics." *Journal of Nursing Law* 4, no. 1 (1997): 21–34.

———. "Ethical Distress in Nursing." *Journal of Professional Nursing* 13 (1997): 280.

———. "Clinical Sidebar by Miriam E. Cameron." From "Spirituality and Chronic Illness" by D. P. O'Neill and E. K. Kenny. In *Image: Journal of Nursing Scholarship* 30 (1998): 275–79.

———. "Reflections on a Trip to Tibet." *Journal of Professional Nursing* 14 (1998): 33.

———. "Completing Life and Dying Triumphantly." *Journal of Nursing Law* 6, no. 1 (1999): 27–32.

———. "An Ethical Perspective: Traditional Tibetan Health Care." *Journal of Nursing Law* 6, no. 2 (1999): 33–42.

———. "Value, Be, Do: Guidelines for Resolving Ethical Conflict." *Journal of Nursing Law* 6, no. 4 (2000): 15–24.

———. "Yoga." In *Complementary/Alternative Therapies for Nursing,* 4th ed. Edited by M. Snyder and R. Lindquist. New York: Springer Publishing Company, 2001.

Cameron, M. E., P. Crisham, and D. E. Lewis. "The Basic Nature of Ethical Problems Experienced by Persons with Acquired Immunodeficiency Syndrome." *Journal of Professional Nursing* 9 (1993): 327–35.

———. "The Content of Ethical Problems Experienced by Persons Living with AIDS." *Journal of the Association of Nurses in AIDS Care* 5, no. 5 (1994): 32–42.

Cameron, M. E., and H. A. Park. "An Ethical Perspective: Equity versus Economics in South Korea." *Journal of Nursing Law* 6, no. 3 (1999): 47–54.

Cameron, M. E., and M. Schaffer. "Tell Me the Right Answer: A Model for Teaching Nursing Ethics." *Journal of Nursing Education* 31 (1992): 377–80.

Cameron, M. E., M. Schaffer, and H.A. Park. "Nursing Students' Experience of Ethical Problems and Use of Ethical Decision-Making Models." *Nursing Ethics* 8, no. 5 (2001): 432–447.

Moch, S. D., and M. E. Cameron. "Processing the Researcher Experience through Discussion." In *The Researcher Experience in Qualitative Research,* edited by S. D. Moch and M. F. Gates. Thousand Oaks, Calif.: Sage Publications, 1999.

Schaffer, M. A., M. E. Cameron, and E. Tatley. "The Value, Be, Do Ethical Decision-Making Model: Balancing Students' Needs in School Nursing." *Journal of School Nursing* 16, no. 5 (2000): 44–49.